Loss Coverage

Most academic and policy commentary rep..........ts adverse selection as a severe problem in insurance, which should always be deprecated, avoided or minimised. This book gives a contrary view. It details the exaggeration of adverse selection in insurers' rhetoric and insurance economics, and presents evidence that in many insurance markets, adverse selection is weaker than most commentators suggest. A novel arithmetical argument shows that from a public policy perspective, 'weak' adverse selection can be a good thing. This is because a degree of adverse selection is needed to maximise 'loss coverage', the expected fraction of the population's losses which is compensated by insurance.

This book will be valuable for those interested in public policy arguments about insurance and discrimination: academics (in economics, law and social policy), policymakers, actuaries, underwriters, disability activists, geneticists and other medical professionals.

GUY THOMAS is an actuary and investor, and an honorary lecturer at the University of Kent. His academic publications have received prizes from the Institute and Faculty of Actuaries and the International Actuarial Association. He is also the author of *Free Capital: How Twelve Private Investors Made Millions in the Stock Market*.

Loss Coverage

Why Insurance Works Better with Some Adverse Selection

GUY THOMAS

University of Kent

CAMBRIDGE
UNIVERSITY PRESS

CAMBRIDGE
UNIVERSITY PRESS

University Printing House, Cambridge CB2 8BS, United Kingdom

One Liberty Plaza, 20th Floor, New York, NY 10006, USA

477 Williamstown Road, Port Melbourne, VIC 3207, Australia

4843/24, 2nd Floor, Ansari Road, Daryaganj, Delhi – 110002, India

79 Anson Road, #06-04/06, Singapore 079906

Cambridge University Press is part of the University of Cambridge.

It furthers the University's mission by disseminating knowledge in the pursuit of education, learning and research at the highest international levels of excellence.

www.cambridge.org
Information on this title: www.cambridge.org/9781107100336
DOI: 10.1017/9781316178843

First published 2017

Printed in the United Kingdom by Clays, St Ives plc

A catalogue record for this publication is available from the British Library.

Library of Congress Cataloging-in-Publication Data
Names: Thomas, Guy, author.
Title: Loss coverage : why insurance works better with some adverse selection / Guy Thomas, University of Kent, Canterbury.
Description: Cambridge, United Kingdom ; New York, NY : Cambridge University Press, 2017. | Includes bibliographical references and index.
Identifiers: LCCN 2016048282 | ISBN 9781107100336 (hardback : alk. paper) | ISBN 9781107495906 (paperback : alk. paper)
Subjects: LCSH: Insurance–Social aspects. | Risk.
Classification: LCC HG8026 .T46 2017 | DDC 368–dc23 LC record available at https://lccn.loc.gov/2016048282

ISBN 978-1-107-10033-6 Hardback
ISBN 978-1-107-49590-6 Paperback

To Zivile

Contents

Acknowledgements

My most important thanks are due to my colleagues Pradip Tapadar and MingJie Hao (PhD student 2013–17) at the University of Kent, whose work substantially underpins the central Chapters 4–6 in this book. Although the loss coverage idea was sketched in earlier papers,[1] my colleagues' work has substantially improved the presentation in this book. MingJie has also produced all the better graphs (the scruffier ones with obvious Excel provenance are mine). Our co-author Angus Macdonald of Heriot-Watt University added rigour to recent papers[2] which further underpin Chapters 4–6, albeit little of this rigour percolates the filter of informal presentation in this book.

My friends Andrew Howe and Pradip Tapadar made detailed comments on drafts of every chapter, which substantially improved the final manuscript. Other friends who commented on partial or complete drafts at various stages in this book's development include: Anthony Asher, Claire Bellis, Shauna Ferris, Brad Louis, Duncan Minty, Peter Siegelman, Leonie Tickle, Shane Whelan and David Wilkie.

Not all these readers have seen all chapters, and not all of their advice has been taken. The general tone of this book and all errors and inadequacies remain my own.

[1] Thomas (2008, 2009).
[2] Hao et al. (2016a, b).

Acknowledgments

Part I Introduction

I The Central Ideas of This Book

Key Ideas:
adverse selection; loss coverage

Discrimination is the taboo of our times. We often feel that it is unfair for a person's treatment to be determined by personal characteristics which have historically been used in oppressive ways, which are not perfectly predictive and which we do not choose. This sentiment is vaguely specified and inconsistently applied, but it is also pervasive, and now deeply embedded in our law and culture.

The insurance industry has traditionally claimed – and to a large extent, received – a degree of exemption from this sentiment. Insurance pricing is largely based on statistical discrimination, one of the practices which anti-discrimination laws often seek to restrain. So when first introduced, these laws typically included comprehensive exemptions for insurers. Over the years, some of these exemptions have been whittled away: many countries now limit insurers' use of genetic test results, and in Europe they can no longer charge different prices to men and women. Actuarial and economic orthodoxy generally derides such restrictions, and predicts that unfortunate consequences will flow from them.

A succinct statement of this orthodoxy is given in the policy document *Insurance & superannuation risk classification policy* published by the Institute of Actuaries of Australia, which explains:

> In the absence of a system that allows for distinguishing by
> price between individuals with different risk profiles, insurers

would provide an insurance or annuity product at a subsidy to some while overcharging others. In an open market, basic economics dictates that individuals with low risk relative to price would conclude that the product is overpriced and thus reduce or possibly forgo their insurance. Those individuals with a high level of risk relative to price would view the price as attractive and therefore retain or increase their insurance. As a result the average cost of the insurance would increase, thus pushing prices up. Then, individuals with lower loss potential would continue to leave the marketplace, contributing to a further price spiral. Eventually the majority of consumers, or the majority of providers of insurance, would withdraw from the marketplace and the remaining products would become financially unsound.[1]

The pattern of people with lower risks buying less insurance and people with higher risks buying more insurance is called 'adverse selection'. This is said to lead to a rise in insurance prices and fall in numbers insured, followed by a further rise in prices and fall in numbers insured, and so on; the sequence is often labelled as an 'adverse selection spiral' or 'death spiral'. The lurid vocabulary reflects the fact that in the typical usage, adverse selection is not a quantified phenomenon, but rather a persuasive fable.

This fable has the seductive property of trivial sophistication: it is sufficiently simple for non-specialists to understand, and yet sufficiently sophisticated to make them feel a little smart and insightful for understanding it. But the fable is often an exaggerated and unnecessarily negative description of reality, and hence a distorting and malign influence on public policy. This book seeks to promote a more nuanced understanding of adverse selection in insurance.

---

[1] Institute of Actuaries of Australia (1994).

Three Main Differences

Insurance textbooks typically represent adverse selection as a severe problem in all insurance markets, which should always be avoided, minimised or deprecated. Some typical examples are as follows:

> The business of insurance inherently involves discrimination; otherwise adverse selection would make insurance unavailable.
>
> (Baronoff, 2003, p. 77)

> Adverse selection ... is an ever present fact in the insurance market.
>
> (Dorfman, 2002, p. 29)

> Adverse selection ... plagues insurers worldwide.
>
> (Black et al., 2013)

This book is critical of the orthodoxy illustrated by these quotations. Those who are indignant at my perceived heresies may tend to read into them a more extreme 'straw-man' version of the claims I actually make. I therefore state succinctly here the three main differences from orthodoxy in this book – one empirical and two normative – and some important limits on those differences:

(a) Adverse selection in insurance is usually weaker than most commentary suggests. (But I do not say that adverse selection is always unimportant, or that insurers should not be vigilant about it.)
(b) From a public policy perspective, 'weak' adverse selection in insurance is a good thing. This is because a degree of adverse selection is needed to maximise loss coverage, the expected losses compensated by insurance for the whole population. (But I do not say that adverse selection of any severity is always good.)
(c) To induce the degree of adverse selection which maximises loss coverage, some restrictions on risk classification are a good thing in some insurance markets. (But I do not say that all restrictions are always a good thing, or that all risk classification should be banned.)

The remainder of this book emphasises the differences, and does not dwell on their limits. My presentational style leans towards what the economist Paul Romer recently labelled 'Stigler conviction', following George Stigler's advice 60 years ago that 'new economic theories are introduced by the technique of the huckster ... [but] ... they are not the work of mere hucksters'.[2]

Scope and Focus

The term 'insurance' can encompass many transactions and arrangements between parties of varying status and sophistication. My focus is on personal insurances, particularly those contingent in some way on the insured's life or health – life insurance, annuities, income protection insurance, critical illness insurance and health insurance (medical expenses insurance). For these insurances, higher risks often face not only *prospective* disadvantage, but also some degree of *current* disadvantage (e.g. some degree of current ill-health). To a lesser extent, I also have in mind other personal insurances, such as travel, home and car insurance. I do not focus on insurances where the insured is a corporation of comparable strategic sophistication to the insurer, or where the insured views the contract as part of a speculative investment portfolio, rather than as protection against some unlikely and undesirable contingency.[3]

Intuitions about public policy, and particularly perceptions of fairness in risk classification, are highly sensitive to this scope and focus. A common but unimpressive response to advocacy of restrictions on risk classification in (say) life insurance is a question along the lines, 'Ah, but would you say the same for property insurance? Or marine, aviation or spacecraft insurance?' The insinuation is that if one would *not* say the same for all classes of insurance, then this indicates some inconsistency in one's thinking. But there is usually no inconsistency; the comparison is merely capricious. I see no reason why a preference for some restrictions of risk classification in one social context (say life insurance) should necessarily be

----

[2] Stigler (1955, p. 296).

[3] Life annuities and pensions are sometimes viewed as investments, but a better view is that they represent insurance against the unlikely and (financially) undesirable contingency of outliving one's assets.

accompanied by a preference for identical restrictions in some other very different commercial context (say aviation insurance). In this book, I usually have in mind personal insurances contingent in some way on the insured's life or health.

Adverse Selection and Loss Coverage

While this book critiques orthodoxy about adverse selection from a number of perspectives, the main innovation is the concept of loss coverage. The following paragraphs sketch the argument; more detail is given from Chapter 3 onwards.

Consider an insurance market where individuals can be divided into two risk-groups, one higher risk and one lower risk, based on information which is fully observable by insurers. Assume that all losses and insurance are of unit amount (this simplifies the discussion, but it is not necessary). Also assume that an individual's risk is unaffected by the purchase of insurance, i.e. there is no moral hazard.

If insurers can, they will charge risk-differentiated prices to reflect the different risks. If instead insurers are banned from differentiating between higher and lower risks, and have to charge a single 'pooled' price for all risks, a pooled price equal to the simple average of the risk-differentiated prices will seem cheap to higher risks and expensive to lower risks. Higher risks will buy more insurance, and lower risks will buy less.

To break even, insurers will then need to raise the pooled price above the simple average of the prices. Also, since the number of higher risks is typically smaller than the number of lower (or 'standard') risks, higher risks buying more and lower risks buying less implies that the total number of people insured usually falls. This combination of a rise in price and a fall in demand is usually portrayed as a bad outcome, for both insurers and society.

However, from a social perspective, it is arguable that higher risks are those more in need of insurance. Also, the compensation of many types of loss by insurance appears to be widely regarded as a desirable objective, which public policymakers often seek to promote, by public education, by exhortation and sometimes by incentives such as tax relief on premiums. Insurance of one higher risk contributes more in expectation to this objective than insurance of one lower risk. This suggests that public policymakers might welcome increased purchasing by higher risks, except for the usual story about adverse selection.

The usual story about adverse selection overlooks one point: with a pooled premium and adverse selection, expected losses compensated by insurance can still be *higher* than with fully risk-differentiated premiums and no adverse selection. Although pooling leads to a fall in numbers insured, it also leads to a shift in coverage towards higher risks. From a public policymaker's viewpoint, this means that more of the 'right' risks – those more likely to suffer loss – buy insurance. If the shift in coverage is large enough, it can more than outweigh the fall in numbers insured. This result of higher expected losses compensated by insurance – higher 'loss coverage' – can be seen as a better outcome for society than that obtained with no adverse selection.

Toy Example

The argument above can be illustrated by a toy example, in the same spirit as dice-rolling examples to illustrate probability rules.

Consider a population of just ten risks (say lives), with two alternative scenarios for adverse selection. First, risk-differentiated prices are charged, and a subset of the population buys insurance. Second, risk classification is banned, leading to adverse selection: a different (smaller) subset of the population buys insurance. The two scenarios are represented in the upper and lower parts of Figure 1.1.

In Figure 1.1, each 'H' represents one high risk and each 'L' represents one low risk. The population has the typical predominance of lower risks: eight lower risks each with probability of loss 0.01, and two higher risks each with probability of loss 0.04. In each scenario, the shaded 'cover' above some of the 'H' and 'L' denotes the risks covered by insurance.

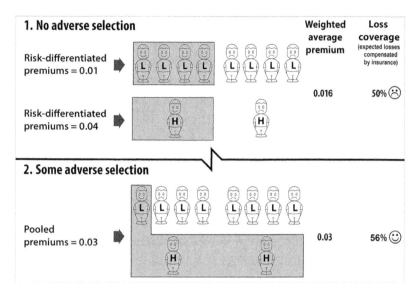

FIGURE 1.1 Two scenarios for risk classification

In Scenario 1, in the upper part of Figure 1.1, risk-differentiated premiums are charged. Higher and lower risk-groups each face a price equivalent to their probability of loss (an *actuarially fair* price). The demand response of each risk-group to an actuarially fair price is the same: exactly half the members of each risk-group buy insurance. The shading shows that a total of five risks are covered. Note that the equal areas of shading over one 'H' and four 'L' represent equal expected losses.

The weighted average of the premiums paid in Scenario 1 is $(4 \times 0.01 + 1 \times 0.04)/5 = 0.016$. Since higher and lower risks are insured in the same proportion as they exist in the population, there is no adverse selection. The expected losses compensated by insurance for the whole population can be indexed by:

$$\text{Loss coverage} = \frac{(4 \times 0.01 + 1 \times 0.04)}{(8 \times 0.01 + 2 \times 0.04)} = 50\% \tag{1.1}$$

In Scenario 2, in the lower part of Figure 1.1, risk classification has been banned, and so insurers have to charge a common 'pooled' premium to both higher and lower risks. Higher risks buy more insurance, and lower risks buy less. The shading shows that three risks (compared with five previously) are now covered. The pooled premium is set as the weighted average of the true risks, so that expected profits on low risks exactly offset expected losses on high risks. This weighted average premium is $(1 \times 0.01 + 2 \times 0.04)/3 = 0.03$.

Note that the weighted average premium is higher in Scenario 2, and the number of risks insured is smaller. These are the essential features of adverse selection, which Scenario 2 accurately and completely represents. But there is a surprise: despite the adverse selection in Scenario 2, the expected losses compensated by insurance for the whole population are now larger. Visually, this is represented by the larger area of shading in Scenario 2. Arithmetically, the loss coverage in Scenario 2 is:

$$\text{Loss coverage} = \frac{(1 \times 0.01 + 2 \times 0.04)}{(8 \times 0.01 + 2 \times 0.04)} = 56\% \qquad (1.2)$$

This book argues that Scenario 2, with a higher expected fraction of the population's losses compensated by insurance, is superior from a social viewpoint to Scenario 1. The superiority of Scenario 2 arises not *despite* adverse selection, but *because of* adverse selection.[4]

This very simple example may not have wholly convinced the reader. But I hope that Scenario 2 – where something good seems to be happening with adverse selection – has at least intrigued you. The key idea is that loss coverage – the expected losses compensated by insurance for the whole population – is increased by a degree of

---

[4] At this point an economist might typically observe that in Scenario 2 three risks are covered compared with five in Scenario 1, and say that this reduction in cover demonstrates that Scenario 2 is 'inefficient'. However, in Scenario 2 the quantum of risk transferred is 0.09 units ($2 \times 0.04 + 1 \times 0.01$), compared with 0.08 units in Scenario 1 ($1 \times 0.04 + 4 \times 0.01$). It seems surprising that an arrangement where more risk is voluntarily traded and more losses are compensated is disparaged as 'inefficient'.

adverse selection. Loss coverage seems a reasonable metric for the social efficacy of insurance, and for comparing alternative risk classification schemes. Hence this book argues that insurance works better with some adverse selection.

Some readers may already have noticed that if the adverse selection progresses beyond Scenario 2 to its logical extreme, so that only a single higher risk remains insured, then loss coverage will be lower than with no adverse selection. This point will be addressed in Chapters 3–6. For now, I merely reiterate that this book's message is one of moderation: it says that insurance works better with *some* adverse selection, not with *any amount* of adverse selection.[5]

Outline

Part I: Introduction

In the remainder of Part I of this book, Chapter 2 describes the history of exaggerated predictions in policy debates about adverse selection, with particular reference to HIV testing, genetic testing, gender classification and racial classification. The documented history of exaggeration motivates the development of a more nuanced account.

Part II: Loss Coverage

Part II covers loss coverage. Chapter 3 uses only elementary arithmetic; Chapters 4–6 are more technical. Readers who are not concerned with technical details may prefer to skip Chapters 4–6, or perhaps just skim the graphs and end-of-chapter summaries.

Chapter 3 gives more detailed and realistic numerical examples than the toy example in this chapter, showing that while loss

---

[5] To anticipate another point which might occur to an economist: the toy example does not encompass the possibility that insurers 'screen' high and low risks by offering contracts with different levels of deductible priced at different rates. My reasons are explained in Chapter 10: essentially, I see little evidence that insurers in the real world actually do this.

coverage is increased by the 'right amount' of adverse selection, it can be reduced if there is 'too much' adverse selection. This chapter also places loss coverage in context, relating it to other concepts in insurance theory.

Chapter 4 gives mathematical definitions for loss coverage, adverse selection and related quantities. It also presents graphical plots of loss coverage against adverse selection. The inverted U-shape of these graphs (indicating that loss coverage is maximised by an intermediate degree of adverse selection) is probably the most important visual image in this book.

Chapter 5 covers mathematical models of insurance markets. These facilitate an exploration of how loss coverage varies with changes in the low-risk and high-risk population sizes, probabilities of loss and demand elasticities.

Chapter 6 considers loss coverage under 'partial risk classification', that is with intermediate classification schemes in between complete pooling and fully risk-differentiated premiums. For comparing different risk classification schemes, I propose a novel metric, the 'separation' of a risk classification scheme, and its complement, the 'inclusivity' of a risk classification scheme.

Part III: Further Aspects of Risk Classification

Part III covers a variety of further aspects of risk classification. This material is more opinionated and less technically dense than Part II, and may be more readable and engaging to casual readers.

Chapter 7 gives a taxonomy of reasons why particular methods of risk classification may be considered objectionable. There are two broad groups of reasons. First, *insufficient inclusivity* – too much or too little pooling of dissimilar risks, resulting in suboptimal loss coverage. Second, *misguided methods* – even if the overall degree of pooling of dissimilar risks produces the highest feasible loss coverage, particular classification methods may be objectionable on various ethical, technical or practical grounds.

Chapter 8 examines empirical evidence for the existence of adverse selection in various insurance contexts, which turns out to be surprisingly weak compared with the strong predictions of orthodox insurance theory. From the perspective of this book's main argument, this is a hopeful state of affairs, since 'weak' adverse selection is needed to maximise loss coverage.

Chapter 9, on myths of insurance rhetoric, explains ways in which adverse selection is often exaggerated and excessively maligned in policy debates. There are four main groups of ways: genuine misperceptions, strategic misrepresentations, rhetorical affectations and cognitive capture.

Chapter 10, on myths of insurance economics, appraises some themes which are pervasive in accounts of adverse selection and risk classification in insurance economics, but for which real-world evidence is lacking. These include the concepts that different levels of deductibles are used by insurers to separate high and low risks; that insurance is 'rationed' for low risks, while full cover is available for high risks; and that tax-and-subsidy schemes are always better from society's viewpoint than risk classification bans.

Chapter 11 considers contexts where one of the main points of this book – that adverse selection is usually weaker than most commentary suggests – may be less valid. These contexts are of two types: (a) the customer has a large 'information edge', defined as the *difference* (not the ratio) of a true probability based on the customer's private information, and a probability used by the insurer to set premiums or (b) the customer can engage in multiple independent transactions, either in parallel (diversification) or in sequence (repetition).

Chapter 12 discusses the concept of moral hazard in insurance. As with adverse selection, moral hazard is typically deprecated, but I argue that there is an optimal non-zero level of moral hazard.

Chapter 13 considers new surveillance technologies and the big data they can collect. To the extent that big data allows insurers to reduce the inclusivity of risk classification, this might reduce loss coverage, if adverse selection is reduced too much. Hence technical advances in the collection and analysis of big data are possible reasons for considering new controls on insurance risk classification.

Part IV: Conclusion

Chapter 14 concludes this book with a summary of the main points, and suggestions for public policymakers, economists and actuaries.

2 Adverse Selection: A History of Exaggeration

Key Ideas:

HIV tests; genetic tests; gender classification; racial classification; increasing discrimination over time

In the examples in Chapter 1, two regimes for risk classification were considered: either insurers charged risk-differentiated prices for high and low risks; or risk classification was banned, so that insurers had to charge a common pooled price to all risks. The latter regime induced some adverse selection, but also higher loss coverage (expected losses compensated by insurance); I argued that this was a better outcome for society as a whole. This surprising phenomenon of 'beneficial adverse selection' does not hold without limit. We shall see from Chapter 3 onwards that maximising loss coverage requires not *unlimited* adverse selection, but the *right amount* of adverse selection. This in turn requires the *right amount* of risk classification. This book treats adverse selection and risk classification as matters of degree.

Many commentators do not treat risk classification and adverse selection as matters of degree, but as matters of dogma. They say that any degree of adverse selection is always detrimental; that more risk classification is always better than less; and that any restriction on risk classification – for example, banning classification on a particular variable, such as gender or genetic tests – will always have dire consequences. Some grain of truth underlies each of these assertions, insofar as *too little* risk classification leading to *too much* adverse selection does indeed produce a bad outcome for society. But each of these assertions is often made in an unqualified and exaggerated form.

This chapter sets the context for the rest of this book by documenting the long history of such exaggerations, which have collectively created the myth of insurance adverse selection as an overwhelming force of darkness. I focus on four risk variables[1] which have often attracted particular controversy: HIV tests, genetic tests, gender classification and racial classification.

Because this chapter is concerned with history, it necessarily quotes from a range of articles, press releases and other policy documents, some as recent as 2014 but others up to two decades old. In many cases the individuals and organisations quoted might no longer endorse their past views, or might today express more nuanced opinions. My purpose in such extensive quotation is not to call for contemporary censure of, or justification from, the authors whom I quote, but rather to substantiate the history of exaggeration which provides the context for this book.

Background: Principles of Insurance Pricing

This section gives a recap on basic principles of insurance pricing and risk classification. Readers with good prior knowledge may prefer to skip this section.

Assume a population of 100 individuals, each facing the same potential loss amount, and each with the same probability of say 15% over 1 year. Insurers can break even by offering insurance over 1 year at a premium of 15% of the potential loss.[2] Because all individuals have the same probability of loss, insurance can be offered to

---

[1] Throughout this book, I shall use the term 'risk variables' (or occasionally, where the context is unambiguous, just 'variables') to refer to the criteria used in risk classification. Some common synonyms are 'risk factors' and 'rating factors'. I prefer 'variables' because in Chapter 13, I shall wish to distinguish between *variables* and *observations*, that is the values which the variables take for a particular person.

[2] In practice, the insurer will allow for investment returns on funds held, and add some margin (sometimes called a 'loading') above 15% for administrative costs and profit. But risk pricing and classification principles are clearer if we abstract from the investment and expenses elements of pricing, and I shall do so throughout this book.

all comers at the same price. Each insurer pools all premiums it collects in single fund, from which payouts are made to 15% of customers who actually incur a loss. Because all individuals have the same probability of loss, insurers are not concerned that those who choose to buy insurance might have different characteristics from those who do not.

Now suppose instead that although all individuals face the same potential loss amount, there are five different probabilities of loss, 5%, 10%, 15%, 20% and 25%, with 20 individuals having each probability of loss. The average probability of loss is still 15%. If insurers offer insurance at a premium of 15%, the insurance may be seen as cheap by individuals whose probability of loss is 20% or 25%, and expensive by individuals whose probability of loss is 5% or 10%. Those who choose to buy may therefore be skewed towards those with higher probabilities of loss. This skew in insurance buyers towards individuals with higher probabilities of loss is called adverse selection.

If insurers facing adverse selection pool the skewed group of individuals with five different probabilities of loss in a single fund and price insurance at the 15% average probability of loss over the whole population of 100 individuals, the insurers will make losses. For a pooled fund to break even, the insurance price needs to correspond to the average probability of loss not for all 100 individuals, but rather for *those who choose to buy insurance at that price*. This is likely to be rather higher than 15%. For example, if *all* the 25% and 20% risks, and *half of* the 15% risks, but *none* of the 5% or 10% risks, choose to buy insurance when a single price is charged, the break-even price is $(20 \times 25\% + 20 \times 20\% + 10 \times 15\%)/50 = 21\%$.

There may be an alternative to this pooling of different risks in a single fund. If insurers can distinguish the higher risks from the lower risks, they can pool approximately similar risks in separate sub-funds (which we shall call *risk-groups*), and charge a different price to each risk-group, set to achieve break-even for the buyers in that risk-group. For example, suppose the 20% and 25% risks are all men under age 30; the 5% and 10% risks are all women over age 50 and the 15% risks are men or women between the ages of 30 and 50. Then if insurers can observe prospective customers' age and gender, they can allocate the risks to three risk-groups for 'low', 'medium' and 'high' risks, and charge different prices to individuals in each risk-group. This classification process is called *risk classification* (or sometimes *underwriting*).

What premiums do insurers need to charge to the 'low', 'medium' and 'high' risk-groups to break even? The break-even premium for the 'medium' risk-group with probability of loss 15% is obviously 15%. For the 'low' and 'high' risk-groups pooling (5% and 10%) and (20% and 25%) risks, respectively, the break-even premiums may be skewed towards the loss probability at the upper end of each risk-group, reflecting some adverse selection within the group. Suppose only two-thirds as many of the 5% risks compared with the 10% risks buy insurance, and the same for the 20% risks compared with the 25% risks. The break-even premiums for the low and high risk-groups would then be 8% and 23% (i.e. slightly above the midpoints of each risk-group, 7½% and 22½%).[3]

Where risks differ very substantially between individuals, insurance may not work well without *some* degree of risk classification. To give an extreme example, life insurance is unlikely to work well in a completely age-blind regime, where the same premium rate is offered to a 20-year-old and a 90-year-old. Under such an age-blind regime, the pooled price which insurers need to charge to break even may be very high, with mainly very elderly people buying insurance. Life insurance may then be largely ineffectual in providing financial security to younger families. So *some* degree of risk classification generally makes insurance work better.

But *how much* risk classification? In the scenario above, the insurer was able to observe customers' age and gender, and thereby

---

[3] The calculations are: (⅔ × 5% + 1 × 10%)/1⅔ = 8%, and (⅔ × 20% + 1 × 25%)/1⅔ = 23%.

separate the risks into three risk-groups: low (5% and 10% risks), medium (15% risks) and high (20% and 25% risks). Now suppose that a new classification technology is developed which enables insurers to separate the risks into five risk-groups, one for each of the five levels of risk from 5% to 25%. Would this be better or worse than using three risk-groups?

From the perspective of a single insurer competing with other insurers in a market where risk classification is unregulated, using five risk-groups is likely to be better than using three risk-groups – or if not better, at least prudently defensive of its competitive position. This is because once *some* insurers adopt the new classification, their lower prices for the 5% risks and 20% risks, compared with the pooled prices of 8% and 23% which other insurers charge to those risks under the three risk-group regime, may attract most of the 5% and 20% risks. Insurers still using the crude 'low', 'medium' and 'high' risk-group regime will then be left with a higher proportion of 10% and 25% risks in their 'low' and 'high' risk-groups than they anticipated, and may therefore make losses in those risk-groups. Thus once some insurers adopt the new five risk-group regime, competitive pressures encourage all insurers to do so.[4]

From a public policy perspective, however, it is not obvious that the new classification technology facilitating five risk-groups rather than three risk-groups gives a better result for society as a whole. The use of five risk-groups will eliminate the adverse selection which previously existed in the 'low' and 'high' risk-groups. But the example in Chapter 1 suggested that some degree of adverse selection can make insurance work better, in the sense that the expected losses compensated by insurance for the whole population is increased (loss coverage is increased). It is possible that moving

---

[4] This is 'competitive adverse selection', which arises when competing insurers use *different* classification methods. It is not the same as 'informational adverse selection', which arises when competing insurers are all subject to the *same* ban on particular classification methods. This important distinction will be elaborated in Chapter 8.

from three risk-groups to five risk-groups reduces loss coverage. Whether this is in fact so depends on the responses of the various risk-groups to changes in the prices they face (technically, the *demand elasticities* of the various risk-groups).

The principles of insurance pricing and risk classification as sketched above suggest that from society's viewpoint, optimal risk classification is a question of degree. We saw in Chapter 1 that *some* adverse selection gives a better outcome for society as a whole; we shall see in Chapter 3 that *too much* adverse selection can make things worse. A common distortion of these principles is to assert that more risk classification is always better than less, and to predict that any limits on risk classification will have dire consequences for society as a whole. As one lawyer has put it, 'actuaries are sometimes like the boy who cried wolf when it comes to adverse selection'.[5] The rest of this chapter presents examples of such exaggerated predictions.

HIV Tests

When David Hurlbert, a San Francisco business consultant, sought to renew his health insurance[6] in 1986, Great Republic Life Insurance Company asked a few extra questions. In the past six months, had he suffered from a sexually transmitted disease? Or an immune disorder? Or had he lost weight recently? The company required its sales force to ask these extra questions of 'single males without dependents ... in occupations that do not require physical exertion'. Hurlbert didn't answer the questions; he sued Great Republic for discriminating against gay men. In a settlement of the litigation in 1990, Great Republic paid a total of $85,000 to Hurlbert and two law firms representing him, and agreed to stop attempting

---

[5] Hall (1999).

[6] Throughout this book, I use the American terminology of 'health insurance' for insurance which reimburses hospital charges, doctors' fees for service, etc. Equivalent terminologies prevalent in the UK include 'private medical insurance' and 'medical expenses insurance'.

to identity customers' sexual orientation as part of its insurance underwriting.[7]

As can be seen from this anecdote, in the 1980s the insurance industry worldwide was alarmed by the rise of HIV and AIDS. Starting in about 1985, premium rates for single men were substantially increased, and HIV tests were required for all policies above a modest size. In health-related insurances, any AIDS-related illness was subject to exclusions (meaning that no benefit would be paid for such illnesses). For many years, most insurers declined to provide any life insurance to men whom they suspected might be gay. Insurers who did offer cover charged premiums at twice or more standard rates.

Insurers attempted to make inferences about applicants' sexual orientation not only from direct questions, but also from circumstantial evidence such as joint house purchase and casual stereotyping of occupations. The company in the anecdote above, Great Republic, directed its agents to highlight applications from 'restaurant employees, antique dealers, interior decorators, consultants, florists, and people in the jewelry or fashion business'.[8] All applicants were asked whether they had ever taken a HIV test. Negative as well as positive HIV test results were used as justification for refusing insurance, on the grounds that where the test was negative, the fact that the individual had sought testing indicated higher risk. The catch-22 nature of this rationale attracted a great deal of criticism, because it seemed likely to discourage people from taking HIV tests, and so promote transmission of the virus. Eventually, in 1994, the Association of British Insurers banned the practice in the UK; since then, questions have referred only to 'testing positive' or 'awaiting the results of a test'.

For justification of these policies, insurers pointed to projections produced by actuarial professional associations. Figure 2.1 shows the

---

[7] 'Who will pay the AIDS bill?' *Newsweek*, 11 April 1988. Settlement details from Li (1996), footnote 83.

[8] Great Republic Insurance Company memorandum, cited in Schatz (1987).

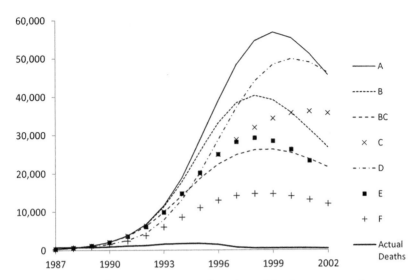

FIGURE 2.1 The 1987 projections of numbers of deaths per annum from AIDS (A highest, F lowest) versus actual deaths (lowest solid line, barely visible above x-axis)
Source: Daykin et al. (1988) for projections and Health Protection Agency (2004) for actual deaths

projections produced by an Institute and Faculty of Actuaries[9] working party in 1987 for the numbers of deaths per annum from AIDS in the UK. Six projections from A (highest) to F (lowest) were given, with peak deaths ranging from 15,000 per annum up to almost 60,000 per annum. The actual numbers of deaths from AIDS in the UK in each year are shown by the lowest line barely visible at the bottom of Figure 2.1. Deaths from AIDS in the UK peaked at less than 2,000 per annum in the mid-1990s – around one-tenth the *lowest* projection (projection F) – and have fluctuated in the range 400–600 per annum since around 2000.

[9] 'Institute and Faculty of Actuaries' is the name currently adopted by the professional body for actuaries in the UK. I use this name throughout this book, to refer to both the current body and its predecessors, the Faculty of Actuaries of Edinburgh and the Institute of Actuaries of London. Prior to their formal merger in 2010, the predecessor bodies had operated largely as one at least since the mid-1980s, with common examinations, working parties and press releases and other publications.

The lowest prediction for deaths from AIDS in the UK was too high by a factor of 10, and the highest prediction was too high by a factor of 30. This in itself is not necessarily worthy of criticism. In its early stages in the mid-1980s, the ultimate spread of the AIDS epidemic was extremely unpredictable. Based on experience at the time, survival periods after diagnosis with AIDS were believed to be very short, with perhaps 10% surviving three years.[10] Although the predicted deaths turned out to be much too high with hindsight, the exaggerated early response to AIDS may have been more justifiable than the response a decade later to the introduction of a small number of genetic tests, which *from an early stage* were clearly likely to be immaterial to insurance.

However, what may be more justifiably criticised in relation to AIDS is the reluctance to acknowledge in the 1990s that earlier predictions had been overstated, and to update insurance practices and recommendations accordingly. Questions about sexual orientation were still being used to reject or rate customers in the early 2000s, by which time it was clear that AIDS was wholly insignificant for insurance in the UK. The Association of British Insurers eventually issued a recommendation against questions about sexual orientation only in 2004. Even today, many insurers continue to apply exclusions so that no payment is made for any HIV-related illness under critical illness and income protection policies, which the Association of British Insurers continues to promote as 'best practice'.[11] There is no justification for this in the pattern or prevalence of HIV-related illness, and no reason why HIV-related illness should not now be treated like any other illness.

In summary, most predictions of the effects of HIV and AIDS on insurance prices in the UK were substantially overstated.

---

[10] Kerr (1989) gives this figure.

[11] Association of British Insurers (2005, 2011). Exclusions are not applied in life insurance for practical reasons: a death certificate may not mention HIV or AIDS, only their sequelae; and the insurer cannot obtain an HIV test result for the deceased.

The exceptional (and now quite unjustified) treatment of HIV-related illnesses continues to this day. The range of predictions promulgated by the Institute and Faculty of Actuaries was between 10 and 30 times too high. HIV and AIDS did not have the large adverse selection effects which were widely predicted.[12]

Genetic Tests

After HIV and AIDS, the next phenomenon to attract adverse selection concerns from the mid-1990s onwards was the perceived threat to insurance companies from not knowing the results of any genetic tests which had been taken by insurance applicants. Figure 2.2 shows the annual number of mentions of the phrase 'genetics and insurance' in English language news items in one online news database. The peak in the early 2000s reflects excessive adverse selection concerns, which later experience has largely negated.

The decline in comment since the early 2000s reflects a consensus in many countries around legislative or quasi-legislative bans on insurers asking questions about any pre-symptomatic genetic tests insurance applicants may have taken. In the UK, a voluntary restriction by insurers has been extended several times, most recently (at the time of writing) to 2019.[13] Laws restricting the ability of insurers to use genetic tests have been enacted in many

[12] The commentary in this chapter refers specifically to HIV infection and AIDS *in the UK*. HIV infection is a bigger problem in sub-Saharan Africa: for example in South Africa, around 11% of the population was estimated to be living with AIDS in 2010. It is also qualitatively different, with transmission being primarily heterosexual and vertical (from mother to child). While the scale of the epidemic is bigger than in the UK, it does not necessarily follow that actuarial forecast errors have had the opposite sign. In South Africa, too, past forecasts appear to have been exaggerated. For example, Actuarial Society of South Africa forecasts for deaths from AIDS in 2010 halved between the 2003 and 2008 model updates. However, the steep fall in updated forecasts is suggestive of an appropriate response to emerging evidence. Source: Actuarial Society of South Africa press release, 9 March 2011. actuaries.org.za, accessed 1 November 2015.

[13] The officially favoured term is not a 'ban' but a 'moratorium'; the document which describes the ban is not an agreement, but a 'concordat'. While this terminology may be technically precise, the effect (and perhaps the intention) of its obscurity is to limit public understanding of the rules.

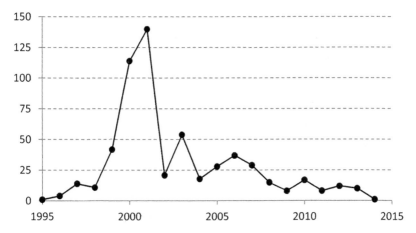

FIGURE 2.2 Annual numbers of mentions of 'genetics and insurance' in English-language news items worldwide
Source: Figures extracted from Nexis UK database

European countries, including Austria, Belgium, Denmark, France, Norway, Sweden and the Netherlands. The prediction by many insurance experts around the millennium that use of genetic test results would imminently become essential for insurance companies' survival now seems exaggerated or misconceived.

The argument often put forward around the millennium was that people with some knowledge of genetic predisposition to illness would routinely seek to buy large amounts of life insurance. For example, a press release from the Institute and Faculty of Actuaries in July 1999 said:

> Bans [on insurers using genetic test results] have already been imposed in some countries, such as Denmark, Netherlands, Norway and a number of states of the USA (e.g. California), leaving the way open for people with knowledge of their genetic condition to take advantage of insurance companies, thus pushing up the cost for everyone.[14]

[14] Institute and Faculty of Actuaries press release dated 26 July 1999. Copy held in author's files.

Actuarial associations in the USA made similar claims. In a letter dated 16 February 2007 lobbying the then Speaker of the House, Nancy Pelosi, against the Genetic Information Non-discrimination Act,[15] the American Academy of Actuaries wrote:

> A ban on the use of genetic information ... would have a direct effect on premium rates, ultimately raising the cost of insurance to everyone.[16]

For people with knowledge of their genetic condition to 'take advantage' of insurance companies, they must pay *less* than they would pay if the insurance companies knew of their condition; the cost of insurance is *not* raised 'for everyone'. The assertion that insurance becomes more expensive 'for everyone' makes no sense – until one understands that for many actuaries, the ontological concept of 'everyone' excludes persons with genetic disadvantages.

Despite the absurdity of such claims, they found a receptive audience among policymakers around the millennium. Indeed the UK government seemed to accept fully actuaries' claims that the use of genetic tests would imminently become indispensable in insurance. Popular opinion was, however, quite hostile to this concept.[17] To bridge the gulf between popular and expert opinion, in 1998 the government established a Genetics and Insurance Committee (GAIC). The GAIC was to consider applications from insurers supported by actuarial evidence for the permission to use particular tests. It was said to be predicated on the following rationales (as expressed by the Department of Health in response to a Parliamentary Committee report in 2001):

> The Government recognises the legitimate concerns of insurance companies over the consequences of 'adverse selection' where

---

[15] The Act became law in 2008.

[16] American Academy of Actuaries. Letter to Nancy Pelosi. www.actuary.org, accessed 20 July 2014.

[17] For example, the *British Social Attitudes 16th Report* (Jowell et al., 1999) found that most respondents were strongly opposed to the use of genetic tests by insurance companies.

individuals with adverse test results take out larger than usual amounts of insurance cover in the expectation of an early claim and a substantial payout.

The Government is aware of insurers' concerns about the risk of adverse selection and supports the continued assessment by GAIC of applications for the use of genetic test results.[18]

The concerns of insurance companies were not in fact legitimate, and the *raison d'être* of GAIC – that genetic discrimination in insurance could be justified by extant actuarial evidence – was wholly misconceived. This was starkly demonstrated by the fact that after a single much-criticised approval for a test for Huntington's disease in life insurance in October 2000, GAIC never received any further applications for test approval from insurers. The actuarial evidence which GAIC's terms of reference envisaged would be presented by insurers simply did not exist, and could not be produced to order, despite very strong ideological motivations for insurers to do so. As a result GAIC became moribund, and was eventually disbanded in 2009.

Even if GAIC had succeeded in approving more tests, it might not have succeeded in its underlying purpose of promoting public acceptance of genetic discrimination. In announcements by or about GAIC, it was never explained why the State's endorsement of genetic discrimination should reassure those who would thereby be disadvantaged. On the contrary, the concept of genetic discrimination endorsed by a State body seemed ominously evocative of eugenic projects such as Nazi Germany's obsession with 'genetically defective' individuals, and analogous sterilisation programmes in the USA and Scandinavia. As an official arbiter of genetic discrimination, GAIC itself was an uncomfortably close analogue of the 'Genetic Health

---

[18] Department of Health (2001).

Courts' established to provide a scientific imprimatur to genetic discrimination in Germany in the 1930s (albeit GAIC's initial powers were fortunately less wide-ranging). In these senses, the concept of State approval via a body such as GAIC might increase rather than reduce alarm about discrimination.[19]

The concept of GAIC may not have originated in government; something like it seems to have originally been proposed to the Department of Health by the Association of British Insurers.[20] I surmise that the concept had its origins in contemporary understanding about genetics and adverse selection in the insurance industry. To assess this understanding, it is useful to examine contemporary articles written for discussion among semiprivate insider groups of experts. Many such articles were even more alarmist than public pronouncements. A portentously titled discussion paper on 'The freedom to underwrite' discussed before a large audience at the headquarters of the Institute and Faculty of Actuaries in 1996 included the following remarks:

> If genetic history is banned on proposals, adverse selection becomes a major issue.
>
> I would agree but it could herald the end of life assurance as we know it.
>
> My own feeling is that the government should outlaw all forms of home and postal testing ... The industry will have terrible problems if legislation does not take place.
>
> Recently, some preserved samples from the body of the US politician, Hubert Humphrey, have been tested. It has been discovered that his bladder cancer could have been diagnosed with genetic testing over ten years before he had any symptoms.

---

[19] The establishment and operation of the Genetic Health Courts in Germany in the 1930s are described in Proctor (1988).

[20] This is based on correspondence I obtained in 2011 by requests to the Department of Health pursuant to the Freedom of Information Act.

Think of the damage individuals could inflict on the industry with such knowledge.

We have to protect ourselves and our existing policyholders from proposers who know the results of genetic or other tests which reveal a poor outlook.

Because of this, I believe that from a theoretical viewpoint and provided offices act responsibly, we are invariably right.[21]

The florid tone of these quotations exemplifies actuaries' paranoia in the mid-1990s about a supposedly existential threat to the insurance industry from people affected by genetic conditions. But questions about genetic tests have now been banned for over 15 years, with no discernible impact on the health of the insurance industry. And in my view, comments such as those quoted above were patently absurd even at the time. It was always clear that the non-disclosure of a small number of genetic tests never represented any realistic threat to the operation of insurance. This is not just hindsight. Here is what I wrote in response to a consultation by the Human Genetics Commission in early 2001:

Recent actuarial studies suggest that even under the most unfavourable assumptions, ignoring genetic tests and family history would have little effect on most insurance markets ... There should be a presumption against insurers' right of access to genetic tests, except for exceptionally large policies, or where insurers can show that ignoring tests would seriously disrupt the financial stability of insurance markets. All evidence to date suggests that under this criterion, little or no access to test results would be justified.[22]

By the middle of the 2000s, insurers' paranoia concerning genetic tests and insurance around the turn of the decade had substantially subsided. The predictions made a few years earlier could

---

[21] Leigh (1996).
[22] Thomas (2001).

now be seen by all to be grossly overstated. In 2001, the Institute and Faculty of Actuaries had predicted:

> There could be a substantial reduction in consumer choice though products becoming dearer or even with the withdrawal of some types of product.[23]

In fact, the lowest premiums for critical illness insurance *decreased* by about 20% over 10 years up to 2012. The lowest premiums for life insurance *decreased* by around 25% over the same period.[24] An exhaustive programme of bottom-up research (that is, considering various genetic conditions and aggregating the results) completed by 2011 in the Genetics and Insurance Centre at Heriot-Watt University suggested that the impact of banning genetic tests in life insurance can be expected to be less than 1% of premiums.[25]

Research and practical experience of genetics and insurance in the UK has not deterred actuaries in other jurisdictions from continuing to make fanciful claims. In 2014, the Canadian senate was considering a proposal whereby insurers would be banned from asking for genetic test results for life insurance cover of up to 1 million Canadian dollars, or benefits payable annually up to 75,000 Canadian dollars (these are similar limits to those which are applied in the UK).

---

[23] Institute and Faculty of Actuaries (2001a).

[24] Smith (2014), sourcing data from Moneyfacts. Life insurance premiums subsequently rose up to 10% in 2013, but this was attributable to a change in the tax treatment of life insurance business at the end of 2012. The mandatory introduction of unisex premiums from December 2012 also makes comparisons more difficult before and after this date. I do not suggest that the ban on genetic tests *caused* premiums to fall in the UK. It is more plausible that the provisions have been a very small upward influence on premiums. But any such influence has been imperceptibly small, and swamped by other influences on premiums.

[25] Macdonald and Yu (2011) summarise the conclusions of this research programme. Simulations by the economists Hoy et al. (2003) and Hoy and Witt (2007) reach essentially similar conclusions, for health insurance and life insurance, respectively.

The Canadian Institute of Actuaries issued a press release commenting as follows:

> A ban on using genetic tests is a bad idea. It hurts the vast majority of Canadians. The research shows that term insurance premium rates could go up by 30% for males and 50% for females.[26]

When considered against the experience in the UK, where life insurance premiums *decreased* by around 25% in the decade after the ban was introduced, the figures of 30% and 50% *increases* appear absurd. Such exaggerations can have real policy consequences: in this case, they were enough to dissuade the Canadian senate from passing the proposed legislation in December 2014.

Gender

Controversy about gender-based pricing predates both HIV testing and pre-symptomatic genetic testing. Differences between insurance risks for men and women are statistically well-evidenced, but generally much smaller than the differences attributable to some genetic predispositions or to HIV infection. Some restrictions on the use of gender in pricing have applied for many years, particularly in pensions. In the USA, higher pension contributions for women (reflecting their longer life expectancy) were outlawed by the Supreme Court as long ago as 1978. In the UK, a unisex requirement applied from 1988 onwards to pensions bought from insurers under 'contracting out' from the State pension scheme.[27] These rules did not apply for non-pension products.

However following a 2011 decision of European Court of Justice, insurers throughout the European Union were banned from charging different prices to men and women on all new policies issued after 21 December 2012. Prior to the ban, different countries

---

[26] Canadian Institute of Actuaries press release dated 14 July 2014. www.actuary.ca, accessed 21 July 2015.

[27] 'Contracting out' refers to arrangements under which part of a person's National Insurance contributions could be diverted to fund a private pension plan. This form of contracting out operated from 1988 until 2012.

adopted different approaches, with several already mandating unisex prices for at least some types of insurance.[28]

The wide variation in pre-existing rules across different European states, all with substantial insurance industries, made it easy to see that banning gender pricing would not create any insuperable difficulty for insurers. Nevertheless prior to the ban, insurers in European states where gender pricing was the norm made many florid predictions of the effects from a ban.

Some examples of such predictions were contained in a document *The use of gender in insurance pricing* published by the trade association Insurance Europe. Sample claims from this document are as follows:

> There are no reasonable alternatives to the use of gender in insurance pricing.
>
> This ... [unisex pricing] would be likely to jeopardise the future of numerous small and medium-sized enterprises (SMEs).[29]

Insurance companies are almost invariably substantial institutions; they are not SMEs. The reference to SMEs appears to be an 'applause light': a largely meaningless allusion which is made only because it is thought policymakers might be more sympathetic to SMEs than to the monolithic reality of most insurance companies. Nearly five years after the ban came into effect, I am not aware of any evidence that SMEs throughout Europe have been devastated by gender-neutral insurance pricing.

In a press release, the Institute & Faculty of Actuaries made the following predictions:

> If gender cannot be taken into account when setting premiums, young female drivers could face premiums of up to 50% higher

---

[28] European Commission (2011). This guidance on implementing the Gender Directive includes as Appendix 1 a comprehensive summary of the prevalence of gender-differentiated and gender-neutral rates across all EU countries prior to the ban.

[29] Insurance Europe (2011).

while young male drivers may benefit from reductions of around 25%.[30]

The Actuarial Association of Europe (previously known as the Groupe Consultatif), a pan-European group of actuarial professional associations, issued a press release claiming that banning gender pricing would increase prices for both men and women:

> The Groupe Consultatif Actuarial Européen has highlighted that gender is an important risk factor for insurance and that a prohibition on its use could increase costs for both men and women overall.
>
> The Groupe Consultatif believes that the impact of self-selection could be even greater for pensions business, leading to an increase in annuity costs for men but no discernible reduction in costs for women.[31]

The claim that prices would increase for both genders was similar in character to claims that restriction on access to genetic tests would raise prices 'for everyone'. In a competitive market, such claims are incoherent. This can be seen in detail from a simple thought experiment involving equalisation of annuity prices for men and women; analogous arguments apply for equalisation of insurance prices.

Suppose that before the gender ban, the price of an annuity of £1 per annum from age 65 is £10 for men and £12 for women, and equal numbers of men and women buy annuities. Assume all annuities are of the same amount (this simplifies the discussion, but is not necessary). After the ban, a first approximation of the pooled price is the simple average of £11. This is cheaper than before for women and dearer than before for men.

---

[30] Institute and Faculty of Actuaries (2010).

[31] Groupe Consultatif press release dated 13 October www.actuaries.org.cy, accessed 30 June 2014.

Suppose that as a result of this relative cheapness and dearness, more women and fewer men now buy annuities. This is adverse selection. Then to cover the total cost of annuity payments, the pooled price will need to be weighted away from the simple average of £11 and towards the previous price for women of £12.

How far towards £12 the price needs to be weighted depends on how far the male/female mix of annuity purchasers shifts from its original 50:50 proportion. But even if most men now decline to buy annuities, the weighted average price, reflecting a mix of predominantly females and fewer males, will still be less than the previous female price.

The claim that the pooled price will be *higher* than the previous price for the higher-cost gender can be true only if the ban is followed by a substantial increase in premiums which is unrelated to what insurers pay out in benefits. This is not plausible in a competitive market: if an insurer tries to enforce such an increase, it will be undercut by rivals. As far as I am aware, the 'more expensive for everyone' outcome has not been documented in any real market, anywhere in the world.

The actual effect of the gender ban can be seen in surveys conducted a few months after the ban. For car insurance, an index produced by aggregator website confused.com and actuarial consultants Towers Watson in October 2013 showed that after the ban, car insurance premiums for 17–20-year-olds had risen by 9% for women, but fallen by 29% for men.[32] Since very much more than half of aggregate premiums in this age group relate to men, this suggests that the average premium over both genders had fallen significantly. As with genetics, I do not suggest that the ban *caused* the average premium to fall, but only that any effect of the ban on the average premium over both genders was imperceptibly small, and swamped by other influences on premiums.

---

[32] Confused.com (2013).

Race

Much less needs to be said about pricing differences by racial origin than the other categories discussed in this chapter. There is evidence of racial discrimination in insurance in the past, but probably no more than would be expected from contemporary social attitudes.[33] In the UK, the Race Relations Act 1968 outlawed racial discrimination in the supply of all goods and services, and the Race Relations Act 1976 outlawed indirect discrimination; neither contained exemptions for insurance. In the USA, the statutory position is more ambiguous: insurance regulation is largely devolved to state level, and around half of states have no specific ban on racial classification in underwriting, at least for some classes of personal insurance.[34]

Nevertheless, in the USA as well as in the UK, nobody now argues that racial classification is important to the operation of insurance. When evidence of past racial classification has come to light in recent years, it appears to have been perceived by insurers as a source of embarrassment, rather than as a practice to be defended with arguments about adverse selection. For example, in the early 2000s a series of lawsuits in the USA alleged that blacks who had bought life insurance policies in the 1960s through 1980s were continuing to be charged 25% more than whites under those policies in the 2000s. Insurers appeared anxious to settle these cases with a minimum of publicity, rather than to defend the practices of the past.[35]

Although insurers no longer overtly defend racial classification, some insurers may continue it covertly. In 2010, the UK consumer organisation *Which?* obtained quotations from 19 insurers for two car

---

[33] In the UK, higher premiums for most insurance for ethnic minorities are reported to have been common and explicit in the 1960s (Leigh, 1996), and the actuarial literature acknowledges that some insurers were still loading premiums for the category 'persons of overseas birth' during the 1980s (Kennedy et al., 1987). In the USA, there is a long history of differential rates, often with expedients such as creating 'preferred' categories of risks, to which almost all blacks were assigned, or requiring additional application forms to be completed by blacks (Heen, 2009; Paltrow, 2000).

[34] Avraham et al. (2014).

[35] Paltrow (2000, 2001).

insurance scenarios. The only difference between the scenarios was whether the 50-year-old applicant had been born in the UK, or born overseas and moved to the UK at the age of 15. Most insurers quoted the same prices for both scenarios. But four brands owned by the FTSE100 insurer Admiral quoted prices an average of 18% higher for the applicant who had moved to the UK as a teenager.[36]

Differentiating premiums on this question is 'indirect' racial discrimination, that is, it is likely that a higher proportion of the white population can satisfy the requirement for a lower premium than ethnic minority populations. Under the Equality Act 2010, indirect racial discrimination could be lawfully justified only if the discriminatory act is a 'proportionate means of achieving a legitimate aim'. This seems unlikely in this example, particularly given the 'immigrated age 15, now age 50' detail of the test scenario, which precludes any argument that a recent immigrant might have lower familiarity with UK driving conditions. As far as I am aware, the point has not been tested in court.

Insurance Discrimination Is Gradually Increasing

Insurers and their advocates often assert that only a very few life insurance applications are not accepted at standard rates. For example in a position statement on genetics and insurance in 1999, the Institute and Faculty of Actuaries said:

> Notwithstanding the underwriting requirements of life insurance companies, it is estimated that over 95% of insurance applications are accepted at standard rates.[37]

Similarly in 2014, the Canadian Institute of Actuaries asserted:

> A significant proportion of policyholders – over 90% in Canada, the US and the UK – are issued insurance at standard rates.[38]

---

[36] 'Which? accuses Admiral of driver discrimination', *The Guardian*, 20 March 2010.
[37] Institute and Faculty of Actuaries (1999).
[38] Canadian Institute of Actuaries (2014).

Figures collated by reinsurer Swiss Re in surveys of its client companies in the UK suggest that the actual average percentage of life insurance applicants accepted at standard rates in 1999 was around 92%. By 2011, this had fallen to 79%.[39] More recently, an informal report from one Australian intermediary indicates an acceptance rate of around 79% of life insurance applications.[40]

Legislative and regulatory developments which purport to limit discrimination by disability, gender and genetics may give the impression of discrimination in insurance gradually reducing over time. The trend in the Swiss Re figures just quoted suggests that this impression is probably wrong. Although discrimination is nominally circumscribed in a few areas, the bigger picture is that in the absence of regulatory limits on risk classification, 'competitive adverse selection' forces each insurer to seek to discriminate more finely than its rivals. The result is that insurers today probably exclude or surcharge a substantially higher proportion of applicants than they did 20 years ago. This process of 'competitive adverse selection' will be discussed further in Chapter 8.

Hindsight Bias?

The preceding sections present examples of overstated predictions of the likely effects of partial restrictions on risk classification. A possible objection is that my critique is informed by hindsight, and that much of the commentary I criticise was more reasonable at the time it was made. To some extent, this must be true: the future is always less known than the past. But many of the more egregious exaggerations of past commentary were contemporaneously identifiable, and indeed were publicly highlighted at the time. For genetics, this is illustrated by the quotation earlier in this chapter from Thomas (2001), my

---

[39] Of the 21% not accepted in 2011 at insurer's standard rates, around 13% were accepted at higher rates, and 8% refused. Source: Somerville (2011).

[40] This is said to be based on 5,000 applications submitted (and not withdrawn) via an Australian aggregator website between 2012 and 2015. www .lifeinsurancedirect.com.au/insurability-2015-11-30, accessed 2 January 2016.

response dated February 2001 to the Human Genetics Commission's public consultation on genetics and insurance.[41]

Summary

The examples on the last few pages have shown that strong claims about the negative effects of any restriction on insurance risk classification – whether related to HIV tests, genetic tests or gender classification – have a long history. This book questions these claims on a variety of grounds. The main point of the book is that some restrictions on risk classification, far from having adverse effects, can actually make insurance work better, in the sense of increasing loss coverage. This is the subject of Chapters 3–6.

---

[41] The full text of the response is still available at www.guythomas.org.uk (search for 'genetics and insurance: an actuarial perspective with a difference').

Part II Loss Coverage

3   Introduction to Loss Coverage

Key Ideas:

loss coverage; social welfare; probabilistic goods; reassurance goods

This chapter examines the usual argument that adverse selection makes insurance work less well. It shows that from a public policy perspective, the absolutism of this argument is misconceived. Some degree of adverse selection in insurance is generally beneficial to society. The optimal level of adverse selection is the level which maximises loss coverage, the expected losses compensated by insurance for the population as a whole.

Although this proposition is unorthodox, there are some analogies which lend it intuitive appeal and plausibility. In many biological contexts, the analogy is hormesis: the phenomenon of stressors which are beneficial to an organism in small doses, but become harmful in higher doses. Examples of hormesis in the human body include the response to most drugs and nutrients (alcohol is a vivid example, but the same pattern applies for substances as ubiquitous and innocuous as water); the response to physical exercise; and the response to stress (cf. 'eustress' and 'distress'). By analogy, we can think of the insurance system being 'stressed' by adverse selection. Small doses 'stretch' the system and make it work better, in the sense of increasing loss coverage, but higher doses make the system work less well.

The argument that some degree of adverse selection makes the insurance system work better will be presented in three ways: first, a verbal summary of the key argument; second, numerical examples; and third, mathematical details. The summary and examples are presented in this chapter, and the mathematics in Chapters 4–6.

The Key Argument

The following verbal summary repeats that given in Chapter 1, with only footnotes and a final paragraph added.

Consider an insurance market where individuals can be divided into two risk-groups, one higher risk and one lower risk, based on information which is fully observable by insurers. Assume that all losses and insurance are of unit amount (this simplifies the discussion, but it is not necessary). Also assume that an individual's risk is unaffected by the purchase of insurance, i.e. there is no moral hazard.[1]

If insurers can, they will charge risk-differentiated prices to reflect the different risks. If instead insurers are banned from differentiating between higher and lower risks, and have to charge a single 'pooled' price for all risks, a pooled price equal to the simple average of the risk-differentiated prices will seem cheap to higher risks and expensive to lower risks. Higher risks will buy more insurance, and lower risks will buy less.

To break even, insurers will then need to raise the pooled price above the simple average of the prices. Also, since the number of higher risks is typically smaller than the number of lower (or 'standard') risks, higher risks buying more and lower risks buying less implies that the total number of people insured usually falls.[2] This combination of a rise in price and a fall in demand is usually portrayed as a bad outcome, for both insurers and society.

However, from a social perspective, it is arguable that higher risks are those more in need of insurance. Also, the compensation of

---

[1] Moral hazard is considered further in Chapter 12.

[2] This right-skewed distribution of the population numbers by risk level is seen in all insurances on human life: health insurance, life insurance, critical illness insurance, etc. In each of these markets, the population of potential insureds is typically characterized by a majority of 'standard' risks and a minority of much higher risks (with probability of loss say 2–4 times or more that for 'standard' risks). There is typically no readily identifiable group of 'super-low' risks with probability of loss less than (say) half that for 'standard' risks. To a lesser extent, a similar skew is typically observed in car insurance, home insurance, etc. If the skew was reversed, limiting risk classification might *increase* numbers insured as well as loss coverage.

many types of loss by insurance appears to be widely regarded as a desirable objective, which public policymakers often seek to promote, by public education, by exhortation and sometimes by incentives such as tax relief on premiums. Insurance of one higher risk contributes more in expectation to this objective than insurance of one lower risk. This suggests that public policymakers might welcome increased purchasing by higher risks, except for the usual story about adverse selection.

The usual story about adverse selection overlooks one point: with a pooled premium and adverse selection, expected losses compensated by insurance can still be *higher* than with fully risk-differentiated premiums and no adverse selection. Although pooling leads to a fall in numbers insured, it also leads to a shift in coverage towards higher risks. From a public policymaker's viewpoint, this means that more of the 'right' risks – those more likely to suffer loss – buy insurance. If the shift in coverage is large enough, it can more than outweigh the fall in numbers insured. This result of higher expected losses compensated by insurance – higher 'loss coverage' – can be seen as a better outcome for society than that obtained with no adverse selection.

Another perspective on this argument is that a public policymaker designing risk classification policies in the context of adverse selection normally faces a trade-off between insurance of the 'right' risks (those more likely to suffer loss) and insurance of a larger number of risks. The optimal trade-off depends on the response of higher and lower risk-groups to different prices (technically, the *demand elasticity* of different risk-groups), and will normally involve at least some adverse selection. The concept of loss coverage quantifies this trade-off, and provides a metric for comparing the effects of different risk classification schemes.

Numerical Examples

Numerical examples can illustrate the argument sketched above. These are similar in nature to the two scenarios illustrating 'no adverse selection' and 'some adverse selection' in the toy example

in Chapter 1. But now I use more realistic numbers, and also intro-
duce a third scenario of 'too much' adverse selection.

Suppose that in a population of 1,000 risks, 16 losses are
expected every year. There are two risk-groups; 200 high risks have
a probability of loss 4 times higher than the other 800 low risks. We
assume that all losses and insurance are of unit amount, and that
there is no moral hazard. An individual's risk-group is fully observable to insurers.

Under the initial risk classification regime, insurers operate
full risk classification, charging actuarially fair premiums to members of each risk-group. We assume that the proportion of each
risk-group which buys insurance under these conditions – the 'fair-
premium demand' – is 50%, which is realistic for life insurance in
the UK and the USA.[3] Table 3.1 shows the outcome, which can be
summarised as follows:

– There is no adverse selection. The average of the insurance premiums,
  weighted by numbers of insurance buyers at each price, is 0.016 (final
  column, fourth line). This is the same as the population-weighted average
  risk (final column, first line). Dividing the first by the second, we index
  the adverse selection as 0.016/0.016 = 1.0, indicating a neutral position
  (i.e. no adverse selection).
– Half the losses in the population are compensated by insurance. We
  heuristically characterise this as a 'loss coverage' of 0.5.

Now suppose that a new risk classification regime is introduced,
where insurers are obliged to charge a common 'pooled' premium to

[3] Extant life insurance markets in the UK and USA operate with few restrictions on
risk classification, and so approximately correspond to the initial risk classification
regime above. The Association of British Insurers (2014) states that 10.8 of 26.4
million (i.e. 41%) of households in the UK in 2012 had some form of life insurance.
The Life Insurance Market Research Organisation (2013) states that 44% of US
households have some individual life insurance. The American Council of Life
Insurers (2014, p. 72) states that 144 million individual policies were in force in
2013, compared with the US adult population of 244 million (aged 18 years and
over at 1 July 2013, as estimated by the US Census Bureau). So 144/244 = 59% of
the adult population have some life insurance (this is an upper bound, because
some policyholders have more than one policy).

Table 3.1. *Full risk classification: no adverse selection (base outcome)*

	Low risk-group	High risk-group	Aggregate
Risk	0.01	0.04	0.016
Total population	800	200	1 000
Expected population losses	8	8	16
Break-even premiums (risk-differentiated)	0.01	0.04	0.016
Numbers insured	400	100	500
Insured losses	4	4	8
Adverse selection			1
Loss coverage			0.5

Table 3.2. *Risk classification banned: moderate adverse selection leading to higher loss coverage (better outcome)*

	Low risk-group	High risk-group	Aggregate
Risk	0.01	0.04	0.016
Total population	800	200	1 000
Expected population losses	8	8	16
Break-even premiums (pooled)	0.02	0.02	0.02
Numbers insured	300	150	450
Insured losses	3	6	9
Adverse selection			1.25
Loss coverage			0.5625

members of both the low and high risk-groups. One possible outcome is shown in Table 3.2, which can be summarised as follows:

– The pooled premium of 0.02 at which insurers make zero profits is calculated as the demand-weighted average of the risk premiums: $(300 \times 0.01 + 150 \times 0.04)/450 = 0.02)$.

- The pooled premium is expensive for low risks, so 25% fewer of them buy insurance (300, compared with 400 before). The pooled premium is cheap for high risks, so 50% more of them buy insurance (150, compared with 100 before). Because there are 4 times as many low risks as high risks in the population, the total number of policies sold falls (450, compared with 500 before).
- There is moderate adverse selection. The pooled premium of 0.02 exceeds the population-weighted average premium of 0.016, giving adverse selection $= 0.02/0.016 = 1.25$.
- The resulting loss coverage is 0.5625. The shift in coverage towards high risks more than outweighs the fall in number of policies sold: 9 of 16 losses (56%) in the population as a whole are now compensated by insurance (compared with 8 of 16 before).

Table 3.2 exhibited moderate adverse selection. Another possible outcome under the restricted risk classification scheme, this time with more severe adverse selection, is shown in Table 3.3, which can be summarised as follows:

- The pooled premium of 0.02154 at which insurers make zero profits is calculated as the demand-weighted average of the risk premiums: $(200 \times 0.01 + 125 \times 0.04)/325 = 0.02154$.

Table 3.3. *Risk classification banned: severe adverse selection leading to lower loss coverage (worse outcome)*

	Low risk-group	High risk-group	Aggregate
Risk	0.01	0.04	0.016
Total population	800	200	1 000
Expected population losses	8	8	16
Break-even premiums (pooled)	0.02154	0.02154	0.02154
Numbers insured	200	125	325
Insured losses	2	5	7
Adverse selection			1.34625
Loss coverage			0.4375

- There is severe adverse selection, with a further increase in the pooled premium and a significant fall in numbers insured.
- The loss coverage is 0.4375. The shift in coverage towards high risks is *not* sufficient to outweigh the fall in number of policies sold: 7 of 16 losses (43.75%) in the population as a whole are now compensated by insurance (compared with 8 of 16 in Table 3.1, and 9 out of 16 in Table 3.2).

Taking the three tables together, we can summarise by saying that compared with an initial position of no adverse selection in Table 3.1, moderate adverse selection leads to higher expected losses compensated by insurance (higher loss coverage) in Table 3.2; but too much adverse selection leads to lower expected losses compensated by insurance (lower loss coverage) in Table 3.3.

This argument that moderate adverse selection increases loss coverage is quite general: it does not depend on any unusual choice of numbers for the examples. It also does not assume any bias by the policymaker towards (or against) compensating the losses of the high risk-group in preference to those of the low risk-group. The same preference is given to compensation of losses anywhere in the population *ex post*, when all uncertainty about who will suffer a loss has been resolved. This implies giving higher preference to insurance cover for higher risks *ex ante*, before we know who will suffer a loss, but only in proportion to their higher risk.

Loss Coverage in Context

The remainder of this chapter makes a range of comparisons and analogies which helps to set the concept of loss coverage in context.

The Hirshleifer Effect

The idea that restricting risk classification and hence inducing a degree of adverse selection can produce a better outcome for society as a whole is analogous to the Hirshleifer effect.[4] This is named

---

[4] Hirshleifer (1971).

after the economist Jack Hirshleifer, who pointed out that too much information about future investment returns can reduce opportunities for risk sharing, because a risk which has been resolved cannot be shared. Although some people can make better decisions when more information becomes available, society as a whole can end up worse off. In insurance, the analogous phenomenon is that the use of too much information for risk classification can reduce risk sharing: although some people get cheaper insurance because of the increased use of information, the overall quantum of risk transferred to insurers falls, so society as a whole ends up worse off.

Loss Coverage and Compulsory Insurance

One way of maximising loss coverage is to make insurance compulsory – either through social insurance, or by laws which compel people to buy commercial insurance. Healthcare is often provided by social insurance, and liability insurances which protect the interests of unidentified third parties or the public at large are often made compulsory (e.g. third-party car insurance, employers' liability insurance). The potential losses compensated by these insurances are largely independent of the personal circumstances of the insured, and so compulsion is a well-targeted approach to achieving policymakers' desired (universal) loss coverage.

In other classes of insurance, such as life insurance, the policy motivations to increase loss coverage may be less conclusive, but are still present to some degree. For example, policymakers may consider that through incomplete information or behavioural bias, most people under estimate their needs for life insurance, and so too little life insurance is bought.[5] However, in life insurance the

---

[5] Evidence for the inadequacy of life insurance holdings and the sharp decline in living standards of surviving spouses is documented in Bernheim et al. (2003) and Auerbach and Kotlikoff (1991). Policymakers may also believe that the wide take-up of insurance promotes economic growth, although the evidence for this is mixed (Ward and Zurbruegg, 2000).

potential loss depends on the personal circumstances of the insured. A compulsory requirement for unmarried persons to purchase life insurance may not increase loss coverage (because there is often no financial loss to a survivor if the unmarried person dies); the cost of premiums to the unmarried person may itself represent an uncompensated loss. One might exclude unmarried persons from compulsion; but some unmarried persons do need life insurance, and equally some married persons do not. Overall, for insurances where the potential loss depends on personal circumstances, compulsion may be a poorly targeted and politically unpopular means of increasing loss coverage. It may be both more effective and more politically acceptable to leave purchasing decisions to individuals, and increase loss coverage by regulating risk classification.

There may be a few classes of insurance where there is little policy motivation to promote the compensation of losses by insurance. A clear example would be insurance against the cost of legal or regulatory penalties; a less clear example might be insurance of pet animals. In these cases, policymakers may view loss coverage as a less important objective than in markets such as liability, health and life insurance. Indeed, policymakers may even seek to reduce loss coverage, by discouraging the insurance. In extreme cases this might mean banning the insurance. In the UK, the Financial Conduct Authority bans the firms which it regulates from insuring against the cost of regulatory penalties.[6]

Loss Coverage versus 'Social Welfare'

There is an extant literature in economics which considers the effect of restrictions on risk classification. Economists typically take a utility-based approach: individuals make insurance choices to maximise their expected utility according to some utility function, and the outcomes of different risk classification schemes are

---

[6] Paragraph GEN 6.1.5 of FCA handbook, www.fca.org.uk

evaluated by *social welfare*, typically defined as the sum of expected utilities over the entire population.[7]

One way of describing the difference in this book's approach compared with the economics literature is that rather than assigning equal weights to *expected utility* levels across low and high risks, I assign equal weights to *loss coverage* levels across low and high risks. Under my approach, if all losses are of unit amount, and high risks have a probability of loss twice that of low risks, then coverage of one high risk is considered to be worth the same *ex ante* as coverage of two low risks.

Another way of describing the difference between loss coverage and social welfare is to note that loss coverage focuses on maximising the benefit of insurance, framed solely as the compensation of losses. Minor details about preferences – who underpays and overpays for insurance, and how much they care (how it affects their utility) – are disregarded, provided that the insurance system as a whole equilibrates.

This disregard seems reasonable in the typical scenario where insurance premiums are small relative to wealth. It is also practical in the sense that loss coverage depends solely on observable claims, whereas social welfare depends on utilities which are never observable. Loss coverage also has the advantage of being a simpler concept, and so more conducive to wide understanding in policy discussions.

Although loss coverage and social welfare are distinct criteria, they can be shown to be tightly related under simple assumptions about utility (and hence insurance demand) functions. Specifically: *for power utility functions (and hence iso-elastic insurance demand),*

---

[7] Sometimes maximum social welfare is instead characterised as the non-existence of a Pareto improvement (a feasible change which makes at least one person better off, and nobody worse off), or *potential* Pareto (or 'Kaldor–Hicks') improvement (a feasible change where the winners could theoretically compensate the losers and still be better off). But since changes to risk classification in the real world usually create both winners and losers, and the winners in practice never compensate the losers, utilitarian formulations are usually more useful. Recent surveys and extensions of the economic literature include Hoy (2006) and Dionne and Rothschild (2014).

either criterion – loss coverage or social welfare – gives the same rank ordering of different risk classification schemes. Those who prefer the criterion of social welfare in principle may then wish to think of loss coverage as an *observable* proxy, under certain assumptions, for social welfare.[8]

Loss Coverage versus 'Coverage'

The criterion of *loss coverage* and the criterion of *social welfare* can be further contrasted with the criterion of simple *coverage,* which is often implicit in informal discussions of risk classification. In informal discussions, adverse selection is often said to be a bad thing because it leads to a 'reduction in coverage' compared with that attained in the absence of adverse selection. Economists typically say that any reduction in coverage is 'inefficient'.[9] But if loss coverage is increased, the quantum of risk transferred to insurers is increased. Why should an arrangement under which more risk is voluntarily traded and more losses are compensated be disparaged as 'inefficient'?

Such discussions of the 'reduction in coverage' arising from adverse selection implicitly treat coverage of one high risk as equivalent to coverage of one low risk. But if the purpose of insurance is to compensate the population's losses, this does not seem a valid equivalence: covering one high risk contributes more in expectation to this purpose than covering one low risk. In other words, these informal discussions are typically predicated on an inaccurate measure of the benefit of insurance.

Another succinct description of the contrast between loss coverage and the common informal reference to just 'coverage' is to note that loss coverage corresponds to *risk-weighted* insurance demand, and coverage to *unweighted* insurance demand.

---

[8] This result is proved in Hao et al. (2016b). The social welfare measure is necessarily standardised to negate the possibility of a 'utility monster' (Nozick, 1974) dominating social welfare. My intuition is that the result will probably be capable of extension to a somewhat wider class of demand functions.

[9] For example, Dionne and Rothschild (2014, p. 185): 'This reduced pool of insured individuals reflects a decrease in the efficiency of the insurance market.'

Probabilistic Goods versus Reassurance Goods

The risk-weighted nature of loss coverage is predicated on the notion that the good provided by insurance is the contingent compensation of losses. This good materialises only in a particular future state of the world, which has different probabilities for higher and lower risks. That is, insurance is a *probabilistic* and *individually heterogeneous* good.

For such a good, one unit of sales to a higher-risk individual is a *different* good compared with one unit of sales to a lower-risk individual. In loss coverage, this difference is reflected in the risk-weighting of coverage. In utilitarian social welfare, it is reflected in higher probabilities attached to losses in expected utility calculations.

While I believe this framing of insurance as a probabilistic good is appropriate when considering public policy at a population and objective level, I acknowledge that at an individual and subjective level, insurance can also be framed as a non-probabilistic good. Insurance goods can be framed as non-probabilistic if the good is conceived as 'peace of mind' or 'freedom from worry'. Think of car insurance, home insurance or life insurance: in every case, at an individual and subjective level, the good might just as well be framed as freedom from worry in the present, rather than as the contingent compensation of losses in the future. Insurance framed as 'freedom from worry' is a non-probabilistic *experience good*. In the specific insurance context, we can call it a *reassurance good* (reassurance being the experience which insurance provides).

If insurance is framed as a reassurance good, one unit of sales to a higher-risk individual is closer to *the same* good as one unit of sales to a lower-risk individual. I say 'closer to' rather than 'equal to' because although both higher and lower risks experience similar reassurance, it might be felt that the quantum of this reassurance increases for higher underlying probability of loss. This is certainly arguable, but it is not obvious that the increase should be in one-to-one proportion to the probability. And it seems at least equally arguable that for any class of insurance (say car, home or life), the quantum of reassurance is invariant to individual variations in probabilities of loss (or alternatively, increasing in less than one-to-one proportion, or at a sublinear rate, in those variations).

I acknowledge that the framing of insurance as a reassurance good may often be psychologically salient to individuals; and that in this framing, the risk-weighting in loss coverage might overstate the benefit of coverage of higher risks. Nevertheless, I believe that the framing of insurance as a probabilistic good is a better basis for public policy. This is for the same reason as I prefer loss coverage to social welfare: I believe that it is more practical to base public policy on observables (such as probabilities of loss), not on individuals' unobservable states of mind (such as feelings of reassurance, or increases in utility).[10]

Loss Coverage and Partial Risk Classification

The discussion above has considered only two possibilities for risk classification: fully risk-differentiated premiums or complete pooling. In practice, partial restrictions on risk classification are common, where only some risk variables (e.g. gender, family history, genetic test results) are banned. Loss coverage is maximised when there is an intermediate level of adverse selection, not too low and not too high. It seems plausible that in some markets, complete pooling generates too much adverse selection; but partial restrictions on risk classification generate an intermediate level of adverse selection, and hence higher loss coverage than under either pooling or fully risk-differentiated premiums. Loss coverage can then provide an explanation or rationalisation of the partial restrictions often seen in practice. Partial risk classification is considered further in Chapter 6.

[10] Lottery tickets are another type of good which fits into the same alternative probabilistic versus non-probabilistic framing, but with two differences. For lottery tickets, the probabilistic good is individually homogeneous (cf. heterogeneous in insurance) and the non-probabilistic good is the experience of 'hope' (cf. the experience of 'reassurance' in insurance).

Different Weights for Different Risk-Groups?

Loss coverage as defined in this book always places equal weight on equal expected losses, irrespective of the part of the population from which they are expected. No preference is given to achieving compensation of losses arising from higher or lower risks. This solution to the trade-off between the interests of higher and lower risks has obvious intuitive and egalitarian appeal. But in some circumstances, a policymaker might wish to give higher priority to compensating the losses of higher (or lower) risks – perhaps because those with higher insurance risks also tend to suffer other economic or social disadvantages. If so, it is straightforward to redefine loss coverage as a weighted average of expected losses over the population, with the weights reflecting the priority the policymaker places on compensation of losses arising from different risks.[11]

Other Public Policy Criteria for Risk Classification

Loss coverage is not the only criterion which a public policymaker may consider when setting policy on risk classification. In some markets, risk classification might provide an incentive for loss prevention: for example, if house insurance premiums are lower for homes with security features such as burglar alarms or better locks, perhaps home owners will be more inclined to install these features.[12] A policymaker might also place value on ensuring the optional availability of insurance to members of higher risk-groups, distinct from the actual take-up of the option. The possible 'spillover' effects of insurance risk classification on privacy, public

---

[11] Technically, this would be rather like a spectral risk measure as defined by Acerbi (2002), but weighted by probability of loss, not size of loss.

[12] Like adverse selection, this notion of risk classification encouraging loss prevention, which I call 'reverse moral hazard', is an intuitively appealing fable. But empirical evidence is weak or contradictory. For example, Schwarze and Wein (2005) found that while deregulation in mandatory third-party car insurance in Germany in the 1990s led to the introduction of many new risk categories, this was *not* associated with either a decline in total damages or a reduction in the average price of insurance.

health and discrimination in other contexts such as employment might also be considered. Restrictions on risk classification sometimes appear to be based on a principled objection to statistical discrimination *per se*, rather than on an assessment of insurance market consequences. These and other objections to risk classification are discussed further in Chapter 7. Nevertheless, to the extent that consequences in the insurance market itself are given weight, loss coverage is a useful metric for those consequences.

Loss Coverage: The Insurer's Perspective

While this book focuses mainly on a public policy perspective, the loss coverage concept can also be viewed from the insurer's perspective. Maximising loss coverage is equivalent to maximising premium income. If profit loadings are proportional to premiums, maximising loss coverage could be a desirable objective for insurers. Even from the insurer's perspective, adverse selection is not always a bad thing! This might help explain why insurers often appear rather slower to make use of every scrap of marginal information for risk classification than economic theory predicts, even when information is observable at zero or at negligible cost and apparently relevant to the risk.

Finkelstein and Poterba (2014) note that UK insurers were very slow to adopt 'postcode pricing' of annuities, despite postcode information being available at zero cost and regional variations in annuitant mortality having been reasonably well known for many years. They offer four possible explanations, but do not consider the possibility that the small amount of adverse selection induced by ignoring postcode information may give higher loss coverage (from the insurers' perspective, higher aggregate annuity premiums). They also note that once one large insurer (Legal and General) adopted postcode pricing in 2007, most other insurers quickly followed. If profit loadings are proportional to premiums, Legal and General's competitive innovation and the resulting 'competitive adverse selection' (as discussed in Chapter 8) may have made insurers collectively worse off.

Loss Coverage versus Preconceptions: Hidden in Plain View

The observation that a larger fraction of the population's losses can be compensated with some adverse selection involves only elementary arithmetic, but as far as I am aware it has not been pointed out before. Given its technical simplicity, this may seem surprising. It becomes less surprising when one reflects on how the insight clashes with extant economic and industry dogma. Economists seem strongly committed to the idea that asymmetric information always makes all markets work less well; in contrast, loss coverage says that that a limited amount of asymmetric information makes insurance markets work better. Similarly, insurers seem strongly committed to the idea that unrestricted risk classification is commercially vital; in contrast, loss coverage says that some restrictions on risk classification are likely to be beneficial, including for insurers themselves. An unrecognised simplicity which clashes with so many people's preconceptions can remain hidden in plain view.

One example where the loss coverage perspective contrasts with an argument made by economists on behalf of insurers is a paper *Why the use of age and disability matters to consumers and insurers*, commissioned by the trade association Insurance Europe from the British economic consultants Oxera.[13] The document presents an example of the effect of banning risk classification by disability in life insurance. The example is hypothetical, with assumed sums assured of £100,000, and all other figures chosen to make a case to policymakers against restrictions on risk classification – but in my view inadvertently making the opposite case. Table 3.4 summarises the figures presented by Oxera as the hypothetical position before a ban on risk classification.

Table 3.5 shows the figures given as the hypothetical position after a ban on risk classification. Oxera notes that the premium for the 'Standard' risks more than doubles after the ban, and suggests that this shows that a ban is undesirable.

[13] Oxera Consulting (2012).

Table 3.4. *Life insurance with risk-based premiums (based on Oxera, 2012)*

Risk	Mortality	Population	Insured population (clientele)	Expected cost per customer (€)	Total claims (€)	Premium rate (€)	Total premium income (€)
Standard	1.4%	800	400	1 400	560 000	1 400	560 000
Double	2.8%	150	75	2 800	210 000	2 800	210 000
High	14.0%	50	0	14 000			
Total		1 000	475		770 000		770 000

Source: Illustrative example of risk-based pricing devised in Oxera Consulting (2012)

Table 3.5. *Life insurance with pooled premiums (based on Oxera, 2012)*

Risk	Mortality	Population	Insured population (clientele)	Expected cost per customer (€)	Total claims (€)	Premium rate (€)	Total premium income (€)
Standard	1.4%	800	200	1 400	280 000	3 333	666 667
Double	2.8%	150	75	2 800	210 000	3 333	250 000
High	14.0%	50	40	14 000	560 000	3 333	133 333
Total		1 000	315		1 050 000		1 050 000

Source: Illustrative example of non-discriminatory pricing devised in Oxera Consulting (2012)

But on Oxera's figures, loss coverage is *increased* by restricting risk classification. Before the ban, the expected number of deaths compensated by insurance is 770,000/100,000 = 7.7. After the ban, the corresponding number is 1,050,000/100,000 = 10.5. Banning risk classification in this example gives an improvement: the shift in coverage towards higher-risk lives more than compensates for the fall in numbers insured.

Of course, since Oxera's figures are hypothetical, it is easy to construct an example corresponding to Scenario 3 earlier in this chapter, where adverse selection 'goes too far' and lower loss coverage results from a ban. But the fact that this was not done suggests that the loss coverage perspective was not considered.

Summary

This chapter has suggested that the usual arguments that adverse selection always makes insurance work less well, and that more adverse selection is always worse than less, are misconceived. Adverse selection implies a fall in numbers insured, and also a shift in coverage towards higher risks. If the shift in coverage outweighs the fall in numbers, the expected losses compensated by insurance are increased – that is the loss coverage is increased. From a public policy perspective, a degree of so-called 'adverse' selection in insurance is a good thing.

4   Basic Mathematics of Loss Coverage

Key Ideas:

adverse selection; advantageous selection; random variables representing cover, Q, and loss, L; 'overlap' of Q and L; loss coverage = E[QL]; adverse selection ratio; loss coverage ratio; demand ratio

The discussion of loss coverage in Chapter 3 was informal. Chapters 4–6 develop more precisely the mathematical relationships between adverse selection, loss coverage, and demand elasticities. Readers who are not concerned with mathematical detail may prefer to skip Chapters 4–6, or perhaps just skim the graphs and end-of-chapter summaries. The full mathematical details are *not* prerequisites for understanding most of the rest of this book.

A Model for an Insurance Market

Throughout Chapters 4–6, I assume a population of risks can be divided into a low risk-group and a high risk-group, based on information which is fully observable to insurers. Just two risk-groups is not, of course, a realistic model of most insurance markets, but it is enough to illustrate principles.[1]

Let μ_1 and μ_2 be the underlying risks (probabilities of loss) for the low and high risk-groups.

Let p_1 and p_2 be the population fractions for the low and high risk-groups, that is the proportions of the total population represented by each risk-group. This means a risk chosen at random from

---

[1] The extension to n risk-groups is straightforward, see for example Hao et al. [2016b].

the entire population has a probability p_1 of belonging to the low risk-group.

Throughout Chapters 4–6, I assume that all losses and insurance cover are of unit size; this simplifies the presentation, but it is not necessary. I also assume no moral hazard, that is, given the risk-group, the probability of loss is not affected by the purchase of insurance.[2]

All quantities defined below are for a single risk sampled at random from the population (unless the context requires otherwise).

The expected loss is denoted E[L] ('L' for 'loss') and given by:

$$E[L] = \sum_{i=1}^{2} \mu_i p_i \qquad (4.1)$$

E[L] corresponds to a unit version of the third row of the tables in the examples in Chapter 3.

In the absence of limits on risk classification, insurers will charge risk-differentiated premiums equal to the probabilities of loss, $\pi_1 = \mu_1$ and $\pi_2 = \mu_2$ for risk-groups 1 and 2, respectively.

The expected insurance demand is denoted E[Q] ('Q' for 'quantity') and given by:

$$E[Q] = \sum_{i=1}^{2} d(\mu_i, \pi_i) p_i \qquad (4.2)$$

where $d(\mu_i, \pi_i)$ is the *proportional demand for insurance* for risk-group i when premium π_i is charged, that is the probability that an individual selected at random from the risk-group buys insurance.[3]

---

[2] Moral hazard is discussed in Chapter 12.

[3] Note that the demand model is at the level of the collective, and says nothing about micro-foundations. That is, the model gives the proportion of the whole risk-group i who buy insurance at price π_i, and says nothing about how or why individual decisions are made. The micro-foundations are not considered further in this book. But they can be substantiated by positing that individuals maximise expected utilities, and that risk preferences vary across individuals; the latter feature implies that some will purchase insurance and some will not, thus generating the proportional demand. For details, see Hao et al. (2016b).

The expected premium is denoted by $E[\Pi]$ ($'\Pi'$ for 'premium') and given by:

$$E[\Pi] = \sum_{i=1}^{2} d(\mu_i, \pi_i) p_i \, \pi_i \qquad (4.3)$$

The expected insurance claim is given by:

$$E[QL] = \sum_{i=1}^{2} d(\mu_i, \pi_i) p_i \, \mu_i \qquad (4.4)$$

Adverse Selection

The phrase 'adverse selection' is typically associated with positive correlation (or equivalently, covariance) of cover Q and loss L; most papers testing for adverse selection in the economics literature use this definition.[4] This section makes this definition precise, in a form which will later help to highlight the relationship between adverse selection and loss coverage.

By the standard definition, the covariance of Q and L is:

$$Cov(Q, L) = E[(Q - E[Q])(L - E[L])]$$
$$= E[QL] - E[Q]E[L]. \qquad (4.5)$$

While the economics literature typically uses covariance $(Q, L) > 0$ as a test for adverse selection, it is more convenient to note that when the covariance is zero, the two terms in Equation (4.5) must be the same. We can then define the adverse selection as:

$$\text{Adverse selection}, \, A - \frac{E[QL]}{E[Q]E[L]} \qquad (4.6)$$

This enables us to index different types of selective behaviour by insurance customers as follows:

$A < 1$: advantageous selection

---

[4] See for example the summary Cohen and Siegelman (2010), and the discussion in Chapter 8.

$A = 1$: no selection

$A > 1$: adverse selection.[5]

To compare the severity of adverse selection under different risk-classification regimes, we need to define a reference level of adverse selection. Adverse selection under alternative schemes can then be expressed as a fraction of adverse selection under the reference scheme. A convenient reference scheme is risk-differentiated premiums (actuarially fair premiums). Then using subscript 0 to denote quantities evaluated under risk-differentiated premiums, we define the *adverse selection ratio* as:

$$\text{Adverse selection ratio} = \frac{A}{A_0} \tag{4.7}$$

In words, adverse selection ratio is the ratio of the expected claim per policy under the actual risk classification scheme to the expected claim per policy under risk-differentiated premiums.

Adverse selection ratio can also be thought of as the ratio of the *demand-weighted average premiums* required for insurers to break even under each risk classification scheme.

Loss Coverage

Loss coverage in this model is defined as the expected insurance claim (as previously evaluated in Equation (4.4)):

$$\text{Loss coverage} = \text{E}[QL] = \sum_{i=1}^{2} d(\mu_i, \pi_i) p_i \, \mu_i \tag{4.8}$$

---

[5] Note that $A \neq 1$ is possible under actuarially fair premiums, if higher and lower risk-groups exhibit different demand responses to their respective actuarially fair premiums. It may seem counter-intuitive that adverse selection can be present under actuarially fair premiums, but it is a consequence of our definition, which allows a difference in insurance take-up by higher and lower risk-groups under actuarially fair premiums to 'count' as adverse selection. However, adverse selection *ratio* as defined in the next paragraph is standardised so that it is, by definition, equal to the 'null' value of 1 under actuarially fair premiums.

The product of random variables Q and L can alternatively be thought of as the following 'indicator' random variable:

$QL = \{1$ if the individual both incurs a loss and has cover, 0 otherwise$\}$

(4.9)

Loss coverage can then be thought of as indexing the 'overlap' of cover Q and losses L in the population. It represents the extent to which insurance cover is concentrated over the 'right' risks (those most likely to suffer loss). It measures the efficacy of insurance in compensating the population's losses.

The right-hand side of Equation (4.8) also shows that loss coverage can be thought of as the *risk-weighted insurance demand* for the randomly selected member of the population.

This concept of loss coverage as *risk-weighted insurance demand* can be contrasted with *unweighted insurance demand*, which corresponds to the 'number of risks insured' often referenced in informal discussions of adverse selection.

Loss Coverage Ratio

When comparing alternative risk classification schemes, it is often helpful to define loss coverage to be 1 under some suitable reference scheme. Loss coverage under alternative schemes can then be expressed as a fraction of loss coverage under the reference scheme. It is convenient to use the same approach as for adverse selection above, that is, I use risk-differentiated premiums as the reference scheme. Then using subscript 0 to denote quantities evaluated under risk-differentiated premiums, I define the *loss coverage ratio* (LCR) as:

$$LCR = \frac{E[QL]}{E_0[QL]}$$

(4.10)

Note that in the numerical examples in Chapters 1 and 3, the fraction between 0 and 1 which I heuristically labelled 'loss coverage' was, more precisely, a loss coverage ratio with the reference scheme (i.e. under which loss coverage = 1) defined as compulsory insurance of the whole population. Clearly the choice of reference scheme – risk-differentiated premiums, compulsory insurance or something else – does not matter, provided we use a consistent reference when making comparisons of different proposed risk classification schemes.

Now note that loss coverage ratio in Equation (4.10) can also be expanded into:

$$\text{LCR} = \frac{\left(\dfrac{\text{E}[QL]}{\text{E}[Q]\,\text{E}[L]}\right)}{\left(\dfrac{\text{E}_0[QL]}{\text{E}_0[Q]\,\text{E}[L]}\right)} \times \frac{\text{E}[Q]}{\text{E}_0[Q]} \tag{4.11}$$

Then by noting that expected population losses are the same irrespective of the risk classification scheme (i.e. $\text{E}[L] = \text{E}_0[L]$), we see that the first term on the right-hand side of Equation (4.11) is the adverse selection ratio in Equation (4.7). The second term on the right-hand side of Equation (4.11) is the ratio of demand under the actual risk classification scheme to demand under risk-differentiated premiums, which I call the *demand ratio*. So Equation (4.11) can then be interpreted as:

$$\text{LCR} = \text{Adverse selection ratio} \times \text{Demand ratio} \tag{4.12}$$

We can illustrate this decomposition of loss coverage ratio by applying it to the numerical examples in Chapter 3. The decomposition is shown in Table 4.1. In each of the three columns in the table, loss coverage ratio (the third line) is the product of adverse selection ratio and demand ratio (the first and second lines).

The decomposition of loss coverage ratio into adverse selection ratio and demand ratio is sometimes helpful in correcting casual intuitions and commentary about restrictions on risk classification. Casual intuitions and commentary often reference rising average prices (adverse selection) and falling demand (numbers insured), but without considering how the two effects interact. But

Table 4.1. *Decomposition of loss coverage ratio into adverse selection ratio and demand ratio for Tables 3.1–3.3*

	Table 3.1	Table 3.2	Table 3.3
Adverse selection ratio: $\left(\dfrac{\text{risk-weighted average premium}}{\text{population-weighted average premium}}\right)$	1.0	1.25	1.3461
Demand ratio: $\left(\dfrac{\text{numbers insured under pooled premium}}{\text{numbers insured under risk-differentiated premiums}}\right)$	1.0	0.90	0.65
Loss coverage ratio(product of above): $\left(\dfrac{\text{loss coverage under pooled premium}}{\text{loss coverage under risk-differentiated premiums}}\right)$	1.0	1.125	0.875

depending on the product of the two effects, loss coverage ratio may be higher or lower than 1 (that is, loss coverage may be increased or decreased). The decomposition highlights that predicting or observing a rise in average price and a fall in demand under a new risk classification scheme is not sufficient to demonstrate a worse outcome. The outcome in terms of loss coverage depends on the product of the two effects.

An illustration of the trade-off between loss coverage and adverse selection is provided by Figure 4.1. This graph plots loss coverage ratio against adverse selection ratio, based on the two risk-group model in this chapter with a plausible form for the demand function.[6] It can be seen that the maximum point for loss coverage corresponds to an intermediate degree of adverse selection, not too low and not too high.

The shape of this graph, with the interior maximum showing that loss coverage is maximised by an intermediate level of adverse selection, is the most important image in this book. A similar

[6] Actually the negative exponential function in Appendix A. But any reasonable demand function will give a similar inverted U-shape. My notion of a 'reasonable' demand function is defined by the intuitive axioms in Chapter 5.

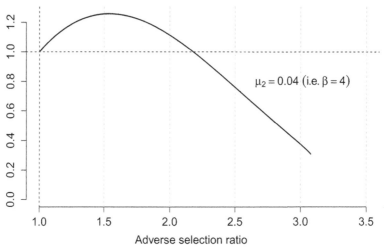

Basis: $p_1 = 0.9$ with negative exponential demand function

FIGURE 4.1   Loss coverage ratio as a function of adverse selection ratio

inverted U-shape is obtained for any reasonable demand function. Note that the highest loss coverage is obtained not *despite* the adverse selection, but *because of* the adverse selection. In moderation, adverse selection is a good thing.

Figure 4.1 is based on a relative risk $\beta = \mu_2/\mu_1 = 4$. If the relative risk is lower, the maximum value of loss coverage is lower, and this maximum is attained with a lower level of adverse selection. This is illustrated in Figure 4.2, which shows the plot of loss coverage ratio against adverse selection ratio for two values of relative risk, $\beta = 3$ and $\beta = 4$. The maximum of the dashed curve for $\beta = 3$ lies below and to the left of the maximum of the solid curve for $\beta = 4$.

Note that the right-hand terminal points of each curve in Figures 4.1 and 4.2 correspond to limiting values, not points at which I arbitrarily chose to stop drawing the curve. These limiting values represent the scenario where all lower risks have dropped out of insurance and only higher risks remain; clearly, adverse selection then cannot increase any more. In Figure 4.2, the terminal point for $\beta = 3$ lies to the left and below the terminal point for $\beta = 4$.

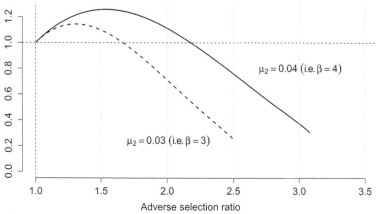

Basis: $p_i = 0.9$ with negative exponential demand function

FIGURE 4.2 Loss coverage ratio as a function of adverse selection ratio, for two relative risks

To understand this, note that when all higher risks have dropped out of the market and only higher risks remain, lower relative risk $\beta = 3$ implies a lower break-even premium (lower adverse selection), and also that a lower fraction of the total risk in the population is covered (lower loss coverage).

Summary

The main points of Chapter 4 can be summarised as follows:

1. Loss coverage:

$$\text{Loss coverage} = \text{E}[QL]$$

$$= \sum_{i=1}^{2} d_i(\pi_i, \mu_i) p_i \, \mu_i$$

Loss coverage is the expected losses compensated by insurance for the whole population. It represents the extent to which insurance cover is concentrated on the 'right' risks (those most likely to suffer loss). It measures the efficacy of insurance in compensating the population's losses.

Loss coverage under alternative risk classification schemes can be compared by loss coverage ratio:

$$LCR = \frac{E[QL]}{E_0[QL]}$$

where subscript 0 denotes a quantity calculated under some base or reference risk classification scheme, e.g. risk-differentiated premiums, or compulsory insurance.

2. Adverse selection:

$$\text{Adverse selection, } A = \frac{E[QL]}{E[Q]\,E[L]}$$

$$\text{Adverse selection ratio} = \frac{A}{A_0}$$

where subscript 0 denotes a quantity calculated under some base or reference risk classification scheme, e.g. risk-differentiated premiums, or compulsory insurance.

3. Decomposition of loss coverage ratio into adverse selection ratio and demand ratio:

$$\text{Loss coverage ratio} = \text{Adverse selection ratio} \times \text{Demand ratio}$$

This decomposition highlights that predicting or observing a rise in average price and fall in demand under a new risk classification scheme is not sufficient to demonstrate a worse outcome. The outcome in terms of loss coverage depends on the product of the two effects.

5 Further Mathematics of Loss Coverage

Key Ideas:

zero-profit equilibrium; loss coverage under iso-elastic demand; loss coverage under alternative demand functions; empirical insurance demand elasticities

Chapter 4 gave mathematical definitions of loss coverage and related quantities. This chapter introduces models of insurance markets which enable us to study how loss coverage varies with changes in the fractions of the population represented by higher risks and lower risks, probabilities of loss and demand elasticities. As with Chapter 4, readers who are not concerned with mathematical detail may prefer to skim just the graphs and end-of-chapter summary.

We focus first on a simple iso-elastic demand function, and then consider more general demand functions.

Two Risk-Groups with Iso-elastic Demand

This chapter uses the same two risk-group model as in Chapter 4. In that chapter, I used a generic function for proportional insurance demand $d(\mu_i, \pi_i)$ to define the quantities $E[I]$, $F[Q]$, $E[\Pi]$ and $E[QL]$ – expected population loss, expected insurance demand, expected premium and expected insurance claim (loss coverage). I did not specify a form for the demand function, nor the detail of how the premiums π_i charged to each risk-group were determined. In the present chapter, I specify a form for the demand function. I also specify the zero-profit equilibrium condition which determines the 'pooled' premium when all risks are pooled at the same price.

Specifying an Insurance Demand Function

To recap, the proportional demand for insurance $d(\mu_i, \pi_i)$ is the proportion of the risk-group with probability of loss μ_i which buys insurance when a premium of π_i is charged to members of that risk-group.

As a preliminary, it is helpful to define the concept of *demand elasticity*. Demand elasticity is defined as:

$$\text{Demand elasticity} = -\frac{\pi_i}{d(\mu_i, \pi_i)} \cdot \frac{\partial d(\mu_i, \pi_i)}{\partial \pi_i} \qquad (5.1)$$

Roughly speaking, this is the percentage change in demand for a very small percentage change in premium. It measures the responsiveness of demand to small changes in premium.

Note that the derivative within the above expression is normally negative (as the premium rises, demand falls). The minus sign ensures that demand elasticity as defined here will normally be positive; this makes the subsequent mathematical presentation tidier.

It is sometimes more convenient to rewrite Equation (5.1) as the *log–log derivative* of the demand function with respect to the premium, that is:

$$\text{Demand elasticity} = -\frac{\partial \log[d(\mu_i, \pi_i)]}{\partial \log \pi_i} \qquad (5.2)$$

What properties should the demand function possess? I suggest the following as intuitive axioms[1]:

(a) *Decreasing in premium:* $d(\mu_i, \pi_i)$ is a decreasing function of the premium π_i for all risk-groups.
(b) *Increasing in risk:* $d(\mu_1, \pi_0) < d(\mu_2, \pi_0)$, that is at any given premium π_0, the proportional demand is higher for the higher risk-group.

---

[1] These axioms are based on those suggested in De Jong and Ferris (2006). They are stated in full to give an intuitive description of reasonable demand functions, but there is some technical redundancy. Axioms (b) and (c), although reasonable, are not strictly required for subsequent development of the model. Also, if axiom (c) is satisfied, then this automatically implies axiom (a): if demand is a decreasing function of (π_i/μ_i), it is also a decreasing function of $c(\pi_i/\mu_i)$ for any constant $c > 0$, and in particular for $c = \mu_i$.

(c) *Decreasing in premium loading:* $d(\mu_i, \pi_i)$ is a decreasing function of the premium loading (π_i/μ_i).

(d) *Capped at 1:* $d(\mu_i, \pi_i) \leq 1$, that is the highest possible demand is when all members of the risk-group buy insurance.

A simple demand function which satisfies these requirements can be obtained by setting the demand elasticity in Equation (5.2) equal to a constant, say λ_i. Solving this differential equation leads to the so-called *iso-elastic* demand function:

$$d(\mu_i, \pi_i) = \tau_i \left(\frac{\pi_i}{\mu_i}\right)^{-\lambda_i} \tag{5.3}$$

where

- $\tau_i = d(\mu_i, \mu_i)$ is the 'fair-premium demand' for risk-group i, that is the proportion of risk-group i who buy insurance at an actuarially fair premium, that is when $\pi_i = \mu_i$.
- μ_i is the risk (probability of loss) for members of risk-group i.
- λ_i is the demand elasticity for members of risk-group i, as already defined.

To interpret the demand formula in Equation (5.3), observe that it specifies demand as a function of the premium loading (π_i/μ_i). When the premium loading is high (insurance is expensive), demand is low and vice versa. The 'iso-elastic' terminology reflects that price elasticity of demand is the same constant λ_i everywhere along the demand curve.

The λ_i parameter controls the shape of the demand curve. This is illustrated in Figure 5.1, which shows plots of demand from higher and lower risk-groups for three different values of λ in the demand function of Equation (5.3).[2]

The demand function in Equation (5.3) clearly satisfies axioms (a) and (c) above. Axioms (b) and (d) appear superficially to require

---

[2] The i-subscript in λ_i is missing here because Figure 5.1 shows the *same* three alternative values of λ, 0.5, 1 and 1.5, for each risk-group. I follow this convention throughout this chapter: wherever the λ_i are the same for both risk-groups, the i-subscript is omitted.

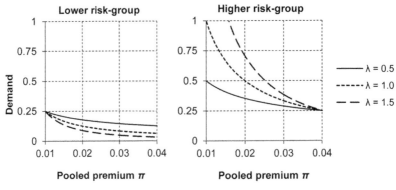

Basis: $p_1 = 0.9; \tau_1 = \tau_2 = 0.25; \mu_1 = 0.01, \mu_2 = 0.04$.

FIGURE 5.1 Iso-elastic demand curves for $\lambda = 0.5$, 1.0 and 1.5

conditions on the fair-premium demands τ_1 and τ_2. In other words, we need to be careful that modelled demand from the lower risk-group is always lower than from the higher risk-group (axiom (b)); and also that modelled demand from the higher risk-group does not exceed 1 at the equilibrium premium (axiom (d)). In Figure 5.1, we can see that the latter point might be a concern for the highest curve in the right panel, the case $\lambda = 1.5$, if the equilibrium-pooled premium happened to be below about 0.016.

However, for the purposes of analysing the mathematical properties of the model, it is convenient to use the following trick. Recall that p_1 and p_2 are the fractions of the total population represented by lower risks and higher risks, respectively. Then define the *fair-premium demand-share* of the lower risk-group as the proportion of total demand which the risk-group represents when actuarially fair premiums are charged to both risk-groups:

$$\text{Fair-premium demand-share: } \alpha_i = \frac{\tau_i p_i}{\tau_1 p_1 + \tau_2 p_2}, \quad i = 1, 2 \qquad (5.4)$$

Clearly α_2, the fair-premium demand-share of the higher risk-group, is just the complement of α_1 (i.e. $\alpha_2 = 1 - \alpha_1$).

We can then analyse the mathematical properties of the model for the full range of possible fair-premium demand-shares $0 \leq \alpha_1 \leq 1$, without worrying about specifying any particular values for the fair-premium demands τ_i and population fractions p_i. It suffices to note that for every possible α_1, there will be *some* hypothetical combination of population structure p_i and fair-premium demand τ_i which satisfies the axioms (b) and (d) above.

Specifying a Zero-Profit Equilibrium Condition

Suppose now that the premiums charged to members of the low risk-group and high risk-group are π_1 and π_2, respectively.

The insurance income[3] (premiums) per member of the population will be the sum of the products of demand and premium for each risk-group:

$$\text{Insurance income} = d(\mu_1, \pi_1)p_1\pi_1 + d(\mu_2, \pi_2)p_2\pi_2 \qquad (5.5)$$

The insurance outgo (claims) per member of the population will be the product of demand and the probability of loss for each risk-group (recall from Chapter 4 that a loss, if it occurs, is always of unit size):

$$\text{Insurance outgo} = d(\mu_1, \pi_1)p_1\mu_1 + d(\mu_2, \pi_2)p_2\mu_2 \qquad (5.6)$$

The right-hand side of Equation (5.6) looks like the definition of loss coverage in Equation (4.8) in Chapter 4. However, loss coverage refers specifically to this quantity *at equilibrium*. The insurance outgo in Equation (5.6) is defined for any premiums, not just equilibrium premiums.

To determine equilibrium premiums, note that the insurer's expected profit (loss, if negative) is expected income less expected outgo, that is Equation (5.5) – Equation (5.6). So any pair of premiums (π_1, π_2) which equates Equations (5.5) and (5.6) is an equilibrium.

---

[3] Strictly this is *expected* insurance income, and similarly the outgo in Equation (5.6) is *expected* insurance outgo. But the 'expected' everywhere can become tedious, so I shall sometimes elide it.

One equilibrium is obvious from inspection: full risk classification (or 'fully risk-differentiated premiums'), that is $\pi_1 = \mu_1$, $\pi_2 = \mu_2$. This represents one extreme.

Another equilibrium – and the main focus in this chapter – is a common 'pooled' premium π_0 for both risk-groups: nil risk classification (or 'pooling') that is $\pi_1 = \pi_2 = \pi_0$. This represents the other extreme.[4] There will always exist some value of π_0 which gives a pooling equilibrium.[5]

Examples

To illustrate the use of this model, set $\mu_1 = 0.01$, $\mu_2 = 0.04$ (i.e. relative risk $\beta = 4$) and $\alpha_1 = 0.9$, that is 90% of the insurance demand under risk-differentiated premiums is from lower risks. These parameter values are used throughout Chapters 5 and 6, except where stated otherwise. The parameters have been chosen by loose analogy with the life insurance market, where typically around 90% of accepted risks are assigned to a large 'standard' risk-group with low mortality, and around 10% of accepted risks are charged a range of higher premiums ranging from +50% to +300% over the standard risk-group's premium. But these values are merely hypothetical and illustrative; they are not presented as a calibrated model of any real market.

Figure 5.2 shows the equilibrium for relatively inelastic demand, $\lambda = 0.5$. Figure 5.2 can be interpreted as follows.

---

[4] Intermediate solutions of 'partial risk classification' where $\pi_1 \neq \pi_2$ are also possible, and will be considered in Chapter 6.

[5] That the pooling equilibrium always exists can be demonstrated as follows. Clearly setting the pooling premium $\pi_0 = \mu_1$ will lead to negative expected profits, because at least some higher risks will buy insurance (and so generate expected losses for insurers) at this cheap price. Setting $\pi_0 = \mu_2$ leads to either zero expected profits, or (provided at least some lower risks buy insurance at this high price) strictly positive expected profits. The expected profit is a continuous function of π_0. Then there is at least one solution in the interval (μ_1, μ_2) such that expected profit is zero (graphically: if the continuous profit function is below the x axis at μ_1 and above the x-axis at μ_2, it must cross the x-axis at least once).

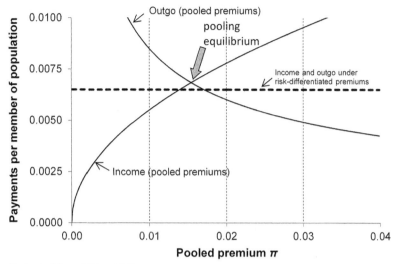

Basis: $\alpha_1 = 0.9; \mu_1 = 0.01, \mu_2 = 0.04.$

FIGURE 5.2 Low elasticity: $\lambda = 0.5$, giving increased loss coverage under pooling

The horizontal dashed line is a reference level representing income and outgo if risk-differentiated premiums are charged: that is, if $\pi_1 = \mu_1$, $\pi_2 = \mu_2$ in Equations (5.5) and (5.6).

The curves represent how income and outgo as defined in Equations (5.5) and (5.6) vary with the level of a common ('pooled') premium which is charged to both risk-groups.

On the left-hand side of the graph, where the premium π is low, demand for insurance at this price is high, and so outgo is high. Because of the very low premium, income is low (despite the high demand); the market is far from equilibrium and insurers make large losses. Insurers will therefore increase the pooled premium, and some customers will leave the market. As customers leave the market, outgo decreases monotonically (the downward sloping curve), but income increases because the number of customers leaving the market is outweighed by the increase in premium collected for each remaining customer. So for demand elasticity $\lambda < 1$, the curve of

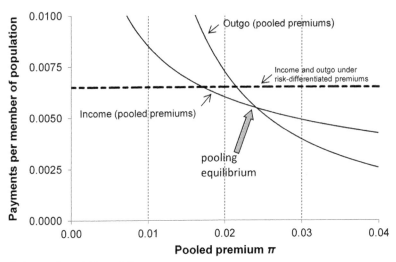

Basis: $\alpha_1 = 0.9; \mu_1 = 0.01, \mu_2 = 0.04$.

FIGURE 5.3 High elasticity: $\lambda = 1.5$, giving reduced loss coverage under pooling

total income slopes upwards.[6] The intersection (shown by the arrow) of the curves for income and outgo represents a pooling equilibrium. The premium at this intersection is the equilibrium pooled premium π_0.

Note that the arrowed intersection is at a higher level of income and outgo than under full risk differentiation. In other words, with the low demand elasticity $\lambda = 0.5$ assumed here, loss coverage under pooling is increased compared with that under risk-differentiated premiums.

Figure 5.3 shows the result for more elastic demand $\lambda = 1.5$, with all other parameters as in Figure 5.2. Note that the equilibrium is at a lower level of income and outgo than when risk-differentiated

---

[6] On the other hand, the curve of total income slopes *downwards* for $\lambda > 1$, as can be seen in Figure 5.3. This is because demand elasticity above 1 means that the number of customers leaving the market when the premium rises is *not* outweighed by the increase in premium collected for each remaining customer.

premiums are charged. In other words, with the higher demand elasticity $\lambda = 1.5$ assumed here, loss coverage under pooling is reduced compared with that under risk-differentiated premiums.

General Results for Iso-elastic Demand with Common Elasticity λ

This section states and illustrates general results for adverse selection, insurance demand (cover) and loss coverage under the iso-elastic demand function as per Equation (5.3), with a common elasticity parameter λ for both risk-groups. Mathematical proofs are omitted in this book, but have been published in Hao et al. (2015, 2016a). In interpreting these results, note that a loss coverage ratio (LCR) above one (LCR > 1) signifies a 'good' outcome from restricting risk classification, and LCR < 1 signifies a 'bad' outcome.

The results stated below are illustrated in Figures 5.4–5.6.

(a) Adverse selection ratio increases monotonically with demand elasticity, to an upper limit where the only remaining insureds are high risks. This is shown in the upper panel of Figure 5.4 for two different relative risks $\beta = 3$ and $\beta = 4$. Note that the asymptotic limiting values of adverse selection ratio are equivalent to the pooled premium when all lower risks have left the insurance market, divided by the weighted average premium under risk-differentiated premiums.

(b) The corresponding change in demand ratio is shown in the lower panel of Figure 5.4. Recall from Chapter 4 that demand ratio represents insurance demand when risk classification is restricted divided by insurance demand under fully risk-differentiated premiums. Demand ratio is therefore a measure of the *reduction in cover* which arises from adverse selection; it is the realisation in our model of what economic rhetoric typically describes as 'efficiency losses' or 'inefficiency' arising from adverse selection.

(c) In contrast to adverse selection ratio and demand ratio, LCR as a function of demand elasticity has an interior maximum, as shown in

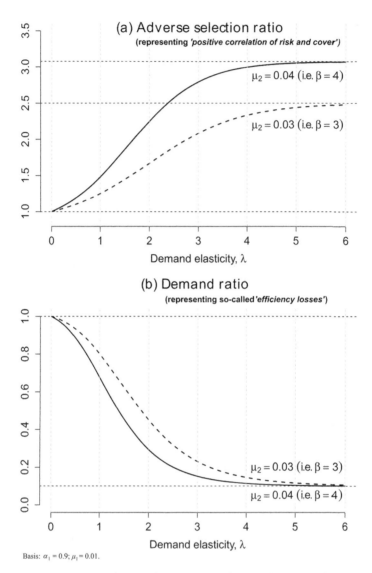

FIGURE 5.4 Adverse selection ratio and demand ratio as a function of demand elasticity, for two relative risks

the upper left region of Figure 5.5. In other words, *loss coverage is maximised with a non-zero level of adverse selection,* irrespective of whether adverse selection is characterised as 'positive correlation of cover and losses' (as in this book, and as in most econometric tests for

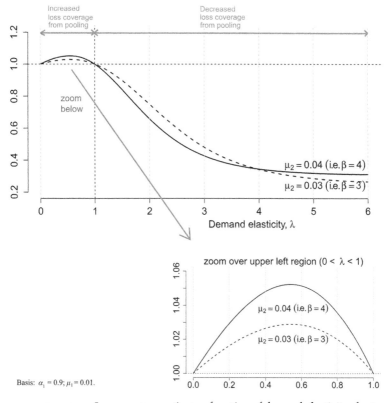

FIGURE 5.5 Loss coverage ratio as a function of demand elasticity, for two relative risks

adverse selection) or as 'reduction in cover' (what economic rhetoric calls 'efficiency losses').[7]

---

[7] This addresses an objection which is sometimes made by economists regarding graphs such as the upper panel in Figure 5.4. The objection says that positive correlation of cover and losses is only a *test* for adverse selection, not a *definition* of adverse selection, and that economists' concerns with adverse selection focus on the 'inefficient' reduction in cover when risk classification is restricted, rather than the correlation of cover and losses *per se*. The lower panel of Figure 4 shows that even if we define adverse selection as 'reduction in cover', we get the same pattern: loss coverage is maximised with a non-zero level of adverse selection. At this point economists sometimes further remark that the concept of inefficiency arising from adverse selection really relates neither to 'positive correlation' nor to 'reduction in cover', but instead has some other definition. My response to such constantly changing definitions of adverse selection is given in the final paragraph under 'Suggestions for Economists' in Chapter 14.

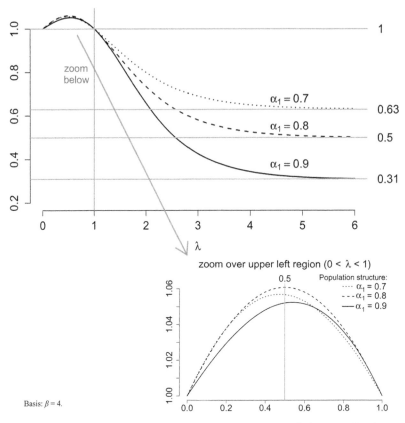

FIGURE 5.6 Loss coverage ratio as a function of demand elasticity, for three population structures

(d) For iso-elastic demand, demand elasticity of 1 always gives LCR of 1, as shown in Figure 5.5 (i.e. both curves pass through the coordinate (1,1)). Lower values of demand elasticity give LCR above 1, and vice versa, that is

$$\lambda \overset{<}{\underset{>}{\gtrless}} 1 \Rightarrow \mathrm{LCR}(\lambda) \overset{>}{\underset{<}{\lessgtr}} 1 \qquad (5.7)$$

So for the iso-elastic demand function, $\lambda = 1$ represents a critical value of demand elasticity, which determines whether loss coverage is increased or reduced by pooling all risks in a single class, as compared with loss coverage under risk differentiated premiums.

(e) For high values of λ, loss coverage flattens out at a lower limit where the only remaining insureds are high risks. This is shown towards the right side of the main graph in Figure 5.5.

(f) The smaller graph on the lower right in Figure 5.5 zooms over the upper left region of the main graph, that is the region where $0 < \lambda < 1$. It can be seen that as demand elasticity increases from zero, LCR increases from 1 to a maximum at around demand elasticity $\lambda = 0.5$. A higher relative risk β gives a higher maximum value of LCR. Note that in this region $0 < \lambda < 1$, the common characterisation of adverse selection as 'inefficient' seems unreasonable. With adverse selection, more risk is being voluntarily traded, and more losses are being compensated.

(g) The value of the maximum for LCR in the zoomed region in Figure 5.5 is higher for $\beta = 4$ than for $\beta = 3$. The maximum is also affected by the population structure. To be precise, the maximum depends on the *fair-premium risk-share*, say w (note: not the same as the *fair-premium demand-share α_i* previously defined in Equation (5.4)), i.e. the fraction of total insured risk which lower risks represent when actuarially fair premiums are charged:

$$w = \frac{\alpha_1 \mu_1}{\alpha_1 \mu_1 + \alpha_2 \mu_2}. \tag{5.8}$$

(h) Figure 5.6 shows loss coverage for three population structures, all with relative risk $\beta = 4$. The smaller graph on the lower right zooms over the region $0 < \lambda < 1$. The curve with the highest maximum for LCR is that corresponding to population structure $\alpha_1 = 0.8$; this corresponds to a fair-premium risk-share of:

$$w = \frac{0.8 \times 0.01}{(0.8 \times 0.01 + 0.2 \times 0.04)} = 0.5 \tag{5.9}$$

(i) For the iso-elastic demand function used in this chapter, it can be shown that if both demand elasticity and population structure can vary, the maximum value for LCR occurs when $\lambda = 0.5$ and $w = 0.5$. This maximum value for LCR is:

$$\max_{w,\lambda} \mathrm{LCR} = \frac{1}{2} \left(\sqrt[4]{\beta} + \frac{1}{\sqrt[4]{\beta}} \right) \tag{5.10}$$

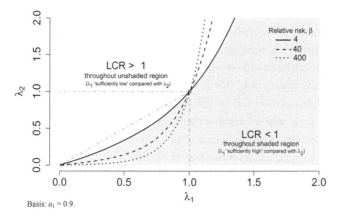

FIGURE 5.7 Regions of (λ_1, λ_2) space where loss coverage ratio is greater or less than 1

(j) The form of Equation (5.10) combined with the requirement for $w = 0.5$ suggests that pooling will be particularly beneficial to loss coverage when there is small risk-group with very high risk (since this combination allows high relative risk β to be combined with fair-premium risk-share $w \approx 0.5$). One obvious example is a small fraction of the population with an adverse genetic profile.[8]

General Results for Iso-elastic Demand with Different Elasticities $(\lambda_1 \neq \lambda_2)$

When the elasticity parameters λ_1 and λ_2 for the low and high risk-groups are different, it becomes harder to make concise general statements about how they affect loss coverage. The general pattern of results is shown in Figure 5.7. This shows the regions in the (λ_1, λ_2) plane where LCR is above or below 1 (i.e. pooling gives higher or

---

[8] The result in Equation (5.10) is proved as Result B.3 in the appendix of Hao et al. (2016a). A similar conclusion that pooling is particularly beneficial in the presence of a small group with high risk is reached via a different argument by the economist Michael Hoy (2006).

lower loss coverage than risk-differentiated premiums). The graph can be explained as follows.

(a) First, ignore the two dashed curves in Figure 5.7 and focus just on the solid curve for $\beta = 4$ (a relative risk of 4, e.g. $\mu_1 = 0.01$, $\mu_2 = 0.04$). This curve demarcates a left-hand unshaded region containing all combinations of (λ_1, λ_2) for which LCR > 1, and a right-hand shaded region containing all combinations for which LCR < 1. Note that LCR > 1 is associated with movement towards the upper left of the graph: that is, to give LCR > 1, λ_1 needs to be 'sufficiently low' relative to λ_2.

(b) Second, note that λ_1 *sufficiently low relative to* λ_2 does not necessarily mean λ_1 *lower than* λ_2. In particular, in the lower part of the unshaded area inside the unit square in Figure 5.7 (the narrow segment *below* the dashed 45° line, but *above* the solid curve), λ_1 is slightly higher than λ_2, and yet still 'sufficiently low' to give LCR > 1.

(c) Third, focus now on the two dashed curves in Figure 5.7. The dashed curves illustrate how the solid curve demarcating the left-hand LCR > 1 (unshaded) and right-hand LCR < 1 (shaded) regions shifts as the relative risk β changes. Note that as relative risk β increases, the curve demarcating the regions becomes more convex, so that a greater range of combinations of λ_1 and λ_2 inside the unit square gives LCR > 1. But the effect is small: increasing the relative risk from 4 to 40 times or even 400 times makes only a small difference to the curve.

Comparison with Empirical Demand Elasticities: $\lambda < 1$ is Realistic

The results summarised in Figures 5.4–5.7 suggest that under iso-elastic demand, pooling will give higher loss coverage than fully risk-differentiated premiums:

(a) in the equal elasticities case, whenever demand elasticity is less than 1;

(b) in the different elasticities case, whenever $\lambda_1 < 1$ and $\lambda_1 < \lambda_2$ (in Figure 5.7, the part of the unshaded region vertically above the $\lambda_1 = \lambda_2$ diagonal and to the left of $\lambda_1 = 1$);

(c) for some values outside this range, provided λ_1 is 'sufficiently low' relative to λ_2 (in Figure 5.7, other parts of the unshaded region).

Table 5.1. *Estimates of demand elasticity for various insurance markets*

Market and country	Estimated demand elasticities	References
Yearly renewable term life insurance, USA	−0.4 to −0.5	Pauly et al. (2003)
Term life insurance, USA	−0.66	Viswanathan et al. (2007)
Whole life insurance, USA	−0.71 to −0.92	Babbel (1985)
Health insurance, USA	0 to −0.2	Chernew et al. (1997), Blumberg et al. (2001), Buchmueller and Ohri (2006)
Health insurance, Australia	−0.35 to −0.50	Butler (1999)
Farm crop insurance, USA	−0.32 to −0.73	Goodwin (1993)

How do these limits compare with demand elasticities in the real world? There is some evidence that insurance demand elasticities are less than 1 in many markets. Table 5.1 shows some relevant empirical estimates. (For convenience the elasticity parameter in this chapter was defined as a positive constant, but estimates in empirical papers are generally given with the negative sign, so the table quotes them in that form.) These estimates suggest that if the iso-elastic demand model is reasonable, loss coverage might often be increased by restricting risk classification.[9]

[9] The estimates in Table 5.1 are *product elasticities*, which pertain to demand for insurance *from the whole market*. Anecdotally, pricing actuaries sometimes make reference to much higher demand elasticities. For example, the demand elasticity for a particular car insurer quoting rates on an aggregator platform (e.g. gocompare or confused.com) may be as high as 10 or 20. These are *brand elasticities*, which pertain to demand for insurance *from a particular insurer*. It is plausible that brand elasticities may be much higher than product elasticities, but it is the latter that are relevant when considering restrictions on risk classification applied equally to all insurers.

Loss Coverage under Alternative Demand Functions

The 'iso-elastic' property of the demand function used above implies that demand elasticity does not change as the premium changes. This is mathematically tractable, but it is arguably unrealistic: the usual pattern for most goods and services is that demand elasticity increases as price increases. To accommodate this pattern, more flexible demand specifications are needed.

One such specification is to assume that demand elasticity is a linearly increasing function of the premium, and the same irrespective of the individual's risk-group. This leads to the *negative exponential* demand function. If we relax the constraint of *linearity* in the increase of elasticity with premium, we then have the *generalised negative exponential* demand function.

The mathematical details of these demand functions are given in Appendix A. In the present chapter, I just show Figure 5.8, which plots loss coverage ratio against demand elasticity for three demand functions: iso-elastic (as used so far in this chapter), negative exponential and generalised negative exponential with a key parameter

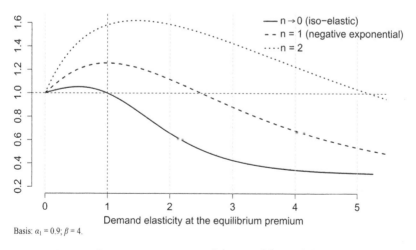

Basis: $\alpha_1 = 0.9$; $\beta = 4$.

FIGURE 5.8 Loss coverage ratio as a function of demand elasticity, for three versions of generalised negative exponential demand

n set to 2 (this parameter n is the 'elasticity of elasticity', also known as the 'second-order elasticity').

I first need to clarify a technical point about the definition of 'demand elasticity' on the x-axis in Figure 5.8. With iso-elastic demand in Figures 5.4–5.6, I plotted loss coverage ratio against a single λ parameter. This parameter represents the elasticity parameter value (common to both risk-groups) of $\lambda_1 = \lambda_2 = \lambda$; and because of the iso-elastic property, it also represents the *actual* demand elasticity at *any* premium. For the alternative demand functions, demand elasticity varies as a function of the premium. But because the alternative demand functions assume that demand elasticity is the *same* increasing function of premium for both risk-groups (the details are given in Appendix A), we can still define a single measure of elasticity for the x-axis: we just plot loss coverage against the *actual demand elasticity (which is the same for both risk-groups) at the equilibrium premium.*

I now move to results. Figure 5.8 shows the plot of loss coverage ratio as a function of demand elasticity at the equilibrium premium, for generalised negative exponential demand with three parameter values for the second-order elasticity:

– $n \to 0$ (this corresponds to iso-elastic demand);
– $n = 1$ (this corresponds to negative exponential demand); and
– $n = 2$ (this corresponds to generalised negative exponential demand).

The solid curve (the iso-elastic case) in this graph is the same as the solid curve in the earlier Figures 5.5 and 5.6. The dashed and dotted curves (the negative exponential and generalised negative exponential cases, respectively) are above the horizontal line representing LCR = 1 for a wider range of demand elasticities. In other words, the iso-elastic case used throughout the earlier parts of this chapter is actually the 'least favourable' case for restrictions on risk classification.

Taken together, the three curves in Figure 5.8 suggest that the main point of this book is robust to a variety of plausible demand functions. For all these demand functions, loss coverage is higher under pooling compared with risk-differentiated premiums, provided demand elasticity is sufficiently low.

Multiple Equilibria: A Technical Curiosity

In footnote 5, I gave a simple argument to show that a pooled equilibrium premium π_0 always exists (the profit function crosses the x-axis *at least* once), but I did not show that it was unique (the profit function crosses the x-axis *only* once). For some extreme population structures and extreme differences between the risk-groups in demand elasticities, the profit function can generate multiple equilibria. In other words, the zero-profit condition can be satisfied by more than one pooled premium (π_{0A}, π_{0B}, π_{0C}, etc.). This technical curiosity turns out not to be important in practice, because the parameter values required to generate multiple equilibria are implausible. But to demonstrate this implausibility, it is necessary to analyse how multiple equilibria can arise, and establish limits on the parameter values which are required. In view of its technical nature, this is dealt with in Appendix B.

Summary

The main points of Chapter 5 can be summarised as follows.

1. This chapter has introduced models of insurance market equilibrium under restricted risk classification, principally with a simple iso-elastic demand function, but also considering alternative demand functions. Although the results differ in detail, the general pattern is the same for all the demand functions considered (see Figure 5.8). The main point of this book is robust to the different demand functions: loss coverage is higher under pooling than under risk-differentiated premiums, provided demand elasticity is sufficiently low.

2. For iso-elastic demand, demand elasticity of 1 is a critical value, which determines whether loss coverage is increased or reduced by pooling all risks at a common premium, as compared with loss coverage under

risk-differentiated premiums. Demand elasticity of 1 gives loss coverage ratio (LCR) of 1. Lower values of demand elasticity give LCR above 1, and vice versa, that is:

$$\lambda \lesseqgtr 1 \Rightarrow LCR(\lambda) \gtreqless 1.$$

3. For the other demand functions we considered, the critical value of demand elasticity at the equilibrium premium, which determines whether loss coverage is increased or reduced by pooling, is above 1 (the other curves in Figure 5.8 cross the x-axis at $x > 1$). In other words, pooling gives higher loss coverage for a wider range of demand elasticities.

4. There is some evidence that insurance demand elasticities are less than 1 in many markets. Together with (2) and (3) above, this suggests a realistic possibility that in the real world, loss coverage can often be increased by restricting risk classification.

6 Partial Risk Classification, Separation and Inclusivity

Key Ideas:

partial risk classification; separation; inclusivity

Chapters 3–5 considered only two polar cases: fully risk-differentiated prices (where risk classification is unrestricted) and complete pooling (where risk classification is banned). Another possibility – and perhaps a more realistic one – is that insurers are allowed to differentiate prices to some extent, but not so much as to fully reflect differences between high and low risks. For example, suppose insurers are allowed to differentiate life insurance prices by age but not by gender, and obtain some but not all of any relevant medical history. Then even where insurers attempt to differentiate prices by risk, the highest-risk insured lives may be charged prices less than their true risk, and conversely for the lowest-risk. This chapter considers such schemes of 'partial risk classification', in contradistinction to 'nil risk classification' (complete pooling) and 'full risk classification' (fully risk-differentiated prices).[1]

---

[1] My framing of 'partial risk classification' in this chapter is that differences in risks (probabilities of loss) are fully observable, but regulation requires that the differences are only partly reflected in differences in prices. At the individual level, this is not quite the same as 'classification by imperfectly correlated observables' (e.g. Hoy, 1982; Crocker and Snow, 1986). By the latter, I mean the use of variables such as gender in car insurance. Gender is an observable which is correlated with underlying risk, but the correlation is less than 1: not *all* men are high risk, and not *all* women are low risk. However at the aggregate level, 'partial risk classification' as in this chapter produces much the same pattern of outcomes as 'classification by imperfectly correlated observables'. If the true risk-levels are μ_1 and μ_2 and insurers classify by reference to an imperfectly correlated observable into two risk pools, with the price in each pool adjusted over time to converge on zero-profit premiums π_1 and π_2, then $\mu_1 < \pi_1 < \pi_2 < \mu_2$, the same pattern as emerges from my framing in this chapter.

This chapter also introduces a novel metric for the degree to which different risks are pooled into broad risk-groups where all members of each risk-group are charged the same price. I call this metric the *inclusivity* of risk classification. I call the complement of inclusivity, that is one minus inclusivity, the *separation* of risk classification.

Partial Risk Classification

To represent partial risk classification in the two risk-group model as used in Chapters 4 and 5, think of starting from an initial position of fully risk-differentiated prices. Total expected profits are zero, and expected profits on both risk-groups individually are zero. Then suppose that a monopoly insurer (or competing insurers, under suitable regulation) slightly reduces the premium for high risks.[2] Demand from high risks will rise, and there is an expected loss on each high risk. To break even, the insurer then needs to increase the premium for low risks. Demand from low risks will fall, and there is an expected profit on each low risk. At a suitably increased low-risk premium, the expected profits on (a reduced number of) low risks will exactly offset the expected losses on (an increased number of) high risks. There are infinitely many possible solutions (π_1, π_2) of the profit equation like this, each corresponding to a different scheme of partial risk classification. Using other notation as in Chapters 4 and 5, the solutions are given by:

$$\sum_{i=1}^{2} d(\mu_i, \pi_i) p_i \pi_i = \sum_{i=1}^{2} d(\mu_i, \pi_i) p_i \mu_i \qquad (6.1)$$

[2] We need to assume either monopoly or regulation of risk classification because without this, the process of 'competitive adverse selection' (as described more fully in Chapter 8) may tend to push all insurers towards using fully risk-differentiated prices.

The change in high-risk and low-risk demand consequent upon the change in prices implies that loss coverage will also change. Loss coverage under partial risk classification is given by:

$$LC(\pi_1, \pi_2) = \sum_{i=1}^{2} d(\mu_i, \pi_i) p_i \mu_i \qquad (6.2)$$

where (π_1, π_2) are a pair of prices which satisfy the zero-profit condition in Equation (6.1).

This leads to the question: under what risk classification scheme is loss coverage maximised: fully risk-differentiated prices, complete pooling or some intermediate scheme of partial risk classification?

The question can be answered by performing a constrained optimisation of the premiums (π_1, π_2), with loss coverage as the objective function and the zero-profit condition as a constraint. The results depend on the nature of insurance demand, as specified by the demand elasticities. Figure 6.1 illustrates results for the iso-elastic demand function used in Chapter 5. The graph shows which type of risk classification – full, partial or nil – gives the

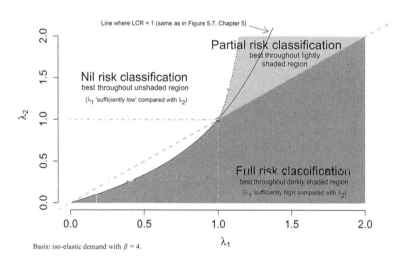

FIGURE 6.1 Risk classification scheme giving highest loss coverage in different regions of the (λ_1, λ_2) parameter space

highest possible loss coverage in each region of the (λ_1, λ_2) parameter space.

Figure 6.1 can be interpreted as follows.

(a) The convex curve from the origin extending into the middle of the lightly shaded region is the line along which LCR = 1, that is where nil and full risk classification give the same loss coverage. (Note that this line is the same line as shown in Figure 5.7.)

(b) In the unshaded left-hand region (i.e. λ_1 'sufficiently low' compared with λ_2), nil risk classification is optimal; and conversely in the darkly shaded right-hand region, full risk classification is optimal. This accords with intuition: other things equal, lower demand elasticity in the low risk-group or higher demand elasticity in the high risk-group should make pooling more beneficial, and vice versa.

(c) Partial risk classification is optimal only in the lightly shaded middle region where both elasticities exceed 1, with λ_2 *somewhat* higher (but not *too much* higher) than λ_1. The nature of the partial risk classification scheme which maximises loss coverage varies progressively as we move horizontally across this middle region, from 'almost nil' at the left boundary to 'almost full' at the right boundary. Details of the boundary conditions are given in the footnote.[3]

(d) At the graph coordinate (1,1) where $\lambda_1 = \lambda_2 = 1$, the three regions in the graph converge: all risk classification schemes give the same loss coverage. This is consistent with a well-known property of iso-elastic demand with unit demand elasticity: total revenues (in this context, premiums) are invariant to price. 'Invariant to price' is equivalent in this context to 'invariant to the risk classification scheme'. Since expected premiums must also equal expected claims (loss coverage) in equilibrium, it follows that loss coverage is then invariant to the risk classification scheme.

(e) The lightly shaded middle region where partial risk classification gives the highest loss coverage is a region where both demand elasticities are higher than one, with λ_2 higher (but not too much higher) than λ_1.

---

[3] The left boundary is given by $\frac{\lambda_1}{\lambda_2} \frac{(\lambda_2 - 1)}{(\lambda_1 - 1)} = \frac{\mu_2}{\mu_1} = \beta$. In the graph as shown, $\beta = 4$ (as indicated by the small '4' printed on the left boundary). For higher values of relative risk than 4, this left boundary rotates very slightly anticlockwise, and vice versa. The right boundary is the 45° line from the origin, i.e. the line given by $\lambda_1 = \lambda_2$.

Separation and Inclusivity of Risk Classification

In the discussion above, I noted that there were many feasible equilibrium partial risk classifications (π_1, π_2). The prices π_1 and π_2 are 'close together' in some risk classification schemes (close to nil risk classification, towards the left of the lightly shaded middle region in Figure 6.1), and 'far apart' in other risk classification schemes (close to full risk classification, towards the right of the lightly shaded middle region in Figure 6.1). Informally, the former type of scheme can be said to have a low 'degree' or 'gradation' of risk classification, and conversely for the latter type. It would be useful to have a metric to index the 'degree' or 'gradation' of a risk classification scheme. The rest of this chapter defines and explores a metric for this purpose, the *separation* of a risk classification scheme and its complement *inclusivity* (i.e. one minus separation).

Two Risk-Groups: Linear Separation

For the two risk-group model used so far in this book, I suggest a simple metric of *linear separation*. Suppose that (π_1, π_2) is a 'partial risk classification' solution of the zero-profit condition given in Equation (6.1), i.e. premiums are neither completely pooled nor fully risk-differentiated, but instead only partly reflect the difference in true risks μ_1 and μ_2. Then the linear separation of risk classification is:

$$\text{Linear separation} = \frac{(\pi_2 - \pi_1)}{(\mu_2 - \mu_1)} \tag{6.3}$$

that is, the distance between the premiums divided by the distance between the true risks.

Interpretation of this metric is intuitive: linear separation is 0 for nil risk classification and 1 for full risk classification, with intermediate values for partial risk classification.

Why Is Separation Interesting?

There are four main ways in which I envisage that separation (or its complement inclusivity) may be a useful concept when discussing risk classification schemes.

(a) *Intuitive description of different 'degrees' of risk classification.* Separation characterises in a direct and intuitive way different versions of partial risk classification – close to fully risk-differentiated prices, close to complete pooling, and all points in between. Characterising these different versions by the resulting adverse selection or loss coverage seems less direct and intuitive.

(b) *Quantification of differences between markets in risk classification.* In car insurance in many countries, there is 'a lot' of risk classification (prices are close to fully risk-differentiated). In health insurance in many countries, there is only 'a little' risk classification (e.g. under Obamacare premiums can vary by a maximum of 3 times for age, and 1.5 times for smoking status). We need a concept to quantify the difference between the typical approaches to risk classification in car insurance and in health insurance. Separation is that concept.

(c) *Quantification of political or ethical objective.* I believe that many people see high inclusivity as politically or ethically desirable for health insurance (and to some extent for life insurance, and sometimes for other types of insurance). This preference often seems quite resistant to arguments about adverse selection or loss coverage; that is, the preference is to some degree independent of the aggregate insurance market outcomes it produces. Since different people seem to have different 'strengths' of this type of preference, we need a metric to quantify it.[4]

---

[4] One statement of this view is given in the insurance chapter of the Human Genetics Commission (2002) report:

It appears to us from our survey of the People's Panel and our consultation that there is a widely held public view that those who are affected by genetic conditions should not feel excluded from the normal benefits of society (employment, participation in public life, and, it might be argued, access to insurance). Over recent decades, the position of disabled people has been steadily improved by legislation ... It would run counter to this commitment if society were to allow new classes of persons to grow up which would be subjected to improper discrimination. (p. 128)

(d) *Object of regulation.* Separation may be a useful metric for regulation of risk classification. For example, the Obamacare rules mentioned above (premiums can vary by a maximum of 3 times for age, and 1.5 times for smoking status) are controls on separation (albeit separation defined by maximum range, rather than the definition I have suggested).

More than Two Risk-Groups: Lorenz Separation

In the real world, realistic risk classification schemes normally involve more than two risk-groups. Each risk-group is identified by the premium charged to all members of the risk-group. Individuals are allocated by the insurer to the risk-group 'closest' to their true risk. Expressed mathematically, risk classification is a function $f(\mu_i)$ which maps true risk (probability of loss) μ_i to premium π_j according to the following rule[5]:

$$f(\mu_i) = \pi_j \Leftrightarrow \operatorname*{argmin}_{k} |\mu_i - \pi_k| = j \qquad (6.4)$$

subject to the 'tie-breaker' that if $|\mu_i - \pi_k|$ is equal for two values of k, we choose the higher π_k.

To generalise the concept of separation for use with more than two risk-groups, we can use the concept of Lorenz curves. Lorenz curves are generally used to represent distributions of income and wealth over the members of a population, but they can also represent distributions of premiums and true risks. The basic idea of Lorenz separation is to compare the shapes of two Lorenz curves, one for premiums and one for true risks. The relevant population for whom the comparison is made are the people who buy insurance.

---

[5] I continue to assume, as in Chapters 4 and 5, that the true risk μ_i is observable by the insurer. Where this is not so, the insurer's *estimate* of true risk will necessarily be used. If there is an error in the insurer's estimate of true risk, this could be called (unintentional) *misclassification*, rather than (intentional) partial classification as in this chapter. Misclassification is not considered in this book (except from the viewpoint of an 'adverse selecting' customer in Chapter 11).

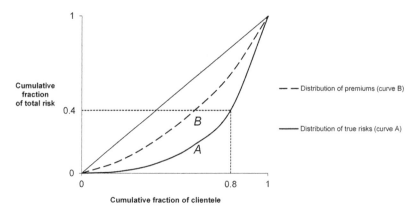

FIGURE 6.2 Lorenz curves denoting distributions of true risks and premiums

I call this population the insurance *clientele*. Two Lorenz curves for premiums and true risks for an insurance clientele are shown in Figure 6.2.

In Figure 6.2, the solid curve labelled *A* represents the distribution of true risks over the clientele. As drawn, the solid curve shows that the lower-risk 80% of the clientele by number account for 40% of the total risk of the clientele: risk is relatively concentrated in the highest-risk individuals (e.g. four individuals with risk of 0.01 and one individual with risk of 0.06). If the solid curve approaches the 45° line, all individuals in the clientele have the same risk. If the solid curve slumps away towards a right-angled shape with corner at the lower right, a single high-risk individual represents all the clientele's risk.

The dashed curve labelled *B* represents the distribution of premiums over the clientele. If the dashed curve coincides with the solid curve, we have full risk classification (fully risk-differentiated premiums). If the dashed curve coincides with the 45° line, we have nil risk classification (complete pooling). If the dashed curve follows an intermediate path, as shown in Figure 6.2, we have partial risk classification.

We then define the Lorenz separation of risk classification as follows[6]:

$$\text{Lorenz separation}, D = \frac{\text{Area from } 45° \text{ line to curve B}}{\text{Area from } 45° \text{ line to curve A}} \quad (6.5)$$

As with linear separation, interpretation of this metric is intuitive: $D = 0$ for nil risk classification (the Lorenz curve for premiums coincides with the 45° line); $D = 1$ for full risk classification (the Lorenz curve for premiums coincides with that for true risks); and D takes intermediate values for partial risk classification. Risk classification schemes with values of D outside the [0,1] range are conceivable, but can generally be disregarded as perverse and unfair.[7]

Lorenz curves are often described by Gini coefficients. The Gini coefficient of the distribution of premiums is the area between the 45° line and the dashed curve, divided by the entire area below the 45° line. Hence writing G_π for the Gini coefficient of premiums and G_μ for the Gini coefficient of true risks, we can write Lorenz separation in Equation (6.5) as

$$\text{Lorenz separation}, D = \frac{G_\pi}{G_\mu} \quad (6.6)$$

For a finite number of observations, the Gini coefficient can be estimated as half the 'relative mean absolute difference', that is the mean absolute difference between all possible pairs of

---

[6] I use D (for 'Distance') rather than S to denote separation, because S is used to denote social welfare in other recent work on loss coverage (e.g. Hao et al., 2016b).

[7] $D > 1$ if the distribution of premiums is 'hyper-separated' (i.e. low risks are assigned premiums even lower than their true risk, and conversely for high risks); $D < 0$ if high premiums are charged to low risks and low premiums are charged to high risks (treating any part of the dashed curve above the 45° line as delineating 'negative area'). While schemes like these can break even if demand elasticities are sufficiently different, I think that in most scenarios, most people would regard them as perverse and unfair.

observations, divided by the mean of the observations.[8] That is, for n observations x_i, the relative mean absolute difference is:

$$\text{Relative mean absolute difference} = \frac{\frac{1}{n^2}\sum_{i=1}^{n}\sum_{j=1}^{n}|x_i - x_j|}{\overline{x}} \qquad (6.7)$$

We can use Equation (6.7) to obtain a formula to estimate the right-hand side of Equation (6.6). First note the following two preliminaries:

(i) In any equilibrium scheme of risk classification, the mean of the premiums (weighted by numbers of risks charged each premium) must be equal to the mean of the corresponding true risks.

(ii) Assume the clientele comprises n individuals with true risks $(\mu_1, \mu_2, ..., \mu_n)$, which the risk classification scheme assigns into $m < n$ distinct risk-groups $(\pi_1, \pi_2, ..., \pi_m)$. So when calculating the relative mean absolute difference of the premiums, each absolute difference $|\pi_i - \pi_j|$ needs to be repeated once for each of the n_i individuals who are paying premium π_i; and then for each of those individuals, the absolute difference with the premium π_j needs to be repeated once for each of the n_j individuals who are paying premium π_j. So each $|\pi_i - \pi_j|$ is repeated a total of $n_i \times n_j$ times, giving an overall total of n^2 absolute differences. This is the same as the number of absolute differences between the n true risks.[9]

Taking (i) and (ii) together, the n^2 and $\overline{x}$ in Equation (6.7) are the same when we calculate Equation (6.7) for either the premiums or the corresponding true risks. So we can omit them in both the numerator and denominator of Equation (6.6), and hence write Equation (6.6) as:

$$\text{Lorenz separation}, D = \frac{\sum_{i=1}^{m}\sum_{j=1}^{m} n_i n_j |\pi_i - \pi_j|}{\sum_{i=1}^{n}\sum_{j=1}^{n}|\mu_i - \mu_j|} \qquad (6.8)$$

---

[8] This was originally shown in Gini (1921).
[9] Each of the n risks has differences with $(n - 1)$ others; the nth difference enumerated in n^2 is the 'difference with itself', which is always zero.

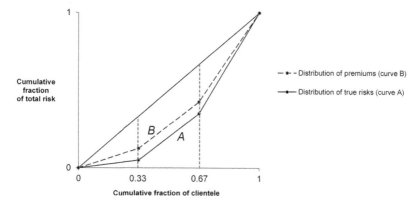

FIGURE 6.3 Lorenz curves when low, medium and high risks are overpriced, fairly priced and underpriced

In words, Lorenz separation is the sum of the absolute difference between each premium and all other premiums (weighted by the numbers paying that premium), divided by the sum of the absolute difference between each true risk and all other true risks. Both numerator and denominator sum over all individuals in the clientele.

Note that Lorenz separation represents a generalisation of linear separation: Equation (6.8) with two risk-groups and two levels of true risk reduces to Equation (6.3).

The geometry of the Lorenz curves provides a visual representation of the cross-subsidies implicit in a risk classification scheme. For example, consider a clientele comprising one-third by number of each of low, medium and high risks, with uniform risk within each of these risk-groups. Suppose the low risks are overpriced, the medium risks are assigned an actuarially fair price and the high risks are underpriced. The Lorenz curves then look something like Figure 6.3 (note that the middle segments of the curves are parallel).

Numerical Example

To illustrate the concept of Lorenz separation for comparing risk classification schemes, consider a population of five risks [0.01,

0.02, 0.03, 0.05, 0.09], and the following alternative schedules of premiums (i.e. risk classification schemes):

Alternative premium schedules:
(a) 5 risk-groups: [0.01, 0.02, 0.03, 0.05, 0.09]
(b) 3 risk-groups: [0.025, 0.06, 0.08]
(c) 2 risk-groups: [0.03, 0.07]
(d) 1 risk-group: [0.07]

Under each premium schedule, the insurer assigns individuals to the nearest premium to their true risk (i.e. in line with the rule given in Equation (6.4) in this chapter). Note that scheme (a) has fully risk-differentiated prices, and scheme (d) has complete pooling. As the risk classification scheme progresses from (a) to (d), we expect adverse selection: that is, the clientele will shift towards the higher risks, and reduce in number. Suppose that the clientele attracted by each premium schedule can be summarised as follows:

Clienteles attracted by the alternative premium schedules:
(a) 4 risks: [0.01, 0.02, 0.03, 0.05]
(b) 4 risks: [0.02, 0.03, 0.05, 0.09]
(c) 3 risks: [0.03, 0.05, 0.09]
(d) 2 risks: [0.05, 0.09]

Note that under scheme (a), fully risk-differentiated prices, the highest-risk individual does not buy insurance, because she perceives the price of 0.09 as unaffordable. As we progress from scheme (a) towards scheme (d), the highest-risk individual joins the clientele, and lower-risk individuals drop out, because they perceive the prices offered to them as poor value. Note that all the premium schedules (a) to (d) are equilibrium schedules, i.e. under each schedule, expected profits are zero for the clientele attracted by that schedule.

Table 6.1 shows values of Lorenz separation calculated using Equation (6.8) for each of the alternative risk classification schemes (a) to (d). Lorenz separation decreases as we move from fully risk-differentiated prices in scheme (a) towards complete pooling in scheme (d).

Table 6.1. *Lorenz separations and loss coverage under four alternative risk classification schemes*

Risk classification scheme (premium schedule)	True risk-levels of clientele attracted by the scheme	Lorenz separation	Loss coverage ratio
(a) [0.01, 0.02, 0.03, 0.05, 0.09]	[0.01, 0.02, 0.03, 0.05]	1	1
(b) [0.025, 0.06, 0.08]	[0.02, 0.03, 0.05, 0.09]	0.870	1.72
(c) [0.03, 0.07]	[0.03, 0.05, 0.09]	0.667	1.54
(d) [0.07]	[0.05, 0.09]	0	1.27

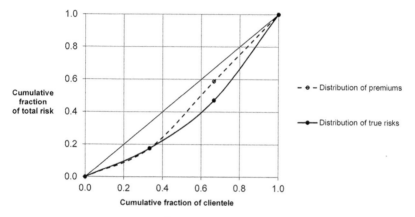

FIGURE 6.4 Lorenz curves for premiums and true risks under risk classification scheme (c) from Table 6.1

Table 6.1 also shows the loss coverage ratio for each of the alternative risk classification schemes (a) to (d). Loss coverage ratio is highest under risk classification scheme (b), which has an intermediate value of separation.

Figure 6.4 illustrates Lorenz separation for risk classification scheme (c) in Table 6.1, that is two risk-groups attracting a clientele of three risks. The solid curve represents the distribution of the three true risks in the clientele. The dashed curve represents the distribution of the two premiums to which the risk classification scheme assigns the three true risks. By inspection, the area between the 45° line and the dashed curve appears to be around two-thirds of the area between the 45° line and the solid curve. This corresponds well to the separation of 0.667 calculated using Equation (6.8) and shown in the third line of Table 6.1.

Separation versus Inclusivity

Separation and inclusivity are complements, and so any reference to one of them immediately implies the other. In this chapter I have usually referenced separation, because this is more mathematically convenient. In the discussion in later chapters, I usually refer to the complement, inclusivity, because this is more verbally convenient. (This usage of a complement for verbal convenience is analogous to usage of the term 'power' in statistical hypothesis testing: the power of a statistical test is one minus the probability of a Type II error.)

Summary

The main points of this chapter can be summarised as follows.

1. This chapter has discussed loss coverage under partial risk classification, where insurers set prices which only partly reflect differences between high and low risks. Typically this will be because of regulation.
2. Loss coverage may sometimes be maximised by neither complete pooling nor fully risk-differentiated prices, but by an intermediate degree of partial risk classification. To quantify the idea of different 'degrees' of partial risk classification, I defined the concepts of separation of risk classification, and its complement, inclusivity (one minus separation).
3. For two risk-groups, linear separation is defined as:

$$\text{Linear separation} = \frac{(\pi_2 - \pi_1)}{(\mu_2 - \mu_1)}$$

4. For any number of risk-groups, Lorenz separation is defined as:

$$\text{Lorenz separation}, D = \frac{G_\pi}{G_\mu}$$

where G_π and G_μ are the Gini coefficients of the Lorenz curves for premiums and true risks, respectively, for the insurance clientele.

5. Lorenz separation can be estimated by the formula:

$$\text{Lorenz separation, } D = \frac{\sum_{i=1}^{m} \sum_{j=1}^{m} n_i n_j |\pi_i - \pi_j|}{\sum_{i=1}^{n} \sum_{j=1}^{n} |\mu_i - \mu_j|}$$

where

 - π_i and π_j are the premiums assigned to insureds in risk-groups i and j
 - μ_i and μ_j are the corresponding true risks
 - n_i and n_j are the numbers of individuals assigned to the i-th and j-th of the m risk-groups
 - n is the number of individuals in the insurer's clientele.

Lorenz separation with $m = 2$ risk-groups reduces to linear separation

6. Inclusivity of risk classification is the complement of separation:

$$\text{Inclusivity} = 1 - \text{separation}$$

Part III Further Aspects of Risk Classification

7   A Taxonomy of Objections to Risk Classification

Key Ideas:

insufficient inclusivity; misguided methods; unfairness; inaccuracy; reinforcement of prejudice; reinforcement of pre-existing disadvantage; controllability; transparency; consent; socially perverse incentives; legitimacy creep; risk classification as blame

Chapters 3–6 have suggested maximising loss coverage as a public policy objective in the design and regulation of risk classification schemes, and explained that this is consistent with a moderate degree of adverse selection. To generate this optimal degree of adverse selection may require some pooling of dissimilar risks. The argument was that an unregulated market could produce an *insufficient inclusivity* of risk classification. Separately from this argument, many people object on various ethical, technical or practical grounds to classification on particular risk variables (e.g. gender, disability, genetic tests, etc.). These objections are about *misguided methods* of risk classification.

Objections of the first type (insufficient exclusivity) are the main focus of this book. Objections of the second type (misguided methods) are more frequently expressed, but to me they seem less general and less compelling. Nevertheless, if this book omitted all reference to 'misguided methods' arguments, it might appear to many readers to miss a large part of the case for some restriction on risk classification. The main bulk of this chapter therefore comprises an account of various 'misguided methods' arguments often made by others.

Insufficient Inclusivity

This type of objection has already been covered in Chapters 3–6. To recap, the argument is that with unregulated risk classification, the inclusivity of risk classification may be too low. Higher inclusivity would make insurance work better for society as a whole, in the sense of producing higher loss coverage.

Also, as noted in Chapter 6, I believe that many people see high inclusivity (low separation) as politically or ethically desirable for health insurance (and to some extent for life insurance, and sometimes other types of insurance). This view often seems quite resistant to arguments about adverse selection or loss coverage; that is, the preference is to some degree independent of the aggregate insurance market outcomes it produces.

If the population distribution of risk is continuous, a crude first impression of the inclusivity of risk classification can be inferred by noting that inclusivity will tend to be inversely related to (a) the *number of risk-groups* and (b) the *number of risk variables* used in risk classification. More precise definitions for the inclusivity of risk classification were given in Chapter 6.

Misguided Methods

The second type of objection, distinct from concerns about inappropriate inclusivity and hence suboptimal loss coverage, is that *particular methods* of risk classification may be objectionable. These arguments can take various forms, which are elaborated in the rest of this chapter.

Unfairness of Statistical Discrimination to Individuals

Statistical discrimination means discrimination based on an individual's group membership, where the discrimination is accurate based on available statistics at the aggregate level of the group (but not always, of course, at the level of the individual). 'Accurate' does not necessarily mean 'desirable' or 'morally justified'; it means only that the discrimination is reliably predictive at the level of the group. For example, many mortality investigations show that women aged 60 as a group survive longer than men aged 60 as a group; but a particular woman aged 60 may not, of course, survive longer than a particular man age 60. The 'statistical' qualifier makes a distinction compared with 'taste-based' or 'prejudiced' discrimination, which is not based on any group statistics.

Despite its accuracy at group level, statistical discrimination is often perceived as unfair to individuals. In car insurance, it seems unfair that a conscientious young man may be charged more than twice as much for car insurance as his equally conscientious twin sister; and it seems even more unfair that an office worker who loses his job through redundancy is then charged 30% to 60% more for car insurance in the following year. Such assessments may be justified by claim statistics at the group level (albeit this is difficult to verify, because the relevant statistics are proprietary to insurers); but even if they were shown to be accurate, this might do little to alleviate the intuition that the discrimination is often unfair in individual cases.

Faced with such perceived unfairness, many people protest that they wish to be treated as individuals, rather than as undifferentiated members of a group defined by the insurer. This preference is ill-defined (what does it mean to be 'treated as an individual'?) and may often be impractical, but it is also often strongly felt. Criticisms of this type represent an ethical objection to the basic principle of statistical discrimination in particular contexts, rather than the technical details of its implementation.[1]

---

[1] The philosopher Kasper Lippert-Rasmussen (2011) gives a critique of the demand to be 'treated as an individual'. He argues that statistical discrimination *does* 'treat people as individuals', and therefore that intuitions about the wrongness of statistical discrimination must be explained in some other way. Nevertheless, his starting point is the same as mine: a recognition that failure to be 'treated as an individual' is a common and fervent complaint against statistical discrimination.

Inaccuracy

Some critics do not object to statistical discrimination in principle, but instead dispute the details of its implementation in practice. For example, it may be argued that it is wrong to charge more for life insurance to moderately overweight people (say those with a Body Mass Index in the range 25–30) not because this is unfair to a few exceptional individuals within this group, but rather because there is a lack of evidence that people with this build on average have higher mortality as a group.[2] If insurers have done their technical work properly, they should usually be able to refute this type of objection. However, in practice underwriting decisions are often based on manuals prepared by one or other of a handful of global reinsurers. Inevitably there will be some areas where the manual merely codifies an opinion expressed on some occasion by a senior underwriter or medical adviser, with no statistical evidence. Several commentators have noted that research projects in recent years to develop a statistical evidence base for use of genetic tests, rather than de-politicising the issues of genetics and risk classification as intended, have instead highlighted the lack of evidence for many other extant underwriting practices.[3]

Reinforcement of Prejudice

The heavy use of some variables in risk classification may reflect their superficial salience and availability coupled with a long history of usage in both insurance and other contexts, rather than their large or reliable contribution to risk differences. This can lead to a perception of prejudice being perpetuated and reinforced. The almost universal use of gender as a variable in personal insurances, despite

---

[2] In a recent systematic review article in the *Journal of the American Medical Association*, Flegal et al. (2013) find that overweight (BMI in the range 25–30) is associated with mortality 0.94 times that of normal weight (BMI in the range 18.5–25). Orthodox life insurance underwriting sources such as Brackenridge et al. (2006) suggest that overweight in this range might sometimes be charged a higher premium.

[3] Van Hoyweghen and Horstman (2009) and Daykin et al. (2003).

generally modest gender differences in risk, possibly arises from its superficial salience and availability. Race may be another example: historically, small life insurance policies ('burial' or 'funeral' insurance) in the USA involved little or no underwriting except that higher rates were charged to African Americans, possibly because skin colour was a salient variable which even the least astute insurance agent could be relied upon to observe.[4] More recently, genetics has been the salient risk variable of the times, often attracting imaginative attributions of risk differences which seem to run well ahead of evidence.

Reinforcement of Pre-existing Disadvantage

This objection is similar to the previous one, except that rather than prejudice being reinforced, the individual's disadvantage is reinforced. If a person is 'higher risk' in life or health insurance, they will typically already have some degree of health disadvantage, and this will often already have led to some degree of poverty. Obviously, there are exceptions: some higher risks for some types of insurance may be wealthy and well, and some lower risks for some types of insurance may be poor and sick. But the typical pattern of association for life and health insurance is obvious and undeniable: higher contingent risk tends to be associated with some degree of current disadvantage. It is this current disadvantage, as much as any prospective contingent disadvantage, that often motivates the sentiment that it is unfair, and perhaps cruel, to impose further disadvantages via risk classification.

Controllability

Controllability refers to the extent to which a risk variable can be influenced by choices or actions of the insured. Intrinsic characteristics such as gender or genetic status are not controllable; habits such as consumption of alcohol (or tobacco or other drugs) and

---

[4] McGlamery (2009).

exercise are controllable, albeit only to some extent and to varying degrees.

Controllability is seen as a desirable property which increases the legitimacy of a risk variable for two reasons: fairness and incentives.

First, regarding fairness, risk variables which are controllable by the insured are generally seen as fairer than those which are not. This is intuitive to most people, and a succinct justification is provided by the veil-of-ignorance argument. That is, choices about social arrangements such as risk classification should be made from behind a veil of ignorance, where you pretend to not know what your own risk status is. Behind the veil of ignorance, any risk-averse person will be attracted to risk classification regimes which avoid the use of uncontrollable risk variables.[5]

Second, regarding incentives, controllability of risk variables may create some incentive for the insured to adopt or maintain behaviour which reduces risk. I call this 'reverse moral hazard'. For example, experience rating in car insurance (described as 'no-claims discounts' in the UK, or 'bonus-malus systems' elsewhere in Europe) may encourage careful driving.

Transparency

A risk variable is useful to an insurer if it is predictive of risk and that predictive relationship is stable. A transparent causal mechanism, such that the risk variable has 'face validity', may increase the

---

[5] The veil-of-ignorance argument is sometimes referred to as the 'ovarian lottery' (imagine you do not know into what identity you will be born), and is commonly attributed to Rawls (1971), as in the phrase 'Rawlsian veil of ignorance'. Essentially the same mental device was earlier suggested by Harsanyi (1955). The veil screens out personal interests, but does not necessarily imply any specific moral conclusions or social arrangements. For Harsanyi, it justified utilitarianism with equal weights assigned to every person's utility. For Rawls, it justified the 'difference principle', a maximin rule for social choices (i.e. social arrangements which produce differences between individuals can be justified only if they make the worst off individual better off). Nevertheless, despite the range of possible moral conclusions, the veil-of-ignorance argument does usefully highlight the necessity of setting aside personal interest in order to think clearly about any social policy.

insurer's confidence in the stability of the relationship. But to the insurer, such transparency is not essential. To the customer, however, a lack of transparency is often objectionable.

As an example of this, investigations by some UK insurers have found that the frequency of cash withdrawals at ATM machines is predictive of full underwriting decisions. Specifically, it has been reported that people over age 40 who make fewer ATM withdrawals have higher probability of being rated or declined after full underwriting for life insurance than people who make more ATM withdrawals.[6] Insurers may therefore be able to shortcut the full underwriting process by using data on an individual's ATM withdrawals, and similar data, sourced from the records of banks associated with the insurer. But this classification is wholly opaque to the customer, and the causal mechanism for it is unclear, which many people may find objectionable.

Consent

Information used in risk classification may sometimes be collected without the customer's consent or even knowledge. The use of banking records from ATM machines as mentioned in the previous paragraph is a possible example of this.

There are some types of data, such as health records, where consent may be particularly salient and sensitive to individuals. In 2014, it was reported that the National Health Service in the UK had sold the entire records of all hospital admissions in England to a group of actuaries for commercial research. Although cursorily anonymised, the records included unique identifier codes for each sequential record, together with month and year of birth, partial postcode, gender and ethnicity, which could make them easy to re-identify by matching with other databases. When the sale of NHS records was publicised on the front page of the *Daily Telegraph* in

---

[6] Hately (2011).

2014, many people regarded it as objectionable because of (among other reasons) the lack of consent.[7]

Socially Perverse Incentives

Risk classification and the consequent differentiation in premiums and possible exclusion from insurance can create financial incentives for individuals to change their behaviour. In many cases, as noted in the discussion of controllability above, these incentives are socially benign: they encourage behaviour which reduces losses, a sort of 'reverse moral hazard'.

But some incentive effects arising from risk classification are socially perverse. The archetypal example is the use of a past pre-symptomatic medical test result to exclude a person from insurance. This discourages the use of the test, and so may impede behavioural change or prophylactic treatment. This was a matter of great concern with HIV testing in the 1980s and 1990s, when some insurers refused life insurance based on the fact that a person had previously sought HIV testing, irrespective of the result of the test.[8] Similar concerns arise with pre-symptomatic genetic testing, where fears about exclusion from insurance discourage the taking of tests which can lead to prophylactic treatment.

Such socially perverse incentives are probably the most compelling reason for restricting insurers' ability to ask about genetic tests. People contemplating whether to undergo genetic tests do appear to be very fearful of the insurance implications. Such fears might be exaggerated, but this matters little if the fears nevertheless influence behaviour in socially perverse ways.

In one survey prepared for the Office of the Privacy Commissioner of Canada, 52% of respondents expressed strong concern that if their doctor recommended that they undergo genetic

---

[7] This incident is discussed further in Chapter 13.

[8] The Association of British Insurers belatedly banned this practice for its members in 1994. After this, underwriting questions referred specifically to testing 'positive' for HIV, or awaiting the results of a test.

testing, they might be asked to provide the results for non-health-related purposes. Of those who expressed significant concern (5–7 on a 7-point scale), 71% said their concerns would be likely to affect their willingness to undergo genetic testing.[9] Another survey found that fear of being excluded from life insurance was rated a moderately or very important factor in the decision as to whether to take the test by 55% of the women who voluntarily attended a clinic for risk assessment of breast cancer; and the women who expressed concern about life insurance were one-third less likely to decide to proceed with the test. The survey's conclusion is stark and compelling: 'For this sample, then, fear of insurance discrimination may lead to underuse of prevention and avoidable cancer deaths.'[10]

Legitimacy Creep

Some objections to risk classification arise not from its direct consequences, but from indirect consequences which may flow from the putative legitimacy of discrimination in insurance. If powerful institutions are permitted to discriminate in one social context, this may tend to normalise analogous discrimination in other contexts. For example, the use of particular information by insurers may tend to normalise similar uses by employers. The questions asked in pre-employment health screening and health conditions placed on job offers often appear to be modelled on those used in insurance underwriting; indeed sometimes they may actually be dictated by an insurer, where death or sickness benefits for employees are insured.

The prospect of this 'legitimacy creep' was the most objectionable aspect of the Genetics and Insurance Committee's (GAIC) project to normalise the use of genetic tests in insurance in the UK. The prospect of a few people being asked to pay more for (or even being excluded from) life or health insurance might not in itself be a devastating disadvantage, even to many of the individuals

---

[9] Phoenix Strategic Perspectives (2013).
[10] Armstrong et al. (2003).

concerned. A far greater concern was the prospect that 'scientific' legitimisation of institutional discrimination would creep into other contexts, such as laws and norms relating to employment, medicine and the rights of disabled people. If merely demonstrating that genetic tests were reliably predictive was sufficient to legitimise their use for private profit in insurance, why should that not also be sufficient for private profit in employment or other relations? Given GAIC's carefully limited terms of reference,[11] there was no obvious Schelling fence on this slippery slope.[12]

Risk Classification as Blame

A corollary of legitimacy creep is that if insurance discrimination has comprehensive legitimacy, no blame can ever be attached to insurers for any negative consequences it may have. Risk classification can then appear to be a practice whereby a powerful institution identifies pre-existing disadvantage such as disability, and then inflicts additional insurance injury, which it proclaims is fair. The infliction of additional injury accompanied by invocations of fairness suggests that risk classification is a form of blame.

This concept does not necessarily attribute to insurers the naïve view that all insurance disadvantages arise from something the insured has done, or that the insured could have avoided the disadvantage by acting differently. Rather it describes a common

[11] GAIC's terms of reference dictated that a test would be approved if it could be shown to reliably indicate extra mortality risk of +50%, the lowest level for which insurers typically charged extra premiums. There was no reference to aggregate consequences for the insurance market, and no reference to social or ethical considerations.

[12] A Schelling fence is a boundary on a 'slippery slope' to which all parties can credibly pre-commit as the limit on the application of some principle (in this case, the principle that demonstration of a genetic test's predictivity justifies its use). It is a variant on the concept of a Schelling point, a coordination solution which people tend to use in the absence of communication. The canonical example is to ask students in New York the question: 'Tomorrow you have to meet a stranger in New York City. Where and when do you meet them?' The most common answer, the Schelling point, is 'noon (at the information booth) at Grand Central Station' (Schelling, 1960).

insurers' view of the location and origin of insurance disadvantage. It characterises insurance disadvantage as an intrinsic property of the individual, rather than as a property which the insurer has chosen to assign to the individual. The insurer is not to blame; the individual is to blame.

This characterisation seems unjustified when one reflects that in most contexts, a great variety of risk classification schemes might be used, with widely varying inclusivity. Society could outlaw risk classification almost entirely (as in health insurance in many jurisdictions), prohibit classification by gender (as in the European Union), proscribe certain genetic information, protect certain disabilities but not others, and so on. Similarly, by custom and practice insurers often disregard some readily available information which seems relevant to risk (despite the competitive pressures towards lower inclusivity in risk classification). The disadvantage allocated to a particular individual by a particular risk classification scheme is then *not* a property of the individual; it is instead a property of the risk classification scheme, imposed at the choice of the insurer (subject to any relevant laws). Insofar as risk classification assigns insurance disadvantage solely to the individual, with an accompanying (implicit or explicit) invocation of fairness, it represents an unjustified assignation of blame.

Summary

This chapter has reviewed objections to risk classification schemes. There were two broad types of objections. First, *insufficient inclusivity*: this can generate too much or too little adverse selection, and hence suboptimal loss coverage. Second, *misguided methods*: even if the overall inclusivity of risk classification is satisfactory, particular methods of risk classification are often argued to be objectionable on a variety of ethical, technical or practical grounds. This book is mainly about the first type of objection, but the second type was reviewed in this chapter for completeness.

8 Empirical Evidence on Adverse Selection

Key Ideas:

informational adverse selection; competitive adverse selection; adverse selection spiral; advantageous selection; empirical estimates; the end of adverse selection?

Chapters 3–6 argued that a degree of restriction on risk classification leading to adverse selection can be beneficial to the population as a whole, provided that the adverse selection does not go 'too far'. This argument implicitly assumes that restrictions can easily induce sufficient adverse selection to go 'far enough'. If adverse selection is in fact a weak and unreliable phenomenon, there might be even less reason to be worried about unintended consequences of restrictions on risk classification. The main problem of adverse selection might then often be that there is not enough of it (in the sense that more adverse selection would produce higher loss coverage).

It turns out that for most insurance markets and contexts, the empirical evidence for adverse selection is indeed weak and equivocal when compared with the strong predictions of insurance theory. Many econometric studies which were conceived in the expectation of demonstrating adverse selection have failed to do so. Unsurprisingly, there are exceptions: some studies do find evidence for a certain amount of adverse selection. But where adverse selection can be demonstrated, it often relates to minor contract features chosen by the insured, rather than the overall amount of cover chosen by the insured. There is almost no evidence for the more florid rhetorical representations, such as the 'adverse selection spiral' which insurance folklore predicts will quickly destroy any insurance market where risk classification is restricted. This chapter reviews some of the empirical evidence on adverse selection.

Interpretations of Adverse Selection: Informational, Competitive and Spiral

The question of whether adverse selection is evident in an insurance market can be interpreted in three ways: informational adverse selection, competitive adverse selection or the 'adverse selection spiral'.

Economists tend to interpret the question as one about information asymmetry between insurers and their customers: do customers know more about their risks than insurers, after whatever risk classification methods the insurers choose to apply? Economists tend to assume axiomatically that any information advantage will be exploited, and therefore be capable of detection by observation of customers' purchasing decisions. This is the main concept of adverse selection used in this book, and in other chapters I refer to it simply as 'adverse selection'. But in this chapter, I shall call this interpretation *informational adverse selection*.

The second interpretation, which is often more salient to actuaries and others concerned with practical insurance pricing, is that adverse selection is about competition between insurers: are innovations in risk classification an important means by which one insurer can gain advantage over other insurers? In this chapter, I shall call this interpretation *competitive adverse selection*.

The third interpretation is that restrictions on adverse selection will lead to an *adverse selection spiral* in which the market eventually collapses. A succinct statement of this concept is given in the policy document *Insurance & superannuation risk classification policy* published by the Institute of Actuaries of Australia, which I quoted in Chapter 1 and repeat here:

> In the absence of a system that allows for distinguishing by price
> between individuals with different risk profiles, insurers would
> provide an insurance or annuity product at a subsidy to some

while overcharging others. In an open market, basic economics dictates that individuals with low risk relative to price would conclude that the product is overpriced and thus reduce or possibly forgo their insurance. Those individuals with a high level of risk relative to price would view the price as attractive and therefore retain or increase their insurance. As a result the average cost of the insurance would increase, thus pushing prices up. Then, individuals with lower loss potential would continue to leave the marketplace, contributing to a further price spiral. Eventually the majority of consumers, or the majority of providers of insurance, would withdraw from the marketplace and the remaining products would become financially unsound.[1]

To clarify the distinction between the first two interpretations, note that when a new risk classification variable is introduced by one insurer, this can lead to competitive adverse selection, even when there is no asymmetry of information between customers and insurers, and hence no informational adverse selection. For example, in recent decades some insurers have introduced 'postcode pricing' (zip code pricing): lower prices for life insurance or higher prices for annuities for customers living in affluent areas. This may lead to competitive adverse selection against insurers who do not use post-codes in pricing. But customers have not suddenly acquired better information than insurers about their own addresses, which have been known to insurers for every policy ever written.[2]

Another way of characterising the distinction between informational adverse selection and competitive adverse selection is to note

---

[1] Institute of Actuaries of Australia (1994).

[2] An alternative framing of competitive adverse selection might be that it is merely a different type of informational adverse selection, one concerned with asymmetry in information (or the use of information) *between an insurer and its rivals*, rather than *between an insurer and its customers*. This framing might fit well within the 'information economics' paradigm. But I shall not pursue it further, because in practice almost all references to information asymmetry in insurance economics seem to relate to customer–insurer asymmetry, rather than insurer–insurer asymmetry.

that the first is about *games customers play with insurers* and the second is about *games insurers play with each other*.[3]

Most empirical tests for adverse selection have been conducted by economists, and so focus on informational adverse selection. Competitive adverse selection seems to be much less formally studied, and so we have to rely mainly on anecdotal examples. For evidence on the 'adverse selection spiral', we again have to rely on anecdotal examples – or rather, the lack of credible examples.

Econometric Tests for Informational Adverse Selection

In testing for informational adverse selection, it is usually difficult to make comparisons between purchasers and non-purchasers of insurance, because insurers generally do not collect data on the losses of non-purchasers. Tests of informational adverse selection therefore generally focus on differences in realised losses and levels of cover between different purchasers of insurance across an insurer's clientele, rather than differences between purchasers and non-purchasers across the whole population. Informational adverse selection implies that purchasers who experience higher losses will have purchased more cover, where 'more' may mean choosing a larger sum insured, or a smaller deductible, or other product features which give greater coverage.

Econometric tests for informational adverse selection are therefore typically based on testing for a positive covariance (or equivalently, correlation) between realised losses and quantity of insurance purchased. There are three main approaches: univariate, bivariate or non-parametric tests.

Univariate Regression Tests

A regression with a single dependent variable (i.e. 'univariate' regression) is carried out:

$$Loss_i = \alpha + \beta \cdot Cover_i + \gamma \cdot X_i + \varepsilon_i \tag{8.1}$$

---

[3] This characterisation was suggested by Macdonald (2004).

where

- $Loss_i$ is a variable representing the *ex post* realisation of the risk of policyholder i
- $Cover_i$ is a variable representing the quantity of insurance purchased by policyholder i
- X_i is a vector of all the characteristics of policyholder i observable by the insurer and potentially relevant to the risk.[4]

Adverse selection is then said to be present in the market if the regression estimates $\beta > 0$ with significance.

Bivariate Regression Tests

The second approach is separate models for losses and amounts of cover (i.e. 'bivariate' regression), with the following two regressions carried out:

$$Loss_i = \alpha_{LOSS} + \beta_{LOSS}(X_i) + \eta_i \qquad (8.2)$$

$$Cover_i = \alpha_{COVER} + \beta_{COVER}(X_i) + \varepsilon_i \qquad (8.3)$$

where $Loss_i$, $Cover_i$ and X_i are defined as before.[5] Then the correlation between the residuals from the two regressions is examined. A significant positive correlation of η_i and ε_i indicates informational adverse selection.

Non-parametric Tests

The third approach avoids the restricted functional forms of the tests above by using non-parametric chi-squared tests for independence.[6] Suppose there are m explanatory variables used in risk classification, each of which can be represented as a dummy (0, 1) variable (e.g. in car insurance 0 for small engine, 1 for large engine). Then we can define 2^m 'cells', and allocate to each cell all individuals in the insurer's clientele who have exactly the same set of

---

[4] Cohen and Siegelman (2010).
[5] Chiappori and Salanie (1997, 2000).
[6] Chiappori and Salanie (2000).

values for *all* the explanatory variables. For example if we have three explanatory variables, we need $2^3 = 8$ cells to cover all possible combinations of the three (0, 1) explanatory variables.

Then for each of the eight cells, a 2×2 table is created from counts of the numbers of individuals having each combination of loss and cover (high–low loss, high–low cover). Then we test the independence of loss and cover, conditional on being in a given cell. If the null hypothesis of independence holds good in every cell, then there is no informational adverse selection.

Relating These Tests to the Model in Chapters 4–6

The concept of informational adverse selection which is evaluated using tests such as those above can be related to the model used in Chapters 4–6, but it is not fully represented in that model.

In the tests above, informational adverse selection is defined as a positive covariance of realised losses and cover in the insurer's clientele, *after* controlling for explanatory variables observable by the insurer (e.g. gender, age, etc.). In other words, informational adverse selection is standardised such that the 'null' corresponds to covariance which is fully explained by the explanatory variables. The rationale for this standardisation is that in most real-world markets, risk classification is largely unrestricted, so insurers can adjust (and economists tend to assume, *will* adjust) premiums to allow for any covariance explained by observable explanatory variables. Covariance which is so explained does not represent an informational advantage of the customer.

Previously in the model in Chapters 4–6, adverse selection was defined as simply a positive covariance of losses and cover in the whole population. There was no concept of controlling for explanatory variables observable by the insurer (there was only one explanatory variable, membership of risk-group 1 or 2, which was observable by all and fully explained the risk). Instead, adverse selection was standardised by the concept of adverse selection ratio, such

Table 8.1. *Comparison of concepts between Chapter 8 and Chapters 4–6*

Concept	Variable or method in Chapter 8	Closest equivalent in Chapters 4–6
Quantum of cover	$Cover_i$	Realisations of Q
Quantum of realised loss	$Loss_i$	Realisations of L
Explanatory variables	Vector X_i (e.g. age, gender, etc.)	Risk-groups 1 and 2
Adverse selection	Positive correlation of $Cover_i$ and $Loss_i$ in insurer's clientele	Positive correlation of Q and L in whole population
Standardisation concept	Control for X_i (i.e. correlation explained by observables is the null)	Use adverse selection ratio (i.e. correlation with risk-differentiated premiums is the null)

that 'null' adverse selection was the value under risk-differentiated premiums.

A comparison of concepts between this chapter and Chapters 4–6 is summarised in Table 8.1.

Limitations of These Tests

Three limitations apply equally to all three of the above approaches – univariate, bivariate and non-parametric – to testing for informational adverse selection.

First, a correlation between realised losses and cover may be a consequence of moral hazard (behaviour after buying insurance) rather than adverse selection (behaviour when buying insurance). Since the two phenomena are generally indistinguishable in the data, tests for informational adverse selection have to be based on an assumption that moral hazard is not a significant factor.

Second, the focus on decisions about amounts within the insurer's clientele, a subset of the population, neglects decisions across the wider population to forgo insurance altogether. This is an understandable consequence of data limitations, but it possibly overlooks an important locus of informational adverse selection.

Third, if customers vary their purchase decisions according to expected losses, but stringent underwriting is fully effective in classifying this behaviour, all three approaches will characterise the situation as one of 'no informational adverse selection'. Actuaries and underwriters might not agree with this characterisation: their perception might be that adverse selection is strong, but is being countered by vigilant underwriting. In other words, actuaries and underwriters sometimes regard informational adverse selection as a behavioural tendency which can be fully offset by underwriting, and so is not normally expected to be observable after underwriting. This expansive concept of adverse selection is not amenable to testing using data from insurance policies after underwriting, so I shall not consider it further.

Evidence on Informational Adverse Selection

Econometric tests of informational adverse selection as outlined in the previous section have typically produced null results.[7] Examples include life insurance,[8] car insurance,[9] health insurance[10] and fire insurance.[11] Outside of insurance, even in the used vehicle market – the canonical example in the 'lemons' model of informational adverse selection[12] – pickup trucks purchased in the second-hand

---

[7] By 'null results' I mean, more precisely, that the tests do not reject a null hypothesis of no adverse selection at typical p-values.

[8] Cawley and Philipson (1999) and Mitchell and McCarthy (2010).

[9] Chiappori and Salanie (2000), Dionne et al. (2001) and Saito (2006). An exception to the general patterns of results was Cohen (2005), which found some coverage-risk correlation for experienced drivers in Israel, but not for inexperienced drivers.

[10] Cardon and Hendel (2001).

[11] Wang et al. (2009).

[12] Akerlof (1970).

market have been found to require no more maintenance than other trucks of similar age and mileage.[13] Some studies have even found a *negative* relationship between risk and insurance purchase – the opposite to that predicted by adverse selection. 'Negative' informational adverse selection (advantageous selection) is discussed later in this chapter.

There appears to be some evidence for informational adverse selection in annuity markets in the UK based on the insured's shrewd choice of contract features rather than the amount of the annuity.[14] Specifically, annuitants who choose contracts with more 'back-loading' of payments – increases in line with the retail prices index, or no initial guaranteed payment period – tend to live longer. Also, annuitants who do not choose a spouse's benefit payable after their own death tend to live longer. The better evidence for selection in annuities compared with insurances may be a reflection of the more likely nature of the contingent events under an annuity, which gives more scope for a large difference between probabilities as assessed by the customer and by the insurer (a large information edge). The idea of the customer's information edge is discussed further in Chapter 11.

There is some evidence for informational adverse selection in crop insurance in agriculture in the USA.[15] Again, this may reflect the relatively likely nature of the events over which selection is exercised, which gives scope for a large difference between customer and insurer probability assessments, and hence a large information edge. Also, a farmer is a 'repeat player' who can learn from experience and smooth results over several years. This is a more promising context for the customer to exploit any superior information than the 'one-shot gamble' of a typical life insurance purchase.

---

[13] Bond (1982).
[14] Finkelstein and Poterba (2002, 2004).
[15] Quiggin et al. (1993), Just et al. (1999) and Makki and Somwaru (2001).

Evidence on Competitive Adverse Selection

As noted earlier, there seem to be no econometric investigations of competitive adverse selection, and so we have to rely on anecdotal evidence.

(a) *Postcode pricing for annuities.* This has already been covered earlier in this chapter, in the section defining informational adverse selection and competitive adverse selection. To recap: the introduction of lower prices for life insurance or higher prices for annuities for customers living in affluent areas may lead to competitive adverse selection against insurers who do not use postcodes in pricing. In the UK, once one large insurer (Legal and General) adopted postcode pricing for annuities in 2007, other insurers quickly followed, possibly because of concerns about competitive adverse selection. Note that there was no question of insurers not knowing their customers' addresses, and thus no possibility of informational adverse selection.

(b) *Nonsmoker discounts for life insurance.* Before the early 1980s, the UK life insurance market functioned well with no distinction by smoking status, despite the link with mortality having become increasingly apparent in the medical literature from the 1950s onwards.[16] But once a few large companies offered a nonsmoker discount, other companies quickly followed, and within a few years almost all companies differentiated life insurance prices by smoking status. It seems plausible that this was a response to competitive adverse selection (although we cannot disprove the alternative that it was merely fashion). Note that customers always had private knowledge of their smoking status, but nobody suggested that this led to adverse selection prior to the competitive innovation.

(c) *Telematics for car insurance.* A possible future example of competitive adverse selection is more widespread use of telematics in car insurance. At present, the installation and data transmission costs of 'black box' tracking mean that insurance priced from telematics data is a niche market; the costs are viable only for policies with high risk premiums (e.g. very young drivers). But if costs fall and a few companies successfully market telematics to the wider market, this may be particularly

---

[16] The first prospective study reported in the *British Medical Journal* was Doll and Hill (1954); and in the *Journal of the American Medical Association*, Hammond (1958).

attractive to conscientious or low-mileage drivers, who anticipate receiving discounts for their lower risk. Higher-risk drivers might then become overrepresented in other companies' clienteles. This competitive dynamic might then pressure all companies to offer a telematics option. As in the postcode and nonsmoker examples, the competitive adverse selection arises from the innovation; there is no change in customers' information about their risk, and no informational adverse selection.

Evidence on 'Adverse Selection Spirals'

The 'adverse selection spiral' concept is very influential in both academic and policy discussions. But it is rare to find well-documented reports of real examples. There are many examples of markets where regulators impose substantial restrictions on risk classification without causing a market collapse. Examples of partial restrictions include the prohibition on using gender, race or genetic test results in many insurance markets. More comprehensive (albeit not quite total) bans on risk classification are common in health insurance. Examples include voluntary health insurance schemes in Ireland and Australia; and in the USA, Obamacare (formally the Patient Protection and Affordable Care Act) allows rating only by age, geographical location and smoking status. The persistence of these schemes indicates that not all restrictions on risk classification lead inevitably to an 'adverse selection spiral'.[17]

One supposed example often cited by academic economists involves, rather parochially, health insurance for employees of Harvard University.[18] The employees were offered a choice between different plans with different benefits, originally with an employer contribution as a fixed percentage of the (different) premiums for different plans. The employer contribution was then changed to the

---

[17] Obamacare also has the 'individual mandate', which helps to reduce adverse selection by applying tax penalties for non-purchase of insurance. Australia and Ireland do not have individual mandates, but in recent years they have introduced some limited risk classification in the form of 'lifetime community rating'. This means that premiums vary only according to age at first entry to insurance.

[18] Cutler and Reber (1998).

same flat contribution irrespective of which plan the employee chose. This led to a rapid migration of younger (presumably healthier) employees from the more expensive plan with better benefits to the cheaper plan with lower benefits. The more expensive plan suffered reducing enrolments and progressively increasing per capita costs, leading to its withdrawal 3 years later.

But this example is essentially a case of selection *against one insurer among many* (competitive adverse selection) in a scenario where different health insurance plans offered differing benefit structures and premiums. It is not the same as the selection *against the whole market* (informational adverse selection) which it is said will lead to collapse of the market when risk classification is banned for all insurers. In the scenario of multiple health plans, the various choices are reasonably close substitutes, and so demand elasticity for any one plan may be high; but in the scenario where risk classification is banned for all insurers, remaining uninsured is often not a close substitute for being insured, and so demand elasticity for insurance from all providers will probably be low.

As well as not being supported by many real-world examples, florid metaphors such as 'adverse selection spiral' or 'death spiral' are not supported by models of insurance markets with restricted risk classification. In the models in Chapter 4–6, with plausible demand elasticities for low and high risks, an equilibrium is reached well before the point where only high risks remain insured. For the market to 'spiral' to the point where only a few very high risks remain insured requires an implausible divergence of demand elasticities for low and high risks.

Advantageous Selection

Sometimes the evidence from empirical tests for informational adverse selection is not merely null, but actually negative: a statistically significant coverage-loss correlation is found, but it has the wrong sign. In other words, people who incur lower losses tend to have bought more insurance (the opposite of the prediction of adverse selection). This was first described as propitious selection, but is now more often called advantageous selection.[19]

Advantageous selection – 'wrong sign' correlation of cover and losses – can be explained by considering a third variable, financial risk aversion. Higher financial risk aversion means that an individual is prepared to pay more for insurance against a given quantum and probability of loss. In some contexts, it seems psychologically plausible that financial risk aversion might be negatively correlated with risk level. This is particularly plausible where risks are partly endogenous, in the sense of being determined by the character of the insured. In other words, 'cautious' individuals may be both more financially risk averse, and more inclined to take more preventive health and other precautions. When all risks are pooled at a single price, financial risk aversion negatively correlated with risk level implies *lower* insurance demand from *higher* risks. This can offset – or sometimes more than offset – higher demand from higher risks for whom the pooled price appears cheap (as in the usual adverse selection story).

Two papers[20] by David Hemenway which introduced the concept of propitious selection give evidence for several examples using US data, including:

– for car drivers, a positive correlation between purchase of noncompulsory liability insurance and a range of health-related risk avoidance activities
– also for car drivers, a positive correlation between purchase of noncompulsory liability insurance and not driving after drinking alcohol
– for motorcyclists, a positive correlation between wearing a helmet and holding medical insurance.

Similarly, it has been shown that those who are most cautious about their health (as measured by participation in preventive health checks) are the most likely to purchase long-term care insurance,

---

[19] 'Propitious selection' was the term introduced by Hemenway (1990), who was the first to draw attention to the phenomenon. 'Advantageous selection' was introduced by De Meza and Webb (2001). The latter terminology has gained currency, probably because of the stronger theoretical backing their paper provided.
[20] Hemenway (1990, 1992).

and yet the least likely to enter nursing homes.[21] Other markets where a negative correlation between insurance coverage and losses has been documented in empirical studies include medigap insurance (drugs coverage in the USA), health insurance in Australia and commercial fire insurance.[22]

Despite these examples, I suspect advantageous selection is probably not a typical aggregate outcome in insurance markets. Weak adverse selection is probably more common. But advantageous selection is, at the very least, common enough to falsify the traditional notion that all selection is always one way.

Empirical Estimates of Demand Elasticity

One reason why econometric studies may fail to detect informational adverse selection could be that customers do have some superior information, but are not very motivated to act upon it. Purchasing decisions may reasonably be more influenced by the customer's perceived need for insurance, such as providing for family or ill health, and by life events such as house purchase, rather than by exploiting small bargains in insurance prices. A slightly lower price or slightly higher risk may not make much difference to buying decisions. In other words, the price and risk elasticities of demand for insurance may be low. Empirical estimates of price elasticity of demand for various classes of insurance are indeed low, typically very roughly around –0.5; some figures were summarised in Table 5.1.

Big Data and Adverse Selection

Most of the evidence in this chapter showing that informational adverse selection is generally a weaker phenomenon than insurance theory suggests is several years old. Informational adverse selection depends on insureds having some information advantage over the insurer in knowledge about their risks. The increasing availability to

---

[21] Finkelstein and McGarry (2006).

[22] Fang et al. (2008) for medigap insurance; Doiron et al. (2007) for health insurance in Australia; Wang et al. (2009) for commercial fire insurance.

insurers of big data from new surveillance technologies as described in Chapter 13 may mean that any information advantages which insureds may have enjoyed in the past may become less prevalent in the future. Hence in the absence of new restrictions on risk classification, informational adverse selection may become even weaker in future than it is in the empirical studies reported in this chapter.[23]

Summary

This chapter has reviewed evidence for three concepts of adverse selection: informational adverse selection (games customers play with insurers), competitive adverse selection (games insurers play with each other) and the 'adverse selection spiral'.

The *adverse selection spiral* is the most rhetorically appealing but least well-evidenced of these three concepts. The idea of a progressive spiral whereby restrictions on risk classification always lead to market collapse is a major theme of insurance folklore. But it is not supported either by equilibrium models of insurance markets with realistic elasticity parameters, or by convincing real-world examples.

Informational adverse selection, which arises from an information advantage of customers which is reflected in their purchasing decisions, is a central concept of insurance theory. Evidence for this concept, while not entirely absent, is surprisingly weak and equivocal compared with the strong predictions of insurance theory. Empirical estimates of insurance demand elasticity are typically low. This suggests that even where customers do have some private information about risk, they may not be very motivated to act on it.

Competitive adverse selection, which arises from the efforts of insurers to gain an advantage over competitors by introducing new ways to differentiate risks, is probably more robust than the two concepts above. Adverse selection in practice is often more about games insurers play with each other, rather than games customers play with insurers.

---

[23] An essay titled 'The end of asymmetric information?' discusses this idea across many contexts, not just insurance (Cowen and Tabarrok, 2015).

9   Myths of Insurance Rhetoric

Key Ideas:

Genuine misperceptions: *naïve cynicism; actuarial paranoia; fallacy of composition; fallacy of the one-shot gambler*
Strategic misrepresentations: *cartoons; barricades; signals*
Other rhetorical devices: *semantic sophistry; one-way hash arguments; presumption of privilege; devaluation of the disadvantaged; affectation of virtue; emo-phobia*
Cognitive capture: *industry funding; career incentives for researchers*

I argued in Chapters 3–6 that from a social perspective, moderate adverse selection in insurance can be a good thing. The empirical evidence reviewed in Chapter 8 showed that in practice, adverse selection in insurance is generally quite weak (which is a hopeful state of affairs, if we think 'moderate' adverse selection is optimal). However in contemporary policy debates, adverse selection in insurance is almost invariably depicted as a bad thing (for evidence, see the quotations in Chapter 2). This chapter examines the rhetoric of adverse selection, highlighting ways in which the phenomenon is exaggerated in scale and excessively maligned in character. The focus is primarily on myths which are prevalent in policy discussions in and around the insurance industry. Some more theoretical myths which are prevalent in academic insurance economics are considered separately in Chapter 10.

There are broadly two groups of ways in which adverse selection is overstated and excessively maligned in public discourse. First, there are genuine misperceptions. Second, there are strategic misrepresentations, where exaggeration is motivated by a desire to persuade, or some other self-interested purpose. These two categories are not mutually exclusive – a genuine misperception can be further exaggerated for strategic purposes – but they provide a convenient way of grouping the various forms of exaggeration which I detail below. I then highlight some further rhetorical devices and affectations which are common in discussions of risk classification. Finally, I discuss the possibility of cognitive capture, whereby industry perspectives may be promulgated by commentators who are ostensibly independent, but in reality 'bought' by corporate funding and other forms of support.

Genuine Misperceptions

Naïve Cynicism

Adverse selection is often described in pejorative terms which suggest that higher risks strategically game the insurance system to obtain some unwarranted benefit. Naïve cynicism is the belief that this 'micro' speculation about the intentions of a few individuals provides comprehensive insight into the 'macro' operation of an insurance system.

Naïve cynicism seems to have psychological roots. In understanding complex human systems such as insurance, the human brain seems particularly adept at focusing on isolated instances of cheating or freeriding, rather than dispassionate observation of the broad sweep of reality.[1] This might be because isolated instances, such as one individual gaining an unwarranted benefit, are much easier to observe and comprehend than the overall performance of complex systems such as insurance.

---

[1] One type of evidence for this focus is that in laboratory experiments which test reasoning skills, people perform poorly in detecting violations of logical rules involving conditionals, but perform much better when the same rules describe social exchanges where rule violations correspond to cheating (Cosmides et al., 2010).

The naïve cynic's obsession with freeriders rather than overall outcomes treats the insurance system as a sort of morality play, in which the most salient actors are the 'good' low risks and 'bad' high risks. This perspective is not helpful because in general, economics is not a morality play. Economic arrangements which produce good 'macro' results may often entail tolerance of some 'micro' features which run against the grain of everyday notions of justice.

Actuarial Paranoia: Prioritising Policing over Epidemiology

In the past three decades, two small groups have attracted disproportionate concern in insurance circles: people with HIV infection and people with genetic predispositions to illness. In the 1980s and 1990s, actuaries became preoccupied with the perceived importance of 'policing' insurers' clienteles so that such people could be surcharged or excluded. Substantial analytical effort and political capital was expended on these preoccupations, as evidenced by contemporary statements (some of which were quoted in Chapter 2), publications and the establishment of professional working parties concerned with AIDS and insurance, and genetics and insurance.[2] However, neither people with HIV nor those with genetic predispositions actually turned out to be financially significant to the overall solvency of insurers in the UK.

A development which *has* turned out to be financially significant to the overall solvency of some insurers in the UK is the widespread reduction in mortality at higher ages, not in a specific subgroup but across the whole population of annuitants and pensioners. For the past quarter century, this development – the management of which is primarily a matter of epidemiology, not policing – has generally been underestimated by actuaries. There

---

[2] The Institute and Faculty of Actuaries AIDS Working Party produced five bulletins with dates ranging from September 1987 to March 1991. Its Genetics Working Party or its predecessors produced various position statements, papers and presentations from around 1998 to 2004, and remains extant in 2017.

was no annuities working party – or rather there was, but only briefly, when it was already too late.[3]

Actuarial paranoia is the tendency of actuaries to direct their efforts disproportionately towards the policing of minorities rather than the epidemiology of populations. It is the professional manifestation of naïve cynicism.

The Fallacy of Composition

Where insurers are permitted to use any risk classification methods, a new risk classification invented by one insurer can be a competitive advantage. An insurer which introduces a new risk classification – either charging less for some type of low risk or charging more for some type of high risk – can gain a least a temporary advantage over other insurers. Other insurers may then be forced to adopt the new classification. This is because if they continue to charge a price undifferentiated to the new classification, they may attract an increasing proportion of the high risks and a reducing proportion of the low risks. This is the 'competitive adverse selection' which was discussed in Chapter 8.

The previous paragraph describes the dynamic of a particular insurer competing against other insurers which may use different risk classification methods. But it is not the dynamic where a regulator bans certain methods of risk classification *for the whole market*. If a classification method is banned for the whole market, there is no possibility of an insurer being disadvantaged because rivals offer prices differentiated by that method. For adverse selection to be a problem under this scenario, there needs to be selection *against the whole market* ('informational adverse selection' in Chapter 8), not just adverse selection *against a particular insurer* ('competitive adverse selection' in Chapter 8). The latter does *not* necessarily

---

[3] The Institute and Faculty of Actuaries established an Annuity Guarantees Working Party from January to December 1997 only.

imply the former. The common elision of these two concepts of adverse selection is a fallacy of composition.

One example of this confusion is contained in a paper commissioned from economic consultants Oxera by the trade association Insurance Europe. One paragraph accurately describes competitive adverse selection against a particular insurer: 'If the insurer does not offer lower premiums to consumers who are less likely to claim, these consumers are likely to shift to an insurer who does recognise their lower likelihood of claiming and charges less for the same product.' But in the next paragraph, this mutates without elaboration into informational adverse selection against the whole market: 'A ban on the use of age and disability would be likely to result in serious problems arising from adverse selection for all of the insurance products considered in this study, and could lead to a breakdown of the market for certain insurance products.'[4]

The Fallacy of the One-Shot Gambler

One justification often given for expecting adverse selection to be devastating to insurers is the idea that anyone with some private knowledge of their higher risk will wish not just to buy insurance, but to buy *very large* amounts of insurance. For example, in 2014 the Canadian Institute of Actuaries lobbied the Canadian senate with a research paper which assumed that 75% of people who receive any adverse genetic test result would immediately purchase convertible term life insurance providing cover of 1 million Canadian dollars. Among other reasons, the paper states that 'They see the price as low enough to constitute a good investment which will benefit their heirs.'[5]

But consideration of plausible probabilities and premiums suggests that in most realistic scenarios, buying large amounts of life insurance on the basis of private knowledge is probably *not* an

[4] Oxera Consulting (2012, p. iii).
[5] Howard (2014, p. 8).

attractive investment. This is for two reasons: (a) life insurance pays out only on low-probability (in gambling terminology, long odds) events, and (b) life insurance purchasers are typically 'one-shot gamblers' who can make their bet on these odds only once.

For example, suppose that an insurer offers me a term life insurance premium based on an assumed risk of dying of $p = 4\%$ over the term of an insurance policy (say the next 25 years), but I have private information (e.g. a genetic or other test result) which tells me my real risk is 5 times the normal level, that is $p^* = 20\%$. If I 'invest' in over-insurance, then my private knowledge means I pay a 'favourable' price (4% rather than 20%). But despite the 'favourable' price, on a one-shot gambler it is still very likely (80% likely, on the true probabilities) that I shall just lose the premium.

This one-shot gambler against long odds seems to me an unattractive investment proposition for a large bet. It would remain unattractive for a wide range of plausible probabilities and premiums. It may be worth buying a 'normal' level of cover *for insurance purposes*, such as protecting my dependants from destitution in the unlikely event of my early death. But the notion of massive over-insurance based on a private genetic test *for investment purposes* generally does not seem attractive for realistic probabilities and premiums.

For a large bet using private information to be attractive *for investment purposes*, I need either (a) a large 'information edge', defined as the *difference* (not the ratio) between the true probability based on my private information and the probability used by the insurer to set the premium or (b) the ability to engage in multiple independent transactions, either in sequence (repetition) or in parallel (diversification). These conditions are *not* satisfied by typical 'private genetic test' scenarios such as that described above.[6]

---

[6] Circumstances where these conditions might be satisfied are considered further in Chapter 11.

Strategic Misrepresentations

The second pattern whereby adverse selection is exaggerated is strategic misrepresentation, where exaggeration is motivated by a desire to persuade, or some other self-interested purpose. Strategic misrepresentations can take the form of cartoons, barricades or signals.

Cartoons (Exaggeration for Effect)

Insurers and their advocates may present exaggerated cartoon-like accounts of adverse selection because they believe that an accurate account would be insufficiently compelling, and so fail to influence public policy in the direction they desire. This is the most straightforward form of strategic misrepresentation.

One manifestation of exaggeration for effect is that references to adverse selection are often qualified by epithets such as 'severe' (as in 'severe adverse selection'), but almost never qualified by epithets such as 'mild', 'moderate', 'slight', 'low' or 'weak'. In January 2016, a Google search on the single string {"severe adverse selection" "insurance"} returned over 5,000 hits. The five search strings {"mild | moderate | slight | low | weak adverse selection" "insurance"} returned around 100 hits in total. The overwhelmingly higher frequency of 'severe' compared with plausible alternative epithets suggests a rhetorical motive, rather than a calibrated assessment of exceptional circumstances.

In other cases cartoons take the form of principles without proportionality, where a technically valid principle or result is presented without relevant context which would highlight its practical insignificance. For example, when the Institute and Faculty of Actuaries acknowledged in 1999 that early actuarial models for genetics and life insurance suggested the effect of banning genetic tests would probably be to raise term life insurance premiums by much less than 10%, it immediately added that this represented 'a material effect on premium rates for term assurances'.[7] It omitted to mention that typical term assurance premiums had fallen by around 25% in the preceding decade, or that the range of the cheapest few quotes at any time from different insurers for any particular term assurance risk varied by around 25%. In the context of these substantial inter-temporal and inter-company variations, an increase of much less than 10% could not reasonably be described as material.

Barricades (Defending Industry Interests)

Insurance lobbyists may believe that by exaggerating the impact of adverse selection and arguing against all risk classification restrictions, they are protecting the industry's interests against external critics. The validity of this 'barricade strategy' depends on the interpretation of 'industry interests'.

On the one hand, if 'industry interests' means the financial interest of shareholders, the barricade strategy may be misconceived. As noted in Chapter 3, maximising loss coverage is equivalent to maximising premium income. The models in this book assume that insurers make zero profits in equilibrium, but in practice insurers hope to earn profits. If these profits are (roughly) proportional to premiums, shareholders should welcome some restrictions on risk classification, at least to the point where loss coverage is maximised. More generally, restrictions on risk classification are generally motivated by social objectives, but as a side effect they reduce the intensity of competition in risk classification. This should tend to raise aggregate industry profits.

On the other hand, if 'industry interests' means specific job roles, the barricade strategy may be valid. In particular, lobbying on risk classification policy is often devolved to personnel presently employed in risk classification. They have a personal interest in maintaining elaborate systems of risk classification, which is quite

---

[7] Institute and Faculty of Actuaries (1999).

distinct from the interests of insurance company shareholders. Upton Sinclair's famous aphorism is apposite: 'It is difficult to get a man to understand something, when his salary depends on his not understanding it.'[8]

One example of this barricade strategy in action is a paper 'Genetics and insurance – some social policy issues' promoted by the Institute and Faculty of Actuaries in 2003.[9] The paper gives a total of eight separate arguments why insurers should be allowed to use genetic tests under the heading *Insurers' lines of reasoning*. Despite the ostensible 'social policy' focus of the paper, there is no equivalent enumeration of arguments for anyone else's lines of reasoning. In the published discussion of the paper, actuaries variously complained that the UK genetics moratorium was 'big enough to drive a lorry through' (p. 842), 'unduly generous' (p. 857) and that 'once you have given that game away you will never get it back' (p. 870). But recall from Chapter 2 that even complete bans on genetics, more comprehensive than the terms of the UK ban, have been estimated to imply an increase of less than 1% of aggregate premiums.[10] In the light of this likely insignificance, many of the actuaries' comments seem overblown.

Signals (Beliefs as Attire)

Insurance requires durable institutions, and this requirement implies a generally conservative culture. This is not a criticism: it is an observation of a necessary characteristic of institutions which are designed to reliably fulfil very long-term contracts. However, an unfortunate corollary of this conservatism is that for an actuary, it is only right to be right when other actuaries are also right. Being right early, when other actuaries are not yet right, is not just uncomfortable at the time; it also carries no credit when one's earlier rightness is subsequently revealed.

---

[8] Sinclair (1934, p. 107).
[9] Daykin et al. (2003).
[10] Macdonald and Yu (2011).

Belief as attire is not principally concerned with making correct predictions; it is concerned with signalling that you are a 'sound' actuary who holds 'responsible' views. Belief as attire is particularly prevalent in contexts where no penalty arises for being wrong. This is broadly true of insurance insiders who express exaggerated beliefs about adverse selection. Exaggerated beliefs about adverse selection may not do much harm to a profit-making insurer, except to the limited extent that they distract attention from more realistic concerns. Exaggerated beliefs do cause real harm when they influence public policy, but industry personnel promulgating exaggerated beliefs have no accountability for public policy.

The trajectories of actuarial concern about HIV testing and genetic testing in the context of insurance illustrate the phenomenon of beliefs as attire. As recounted in Chapter 2, the predictions typically made by actuaries on these topics in the 1980s and 1990s have turned out to be substantially wrong. But for many actuaries, these predictions were probably made or endorsed largely as attire. There was no subsequent discredit for actuaries who made or endorsed grossly wrong predictions, and no credit for those who made more accurate ones.

Other Rhetorical Devices

Semantic Sophistry

In an official monograph *On risk classification*, The American Academy of Actuaries notes that public policy sometimes imposes limits on risk classification, and then opines that:

> An important consideration to remember in this context is that risk classification classifies risks, not risk subjects. People are not placed into groups; rather their mortality risk or morbidity risk or longevity risk is.[11]

---

[11] American Academy of Actuaries (2011).

Is this the best the American Academy of Actuaries can do? One might as well defend apartheid in South Africa or the Nuremberg laws in Germany by saying that they did not place people into groups, rather their skin tones or grandparental origins were placed into groups.

One-Way Hash Arguments

To a person who has never given much thought to insurance, the concept of adverse selection may not be immediately salient. But most people of reasonable intelligence – including those with no affinity for mathematics beyond basic numeracy – can quickly grasp the concept when it is explained to them. In this sense, adverse selection stories are pitched at an optimal level of complexity: easy enough for almost anyone to grasp, but clever enough for them to feel a little insightful and astute on account of their understanding.

Reality is more nuanced and harder to explain. As we saw in Chapter 8, tests for adverse selection show evidence of adverse selection in a few insurance markets, but not in many others. And as we saw in Chapters 3–6, a modest degree of adverse selection is beneficial, in the sense that it increases loss coverage, but too much adverse selection reduces loss coverage.

The orthodox presentation of adverse selection as a universally negative phenomenon is thus an example of a *one-way hash* argument. A one-way hash is an argument which is flawed or incomplete, but nevertheless intuitive, plausible and appealing to non-experts (especially naïve cynics). Understanding the limitations and half-truths inherent in the one-way hash argument requires a deeper level of understanding, a level which the non expert in a hurry may not be able to attain.

One-way hash arguments are common in lay discussions of complex phenomena which attract political controversy, such as climate change, evolution, environmentalism or adverse selection. The term 'one-way hash' is a metaphor from public-key cryptography, where the one-way hash which encrypts a message relies on the property that given two prime numbers, it is easy to multiply them together to find their product (convince a layman by an over-simplified argument); but given only their product, it is hard to find the two prime numbers (explain to a layman why the oversimplified argument is wrong).

Presumption of Privilege

Commentators on risk classification typically operate under an implicit presumption that they are members of a privileged class who will not be in any way disadvantaged or threatened by risk classification. Analogous presumptions are usually made by analysts working on the technical details of new risk classifications. These presumptions are generally correct – or at least can be made correct – because the advocates and architects of innovation can always disregard or defer any results or proposals which might be disadvantageous or threatening to their own privileged class.

One example of the deferral of socially unwelcome new results was the slowness of insurers in the 1960s and 1970s to charge more to smokers for life insurance. The health hazards of smoking had been recognised in the medical literature at least since the 1950s,[12] but were not recognised in life insurance pricing by UK insurers until the early 1980s. This was possibly because many senior insurance company executives were themselves smokers. I suspect that the delay arose not so much from a reluctance to *financially penalise* smoking, but rather because it would have been embarrassing to *deprecate* smoking, at a time when smoking remained common among the most senior insurance personnel.

Devaluation of the Disadvantaged

Commentators who feel secure in the presumption of their own privilege are often offensive to the less privileged. In particular,

---

[12] The first prospective study reported in the *British Medical Journal* was Doll and Hill (1954) and in the *Journal of the American Medical Association*, Hammond (1958). In Germany, retrospective studies linking cancer and tobacco use were published in the 1930s and 1940s (Proctor, 1999).

commentary on adverse selection is often offensive to people who face higher risks. A few commentators are probably deliberately offensive, but many may not realise that they are being offensive.

In general terms, to give offence is to imply that a person or group has, or should have, low status. When discussing risk classification, insurers and their advocates do this in three main ways. First, they talk about people who face higher risks as non-persons, almost always referring to them collectively rather than individuals. Second, they treat people who face higher risks as objects or problems to be discussed, while excluding them from participation in that discussion. Third, they make clear by the nature of their comments that people who face higher risks are also excluded from the intended audience for their remarks.

One example of such exclusion is the routine assertion by actuarial associations that restrictions on risk classification make insurance more expensive 'for everyone'. Some examples of such claims were quoted in Chapter 2. But the mechanism by which the average price of insurance rises is that coverage shifts towards higher risks, who pay less than they did before. The assertion that restrictions on risk classification make insurance more expensive 'for everyone' makes no sense, until one discerns that for many actuaries the ontological concept of 'everyone' excludes minorities with higher risks.

Another example of offensiveness towards people who face higher risks, or those who are concerned for them, is the assertion that the fears of these parties concerning insurance discrimination are 'irrational'. In a position statement about genetics and insurance, the Institute and Faculty of Actuaries said (emphasis added):

> The profession actively supports research and discussion on questions concerning the applicability of the results of genetic tests. A major route for achieving this will be through the UK Genetics and Insurance Forum, the establishment of which has been promoted by the actuarial profession. The Forum will also

provide a mechanism for informing the public about the relevance of results of genetic tests and defusing *irrational and unfounded concerns* about the reactions of insurance companies and the nature of insurance business.[13]

Terms such as 'rational' and 'irrational' are properly used only when discussing cognitive algorithms *as algorithms*. It is usually imprecise – and in the case of 'irrational', gratuitously offensive – to use these terms to describe a person's concerns.

Affectation of Virtue

Another rhetorical device often used by advocates of risk classification is an affectation of moral virtue on the part of the commentator. Faced with the problems of genetic predispositions to illness, or actual illness, a natural empathetic response is a desire to help, for example by restricting risk classification. The essence of actuarial orthodoxy is that this response is shortsighted: the actuary sternly warns that any attempt to help will lead to a decline in insurance coverage and eventually the collapse of the insurance system. Essentially, actuarial orthodoxy demands immediate pain (discrimination against the ill) for supposed long-term gain (the survival of the insurance system).

Although the implied necessity is almost always overstated, the narrative of immediate pain for long-term gain is appealing to many commentators. Advocacy of immediate pain to secure long-term gain seems to carry a connotation of hard-headed moral virtue. But notice that in general, the commentators are privileged by their affluence and health, while the pain they advocate is to be imposed on disadvantaged others. This makes the connotation of virtue illusory: there is no moral virtue in advocating that pain be imposed on disadvantaged others for the benefit of one's own privileged class.

---

[13] Institute and Faculty of Actuaries (1999).

Emo-Phobia

Affectations of virtue are often associated with a complementary rhetorical affectation which I call *emo-phobia*. This occurs when commentators speaking about risk classification preface their advocacy with a reference to public sentiment or sympathy, followed either literally or structurally by some form of 'but ...' Some examples are given below:

> Clearly genetics is a sensitive area but ...
>
> (Institute and Faculty of Actuaries, 2001a)

> It is clear that patient interest groups will campaign very cogently and convincingly on behalf of their members and the prohibition of insurers using certain genetic tests as an act per se may be of small benefit. But ...
>
> (Institute and Faculty of Actuaries, 2001b)

> It is perfectly natural that when it comes to issues of rights of a disadvantaged group, public sympathies will be with the individual rather than a large corporation. However ...
>
> (Life Insurance Association of Singapore, 2006)

Emo-phobia generally indicates that the speaker wishes to argue against a position which has both popular appeal and moral rightness (e.g. not inflicting further harm on persons already disadvantaged by genetic predispositions), in order to advance some unpopular and selfish interest (e.g. marginal commercial gain for insurance companies). Recognising the weakness of this position, the speaker seeks to disparage popularity and moral rightness as 'emotional' properties.

The appropriate response to an emo-phobe is to say yes, this is an emotive subject, and therefore one in which we should take account of moral imperatives, rather than the narrow interests which you selfishly seek to advance. Good judgement requires not the flattening of emotions, but rather the right emotions: those which are accurately calibrated to the contours of truth.

Cognitive Capture

Academics in mature democracies such as the USA and the UK generally face few formal restraints on their intellectual inquiry. If they wish to criticise risk classification policies or other aspects of insurance practice, they can generally do so without fear of immediate repercussions for their relatively secure employment. Nevertheless, those whose work is amenable to corporate influence and interests can gradually accrue many advantages over those whose lines of enquiry are more independent. These advantages may include: funding of academic posts or research assistance; access to industry data; greater ease of publication in professional and academic journals; invitations and funding to speak at conferences; lucrative consulting opportunities and so on. These effects can lead over time to 'cognitive capture' (sometimes called 'intellectual capture'), analogous to the effects labelled 'regulatory capture' for regulators.[14]

In the proximate context of pension reform, the independent British economist John Kay offered some perceptive reflections on his naivety about cognitive capture in his early academic career:

> There is a book on my shelves published in 1982, called The World Crisis in Social Security. I now feel slightly ashamed of my contribution to that volume. Not because of its content: my criticisms foreshadowed sensible reforms for Britain that were implemented soon after. Rather I feel ashamed for my youth and naivety and my failure to understand the game in which I was being asked to play.
>
> Every pension system has weaknesses and there are always honest but simple scholars who can be encouraged to point them out. Hence my agreeable trip to Washington to debate 'the world

---

[14] A good reference on regulatory capture generally is the book *Preventing regulatory capture: special interest influence and how to limit it* (Carpenter and Moss, 2014).

crisis in social security'. I was joined by others who could tell
of deficiencies in the pension systems of France, of Germany,
and the public system of the US itself.[15]

Kay feels slightly ashamed, despite the technical competence
of his critique of British social security, because he did not understand that he was a tool. He did not understand that the indulgence
of funding for his agreeable trip to Washington was part of a decades-
long campaign to denigrate social security schemes and promote
their replacement with privatised pensions. There are always
research grants and publication opportunities and conference invitations for academics willing to write about the 'crisis' in social security, the 'inefficiency' of risk classification restrictions[16], or the
'competitiveness' of contingent commissions.[17] Academics are in
principle equally free to write about the equity of universal public
benefits, the loss coverage benefits of risk classification restrictions,
or the dishonesty of undisclosed kickbacks from insurers to brokers,
and those who do so usually experience no immediate sanctions. But
those who do so also experience many obstacles in funding and pub-
lishing their work, and over time their careers slowly fall behind
those of colleagues who pay obeisance to corporate influence and
interests. These are not personal complaints, because I am not a
career academic; but it might have been difficult to write this book
if I were.[18]

---

[15] 'Pensions crisis helps create one', *Financial Times* 24 January 2005.

[16] For example the book *Risk classification and life insurance*, where the preface
states that the book was commissioned by the American Council of Life Insurers
(ACLI), and submitted to them for review before publication, because 'The ACLI
was concerned about legislative and judicial activity in this area and its potential
effects on the life insurance industry' (Cummins et al., 1983).

[17] For example the paper 'Economics of insurance intermediaries', sponsored by the
American Insurance Association (Cummins and Doherty, 2006, see further details
at the beginning of Chapter 10).

[18] For broader evidence and discussions of the cognitive capture of economists by
business, see Zingales (2013), Häring and Douglas (2013) and the 2010
documentary film 'Inside Job'.

Summary

This chapter has outlined some reasons why adverse selection is often overstated in policy discussions. There were two broad categories of reasons, which were not mutually exclusive.

First, genuine misperceptions:

- naïve cynicism (obsessive searching for freeriders, neglecting the broad sweep of reality);
- actuarial paranoia (prioritising policing over epidemiology);
- fallacies of composition, which confuse analysis of the position of one insurer in a competitive market with analysis of the whole market; and
- the fallacy of the one-shot gambler.

Second, strategic misrepresentations:

- cartoons (exaggeration for effect);
- barricades (the belief that arguing against risk classification restrictions defends industry profits (which is unlikely) or specific job roles (which is more likely)); and
- signals (beliefs as attire).

I also discussed some common rhetorical devices in discussions of risk classification:

- semantic sophistry;
- one-way hash arguments;
- presumption of privilege;
- devaluation of the disadvantaged;
- affectation of virtue; and
- emo-phobia.

Finally, I discussed the possibility of cognitive capture of academics by industry funding, which tends to favour the exaggeration of adverse selection and other industry-approved perspectives.

The above misperceptions and misrepresentations relate mainly to general policy discussions of risk classification in insurance by actuaries, regulators, academics, politicians and others. In the academic discipline of insurance economics, there are a number of more esoteric myths and biases. These are the subjects of Chapter 10.

10 Myths of Insurance Economics

Key Ideas:

chameleon models; Rothschild–Stiglitz model; uniform endowments; efficiency losses; deductibles as screening devices; rationing of insurance for low risks; unrestricted cover for high risks; asymmetric assumptions about information; asymmetric assumptions about behaviour; semantic stretches; concern trolling

> Do these theoretical speculations tell us anything about the real world? In the absence of empirical work, it is hard to say.
>
> (Rothschild and Stiglitz, 1976)

> This section uses a modified version of Rothschild and Stiglitz (1976) to show that contingent commissions can be beneficial to policyholders ... Despite recent allegations that contingent commissions are a 'kickback' that compromises the intermediary's obligations to its clients, such commissions can be beneficial to clients.
>
> (Cummins and Doherty, 2006)

The first quotation above is a very reasonable observation from the final paragraph of Rothschild and Stiglitz (1976), which is probably the best-known paper about adverse selection in insurance economics. In this conclusion, Rothschild and Stiglitz acknowledged that the paper's main theoretical constructs – that insurers cannot distinguish between high and low risks, that insurers use 'menus' of alternative contracts to 'screen' for high and low risks and that insurance for low risks is 'rationed' – had not been substantiated by any real-world evidence. Four decades later, this still remains broadly true.

The second quotation is from a paper about the economics of insurance brokers. This paper uses a modified version of the Rothschild–Stiglitz model to make a policy argument that contingent commissions, which Eliot Spitzer (then New York Attorney General) and other regulators were seeking to ban, should continue to be permitted 'because they can benefit policyholders by reducing adverse selection'. Both papers were published in top journals: the first in the *Quarterly Journal of Economics* (the oldest English language journal in economics, associated with Harvard University) and the second in *The Journal of Risk and Insurance* (the leading 'field journal' for insurance economics).

Contingent commissions are payments from insurers to insurance brokers which are contingent on either the volume of business introduced by the broker, or the profitability to the insurer of that business, or both. They are controversial because they may encourage the broker to act contrary to the policyholder's interests. If the broker stands to benefit from the insurer's profitability on the introduced business, the broker may be less proactive in advising and assisting the policyholder, for example in pursuing any ambiguous or disputed claims. In many jurisdictions including the USA and the UK, the broker is in law an agent of the policyholder; but contingent commissions align the broker's financial interests with the insurer, and so create an obvious conflict of interest. This seems a strong *prima facie* argument that contingent commissions should simply be banned.[1]

Taken together, the two quotations encapsulate a common pattern of interaction between theories and applications in insurance economics. In the first, unrealistic assumptions are used to build a theory with striking predictions; the main attractions are the ingenuity and internal consistency of the analysis, and there is an admitted neglect of (and perhaps indifference to) whether any of the

---

[1] Schwarcz (2007) advocates a complete ban on contingent commissions in consumer insurance. The distinction from commercial insurance is predicated on the notion that commercial customers may be more sophisticated, and hence alert to the insurance brokers' conflict of interests.

predictions are actually true. In the second, the ingenious theory from the first is applied to make strong policy recommendations on a real-world insurance issue; the lack of empirical support is now forgotten, but the policy recommendations conveniently serve the interests of a financial sponsor.[2]

The different roles of the Rothschild–Stiglitz model in each paper constitute an example of a *chameleon model*: a theoretical model built on assumptions with dubious connections to the real world, which is nevertheless used to make confident policy recommendations for the real world. If the unrealistic assumptions are directly challenged, the modeller will typically retreat behind the excuse that confident recommendation is 'just a theory', and not necessarily intended for wide application (even though the presentation of the original recommendation encouraged wide application).[3]

This chapter's critique of insurance economics, and particularly the standard account of adverse selection, is directed at the canonical textbook models. For most of my criticisms, it may be possible to find a few papers in the economics literature which address the point (and sometimes I cite authors who do). But where a particular approach or assumption is espoused in every textbook and taught in every classroom, the fact that a different approach or assumption may occasionally have been pursued by a few researchers does not negate a critique of the standard account.

The Rothschild–Stiglitz Model

Before offering a critique, I first need to give some indication of what I mean by the 'standard accounts' of adverse selection in insurance economics. The textbooks by Rees and Wambach (2008) or Zweifel

---

[2] The acknowledgements in the second paper disclose financial support from an insurance brokers' trade association. The insurance brokers eventually got what they wanted: the restrictions on contingent commissions for large brokers which had been introduced following Spitzer's initiatives in 2005 were relaxed in 2010. See 'Large brokers freed to go after contingent commissions – but will they?' *Insurance Journal*, 17 February 2010.

[3] The prevalence of chameleon models in economic policy analysis generally is discussed in Pfleiderer (2014).

and Eisen (2012) are contemporary examples. Probably the best-known account of adverse selection in insurance economics is the paper I have already quoted, Rothschild and Stiglitz (1976). There are some much-cited earlier papers such as Arrow (1963) and Akerlof (1970), but the focus of these is on medical care (Arrow) and adverse selection in markets in general (Akerlof), rather than on adverse selection in insurance. I discuss the divergence between Rothschild and Stiglitz (1976) and the real world of insurance in some detail, not because this paper is especially unrealistic, but rather because it is especially esteemed: it is the first (and often only) model of insurance which students of economics encounter, it has over 5,000 citations in Google Scholar, and it is the first paper mentioned in the citation for Stiglitz's 2001 Nobel prize. Of course I do not question the theoretical soundness of such a celebrated paper, but I do question the paper's relevance to the real world of insurance (as the original text does, and so also to some extent Stiglitz in his Nobel lecture[4]).

The Rothschild–Stiglitz model assumes two risk-groups, with high and low probabilities of loss. Every individual faces a potential loss of the same amount, and every individual knows her own probability of loss. Insurers know what proportions of the population high and low risks represent, and know the high and low probabilities of loss, but cannot distinguish high risks from low risks at the individual level. (Note that this is immediately contrary to the facts in most insurance markets, where insurers almost invariably do obtain at least some information on individual risks, but may not know the population proportions – an interesting thought experiment, but a questionable starting point from which to derive recommendations for public policy.) Insurance contracts are assumed to be exclusive,

---

[4] Stiglitz (2001, p. 500):

> Moreover, though there is considerable evidence for the kinds of selection processes discussed above, there is also considerable evidence that the market is far from as rational as the theory would suggest ... competition is far more limited than we postulated; there are, for instance, significant search costs, and considerable uncertainty about how easy it is to get the insurance company to pay on a claim.

that is each person can buy only one contract from one insurer (e.g. as in real car insurance and health insurance, but not in life insurance).

The theory predicts that a 'pooling equilibrium' – that is, one where insurers charge a single price representing a demand-weighted average of the low and high risks – will not be stable. This is because some enterprising insurer can always offer a contract at the lower actuarially fair price appropriate to the low risks, with contract features which ensure that only the low risks find it attractive (this will be explained in the next paragraph), and so 'cream-skim' the low risks, thus 'breaking' the pooling equilibrium.

In response to this unstable situation, the theory predicts that all insurers will offer a choice of two contracts, each with its own level of deductible – in effect, a choice of levels of cover.[5] Each contract can be bought by anyone, but is designed to be attractive only to high risks or only to low risks, and is priced at the actuarially fair premium rate for its target risk-group. Specifically, because high risks derive more expected utility from each dollar of insurance cover than low risks, they are more willing to 'pay up' for a full-cover contract (i.e. a zero deductible). Therefore if the insurer offers a full-cover contract at the high-risk fair premium rate, and a partial-cover contract at the low-risk fair premium rate, each group will self-select into the 'correct' contract. Hypothetically, if the low-risk and high-risk probabilities of loss are 0.1 and 0.2, the contract offers might look like this:

- contract targeted at high risks: full cover (zero deductible) at 0.2 premium rate
- contract targeted at low risks: partial cover (large deductible) at 0.1 premium rate

Then high risks prefer to pay the 0.2 rate for full cover (because their high risk means they place higher value on each dollar of cover); low risks prefer to pay the 0.1 rate for partial cover.

---

[5] The original exposition in Rothschild and Stiglitz (1976) does not explicitly define deductibles, but instead specifies insurance contracts by a vector (α_1, α_2), where α_1 is the premium paid and α_2 is the payout if a loss occurs. But many later authors (including Stiglitz in his Nobel lecture) use the expository concept of deductibles, and hence I do so here.

In this 'separating equilibrium', high risks and low risks self-select into separate groups, by choosing the contract priced at the actuarially fair premium rate for their own risk. But because the low-risk contract is offered only with a large deductible, and contracting is exclusive (i.e. nobody can buy more than one contract), the low risks cannot obtain full cover at their actuarially fair premium rate. This alleged 'rationing' of cover at the low-risk price, implying a forced reduction in cover for low risks, is the key 'inefficiency' which is said to arise from adverse selection.

Rothschild and Stiglitz also predict that if the high risks represent only a very small fraction of the population, a further problem will arise. In this scenario, the pooling price is only slightly above the low-risk price. Loosely speaking, the low risks will then not have a strong preference for either of the two possibilities: a slightly more expensive, full-cover contract which pools them with the high risks or a slightly cheaper partial-cover contract priced just for low risks. The lack of clear preference means that neither the separating equilibrium nor a pooling equilibrium is stable, so no stable equilibrium exists.[6] With no stable equilibrium, the predictions of the model are indeterminate; perhaps different insurers offer different types of contract, or alternate erratically between offering pooling and separating contracts. Subsequent papers have introduced a range of subtly different concepts of market equilibrium designed to resolve this so-called nonexistence puzzle.[7]

[6] The 'loosely speaking' argument I give here – that low risks lack a strong preference between pooling and separation – is merely suggestive of instability. Rothschild and Stiglitz make this argument rigorous, but I omit the details for brevity.

[7] Rothschild and Stiglitz (1976) used a Nash equilibrium, where each insurer assumes that other insurers' contract offers are independent of its own offer. Wilson (1977) considers 'anticipatory equilibrium', where firms are forward-looking and anticipate the actions of rivals, rather than the myopic firms in Rothschild and Stiglitz (1976). Miyazaki (1977) applies this to the labour market and shows that the equilibrium is the solution of a constrained optimisation problem. Spence (1978) generalises for an arbitrary number of risk groups. The forward looking equilibrium concept in these three papers is sometimes described as the 'MWS equilibrium' in deference to the authors' surnames. Further alternative concepts of insurance market equilibrium are discussed in Riley (1979), Grossman (1979) and Dasgupta and Maskin (1986).

Within the Rothschild–Stiglitz framework, the distinction between cover and loss coverage (*unweighted* insurance demand and *risk-weighted* insurance demand) which is emphasised in this book is of limited interest. This is because the Rothschild–Stiglitz model implicitly compares the outcome under adverse selection with an idealised (but in the real world, unrealistic) scenario in which all individuals buy full cover at their actuarially fair premium rate. When risk classification is not feasible and adverse selection ensues, lower risks are worse off because they are 'rationed', while higher risks are no better off. In this framework, adverse selection is unambiguously a bad thing: it makes no difference for higher risks, and reduces cover for lower risks, leading to reductions in both insurance demand (cover) and loss coverage. So in this framework the possibility that loss coverage rises when cover falls cannot arise, and hence the loss coverage concept is of limited interest.[8]

Rothschild–Stiglitz and the Real World

The Rothschild–Stiglitz model of insurance markets outlined above has been enormously influential, and is frequently applied to make policy recommendations on real-world issues (as exemplified in the second quotation at the start of this chapter). For such a dominant and widely accepted theory, it is remarkably hard to find real-world evidence for the alleged phenomena the theory predicts.

I know of no evidence that the concept of separating risk-groups by a menu of deductibles priced at different rates is salient, or even recognisable, to actuaries and others involved in insurance pricing or marketing. I know of no evidence that cover for low risks is 'rationed' by mandatory larger deductibles for polices priced for

---

[8] It is not of *no* interest, because even in the Rothschild–Stiglitz model, loss coverage gives a different (and in my opinion, better) measure of inefficiency arising from adverse selection than the conventional 'reduction in cover'. Specifically, inefficiency as measured by reduction in loss coverage is always *smaller* than inefficiency as measured by reduction in cover (because the *risk-weighted* nature of loss coverage means that less weight is placed on the reduction in cover arising from 'rationing' of low risks).

low risks compared with high risks, or any equivalent mechanisms. I know of no evidence that markets where high risks represent a very small fraction of the population are notoriously problematic or unstable. Overall, the Rothschild–Stiglitz model and its derivatives bear astonishingly little resemblance to any observable reality of insurance markets; but 40 years after their introduction, they remain the canonical representation of insurance pricing in economics textbooks.

The exposition of Rothschild–Stiglitz above described the contracts targeted at low risks as providing 'partial' cover, but did not explicitly state the size of the deductible. For the theory to work, the deductible needs to be incentive-compatible: that is, small enough so that low risks prefer the low-rate contract with deductible, and large enough so that high risks prefer the high-rate contract with no deductible. This may be another problem with the model: my back-of-an-envelope estimates suggest that the required deductible might typically be well over 50% of the loss, which is much larger than the small deductibles typically observed in practice.[9]

Much subsequent work building on Rothschild and Stiglitz, rather than moving closer to reality, has developed ever-more exotic concepts of equilibrium, such as anticipatory equilibria, mixed strategies and other obscure game-theoretic formulations. But as far as I am aware, there is no empirical work testing these concepts against data and identifying which if any of them describes the operation of any real insurance markets. This continuing absence of the empirical work probably reflects the fact that the central constructs of the models – inability of insurers to assess risks, menus of deductibles offered at different premium rates, 'rationing' of low risks – are

---

[9] For example if we assume initial wealth = 2, potential loss = 1, probabilities of loss of 0.1 (low) and 0.2 (high) and logarithmic utility, I calculate that a suitable deductible to induce separation of the risk-groups is around 75% of the loss. An economist friend told me that he once did some calculations which estimated the required deductible at around 70% of the loss.

myths which are barely recognisable in any form in real insurance markets. It is hard to conduct empirical studies on unicorns.

Apart from the exaggerated credence afforded to the theoretical constructs promulgated in Rothschild and Stiglitz (1976) and its large derivative literature, insurance economics embraces some other myths, biases and omissions in its account of adverse selection in insurance. The following sections elaborate on this.

Myth: Adverse Selection Always Implies 'Efficiency Losses'

Economists generally describe the reduction in cover when risk classification is restricted as involving 'inefficiency' or 'efficiency losses'. One recent survey article on the economic effects of risk classification bans summarises this argument as follows (emphasis added):

> To illustrate, observe that risk-pooling arising from legal restrictions on risk classification may lead to a situation where lower-risk individuals are charged higher than actuarially fair premiums and higher-risk individuals are charged lower than actuarially fair premiums. While these financial inequities (may) reduced classification risk (and/or improve social equity), the higher-than-fair premiums for lower-risk individuals may cause them to forgo insurance entirely, particularly when the proportion of high-risk individuals is large. *This reduced pool of insured individuals reflects a decreased efficiency of the insurance market.*[10]

This description is valid in the limited sense that technical terms such as 'efficiency' can ultimately be assigned arbitrarily. But in my opinion this is not a sensible concept of 'efficiency', because it ignores the benefit from the shift in coverage towards higher-risk individuals when risk classification is restricted. As we saw in Chapters 3–5, if the shift in coverage more than outweighs the

---

[10] Dionne and Rothschild (2014, p. 185).

reduced pool of insured individuals, expected losses compensated by insurance will rise (loss coverage will rise). Why should an arrangement under which more risk is voluntarily traded and more losses are compensated be disparaged as 'less efficient'?[11]

Perhaps reliance on Rothschild–Stiglitz as a chameleon model encourages the mis-characterisation of adverse selection as always inefficient. In Rothschild–Stiglitz, adverse selection manifests as reduced cover for low risks, with no change in cover for high risks; I agree that this is always inefficient. But as discussed in the previous section, Rothschild–Stiglitz bears little resemblance to the observable reality of extant insurance markets.

Myth: Small High-Risk Group, Big Problem

A curious feature in the Rothschild–Stiglitz model is that the 'non-existence puzzle' regarding equilibrium arises only when the high-risk group is a very *small* fraction of the population. Intuitively, it seems unlikely that neglecting to identify and surcharge a very small high-risk fraction of the population would make much difference to the aggregate outcome. Empirically, bans on life and health insurers using results of genetic test for rare but severe monogenic diseases have not led to any obvious market instability. But the Rothschild–Stiglitz model has sometimes been used to argue that restriction on risk classification is *more* likely to cause serious problems where the restriction benefits only a *small* group. One book titled *Risk classification in life insurance* warns that:

> Restrictions on the use of various impairments or handicaps in insurance pricing have occurred on a piecemeal basis at the state level. Restrictions prohibiting the use of a particular variable are potentially troublesome, if this variable in fact has an effect on mortality. In this regard, it is important to reemphasize the result

---

[11] Of course, if adverse selection is high enough, loss coverage will fall when risk classification is restricted. It would be reasonable to describe this as 'less efficient'. But this implies a different concept of efficiency to the one normally used by insurance economists.

from chapter 3 that the chance of market failure increases when the prohibited classification is relatively small.[12]

For life insurance – the ostensible subject of the text from which the above quotation is taken – this is an egregious example of a chameleon model. The Rothschild–Stiglitz model from which the purported 'result' is derived is unrealistic for most insurance markets, and particularly unrealistic for life insurance (where nonexclusive contracting is the norm, and the concept of partial cover is meaningless). Small groups of very unfortunate people can generally be helped at modest cost, precisely because they are small; to suggest otherwise is a particularly cruel case of economic dogmatism.

Myth: Deductibles as Screening Devices

This myth originated with Rothschild and Stiglitz (1976) as discussed above, and has since become a pervasive concept in insurance economics, but there is little evidence for it in the real world. Often, where a deductible features in the contract design, a modest level of deductible is compulsory. Some limited choice of optional higher deductibles may be offered, but this is usually a late and minor choice in the insurance sales process; the choice is not prominently promoted as a key contract feature. Also, if insurers used deductibles for screening risks, one would expect the setting of an appropriate menu of deductibles to induce the desired self-selection to be a salient concept to actuaries and others involved in insurance pricing. As far as I am aware, this concept is entirely absent from actuarial literature and lore.[13] A textbook recently written to meet the Core European Syllabus for actuaries even specifically counsels

---

[12] Cummins et al. (1983).

[13] Recent actuarial textbooks which give comprehensive coverage of premium rating, but with no allusion to the concept of menus of deductibles as screening devices, include: *Pricing in general insurance* (Parodi, 2014), which runs to 560 pages; *Fundamentals of general insurance actuarial analysis* (Friedland, 2013), which is the recommended reading for the Society of Actuaries general insurance ratemaking and reserving examination and *Risk modelling in general insurance* (Gray and Pitts, 2012).

against any thought of including the level of deductible as a risk variable, warning that this is 'not a good idea'.[14]

More plausible motivations for the deductible as a contract feature are: to save administrative costs on small claims; to deter moral hazard and fraud by making the policyholder bear the first part of any loss; and to provide a simple dimension of limited flexibility in premium quotations for customers who expect to negotiate on price. Specifically, customers who ask for a discount can be offered a revised quote with a larger deductible. The lower price will often satisfy the customer, who may feel gratified by the apparent fruits of her negotiating skill; the customer will probably not realise that the reduction given is less than its actuarial expected cost.

Myth: 'Rationing' of Insurance for Lower Risks

A predicted corollary of the use of deductibles as screening devices is that insurance for lower risks is 'rationed': the imposition of a deductible means that under exclusive contracting (i.e. each person can hold only one valid policy, as in car insurance and health insurance), lower risks cannot buy as much cover as they would like. Again, this myth originated with Rothschild and Stiglitz (1976) as discussed above, and has since become a pervasive concept in insurance economics; the enforced limitation of cover which it implies is the main 'inefficiency' which allegedly arises from adverse selection.

---

[14] Ohlsson and Johansson (2010, p. 65) note that using the deductible as one of several multiplicative risk variables in a pricing model is problematic if the claim severity varies between risk cells. Suppose there are two choices of deductibles: 200 and 400. Suppose there are two customers: the first with mean claim severity of 500 before deductible and the second 1,000. The net mean severities for the first customer are then either (500 − 200) = 300 or (500 − 400) = 100, depending on the level of deductible chosen. For the second customer, the corresponding figures are 800 and 600. The ratios between these amounts – the expected 'extra claim cost' arising from the choice of a smaller deductible – are then 300/100 = 3 times and 800/600 = 1.3 times, respectively, for the two customers. But if the deductible is to act as one of a set of multiplicative risk variables used to assess all customers, these ratios should be the same. This argument is not, of course, relevant in the limited framework of the Rothschild–Stiglitz model, where all claim severities are of the same size; but it does illustrate that pricing actuaries in practice focus on quite different concerns from those imagined by economists.

But the concept is completely unknown to actuaries, at least in my experience. Practical experience points strongly the other way: it is high risks, not low risks, which tend to be offered only partial cover, either of limited amount or with many exclusions.

Interestingly, one theoretical paper which assumes that a monopolistic insurer can predict risk *better* than customers (that is advantageous selection rather than adverse selection) derives the realistic prediction: lower risks are offered full insurance, while higher risks are 'rationed'.[15] A recent working paper which assumes a monopoly insurer with administrative cost loadings or claims processing costs also obtains this prediction.[16] But as I noted in the introduction to this chapter, the existence of a very few papers which make realistic predictions does not invalidate a critique of the standard account which appears in every textbook.

Myth: Unrestricted Cover for High Risks

As just noted, it is high risks, not low risks, which tend to be rationed, that is they find it difficult to buy as much insurance as they would like. Often this rationing takes the form of outright refusal: a person in remission from cancer, for example, will often be refused any health, life or travel insurance. In the Swiss Re survey cited in Chapter 2, the rate of outright refusal of life insurance applications varied between 3% and 11% of applications received for different UK insurers in 2011.

This phenomenon of outright refusal is probably the most important social problem of risk classification. But insurance economics asserts that the problem does not exist: in the standard models high risks can always buy full cover. This myth is particularly egregious, because it does not merely ignore reality but actually *reverses* reality. It is even suggested that high risks are responsible for the alleged difficulties faced by low risks: according to Rothschild and Stiglitz, 'By their very being, high-risk individuals cause an

---

[15] Villeneuve (2000).
[16] Chade and Schlee (2016).

externality: the low-risk individuals are worse off than they would be in the absence of the high-risk individuals'.[17] The insinuation of blame against high risks for imaginary difficulties faced by low risks – difficulties for which no evidence exists in any real insurance market – is a particularly malign piece of dogma.

A recent paper[18] which does engage with the fact of insurers' refusal to quote prices for many higher risks in life insurance explains this by the usual bogeyman of 'asymmetric information'. The idea is that people with serious health conditions – rather than people in general – have superior information about their health risks. That is, life insurers assume that a person in remission from cancer (say) knows accurately how their risks compare with other people in a similar position, and so life insurers refuse to quote even a high price to such people because of their assumed superior information.

This explanation has been enthusiastically received (as evidenced by its publication in the top journal *Econometrica*), probably because it aligns with many economists' theoretical fetish with asymmetric information as the explanation for all manner of ills. But I have never heard actuaries or underwriters voice concern about the superior private information of higher risks compared with other risks. I think there are two less theoretically exciting but more plausible explanations for blanket refusal to quote for high life insurance risks. First, administrative costs: it is expensive for an insurer to investigate and quote on unusual risks. Second, low take-up rates: when an insurer quotes a high price for a nonstandard risk, the potential customer – who has probably already been quoted a standard price for her age as an indication – will very often balk at the revised quotation.[19] High administrative costs combined with a

---

[17] Rothschild and Stiglitz (1976, p. 629).

[18] Hendren (2013).

[19] The actuary and medical adviser De Ravin and Rump (1996) discuss the low completion rates on quotes for high life insurance risks. They cite a completion rate as low as 1.7% of initial enquiries for an experimental scheme established in Canada to insure life insurance risks in the range 4–10 times of standard mortality (De Ravin and Rump, 1996, p. 31).

high proportion of quotes not taken up make quoting on unusual risks a commercially unrewarding endeavour; most insurers prefer simply to decline to have anything to do with high and unusual risks. I think this is probably a matter of commercial practicality, rather than a sophisticated response to different expected information asymmetries for high and low risks.[20]

Myth: Uniform Endowments

Economic models of adverse selection generally assume that *except* for their different risk levels, higher-risk and lower-risk individuals are alike in all respects. In particular, higher and lower risks are assumed to have similar endowments of wealth, health and other advantages. The assessment of 'higher risk' relates to a contingent future; it is not associated with any current disadvantage.

This typically does not correspond to reality. If a person is 'higher risk' in life or health insurance, they will typically already have experienced some misfortune, and this misfortune will often already have led to some degree of poverty or other disadvantage. Obviously there are exceptions: some higher risks for some types of insurance may be wealthy and well, and some lower risks for some types may be poor and sick. But the typical pattern of association for life and health insurance is obvious and undeniable: higher contingent risk tends to be associated with some degree of current misfortune. It is this current misfortune, as much as any prospective contingent misfortune, that often motivates the sentiment that it is unfair to impose further misfortune in the form of insurance disadvantages. By almost invariably assuming uniform endowments, insurance economics devalues current misfortune.

---

[20] A few insurance brokers do specialise in high and unusual risks – often where the broker has a personal interest, say a family member affected by a particular disease.

Bias: Semantic Stretches for Evidence on Adverse Selection

I noted in Chapter 8 that evidence for adverse selection in insurance in many empirical studies is quite weak. In many empirical studies, null results have been obtained[21]; sometimes evidence of selection is found, but it has the wrong sign (that is selection is 'advantageous' rather than 'adverse'). The expected positive relationship between risk and cover has been found only in a few markets and for narrow types of selection, such as selection on the product features in annuities.[22]

It might be expected that weak and sometimes negative evidence would lead to a reappraisal of the underlying theories. Perhaps adverse selection is seldom detected because insurers typically understand risks better than customers do themselves. But there is little sign of a feedback effect from evidence to new theory. A more common response seems to be semantic stretches which downplay the empirical results, or 'stretch' the definition of adverse selection so that evidence of dubious or marginal relevance can be cited.

One example is contained in a review of econometric tests for asymmetric information in insurance, where the conclusion states:

> Several studies have already contributed to a better knowledge of the impact of adverse selection and moral hazard in various markets. In several cases, the importance of information asymmetries has been found to be limited. This by no means implies, however, that such phenomena are of no importance to insurance.[23]

I agree that adverse selection and moral hazard are not of *no* importance to insurance. However, the immediate repetition of these theoretical dogmas seems an anxious reaction to largely null empirical results. Notice also the double negative ('by no means implies ... no

---

[21] Cawley and Philipson (1999), Chiappori and Salanie (2000), Cardon and Hendel (2001), Dionne et al. (2001) and Saito (2006).

[22] Finkelstein and Poterba (2004).

[23] Chiappori (2000).

importance'): such contrived syntax usually signals a contrived conclusion. A more natural interpretation of largely null empirical results might be that perhaps minor restrictions on risk classification, such as on one type of medical test, are unlikely to cause significant adverse selection. Instead of acknowledging this natural interpretation, the next paragraph of the conclusion reverts to evidence-free warnings of 'market collapse':

> For instance, many countries restrict (and sometimes prohibit) the use of HIV tests for health insurance pricing. For an economist, however, the potential perverse effect of this regulation is to replace explicit discrimination by adverse selection, which may sometimes result in either similar discrimination plus signalling inefficiencies, or even in market collapse.[24]

This passage is an example of 'affectation of virtue', the rhetorical device described in Chapter 9. The economist sternly disparages compassion towards people with HIV, and warns that pain must be tolerated to ensure the soundness of insurance markets. But the virtue is an affectation, because the economist has no intention of bearing any of the pain himself; the pain he advocates is to be imposed on disadvantaged others.

Another example of a semantic stretch to find adverse selection despite lack of evidence is contained in Rothschild (2009), who admits the 'underwhelming' nature of evidence for adverse selection in most insurance markets, but then explains that this is because 'adverse selection can be masked by advantageous selection in empirical studies of standard insurance markets'. Since advantageous selection is merely 'negative adverse selection', this seems rather contrived. It is like saying that a rise in the consumer price index of 2% in a year does not show that inflationary forces in the economy are weak, but rather that inflation can be masked by deflation.

---

[24] Ibid.

Another example of semantic stretch is the so-called passive selection presented as evidence for adverse selection in annuities in Finkelstein and Poterba (2002). These authors note that the longevity of annuitants is greater than that of the general population, and that this is largely explained by the correlation of both longevity and annuity purchase with wealth: the affluent both live longer and have more resources to purchase annuities. In a similar vein, Mitchell and McCarthy (2002) refer to what they term the 'compulsory selection' of annuitants in group-defined contribution pension plans: members of these plans, who are compelled to buy an annuity at retirement, live longer than the general population and have higher wealth than the general population. 'Passive selection' and 'compulsory selection' are then cited as part of a body of evidence for adverse selection in annuity markets. But 'passive' or 'compulsory' selection does not involve individual purchasing choices motivated by private information, which is the essence of adverse selection as described in insurance theory. It seems more in the nature of an incidental correlation, which should probably not be regarded as evidence of adverse selection at all.[25]

Bias: Asymmetric Assumptions about Asymmetric Information

Insurance economics typically assumes that customers are omniscient about individual variations in the risks they wish to insure, while insurers know nothing about individual variations in risks. This 'asymmetric information' is said to be existentially threatening to insurers. Proposals to 'reduce information asymmetry' are a common mantra in policy prescriptions. But in reality, customers often have little quantitative understanding of their risks, while insurers understand a great

---

[25] In another paper (Finkelstein and Poterba, 2004), these authors do present some better evidence of 'genuine' adverse selection in the choice of product features in annuities. Specifically, annuitants who choose annuities with more 'back-loading' of payments – increases in line with a retail price index, and no initial guaranteed payment period – appear to live longer than those who purchase level annuities. But the effect sizes are small.

deal. Insurers are experts in risk assessment, and can combine information from many sources to make risk predictions which are often far superior to any vague intuitions the customer may have.

As well as overstating the information advantage of customers in relation to their individual risks, insurance economics largely ignores the information advantages of insurers in relation to premium calculation, the terms of cover and claims handling.

As regards premium calculation, insurers invariably have a much better understanding than customers of the algorithms by which risks are classified and premiums are calculated. It is usually very difficult for even an expert customer to obtain this information, or even to establish the fact that a nonstandard premium loading has been applied. Insurance economics typically ignores this asymmetry of technical knowledge.

As regards terms of cover and claims handling, insurers almost invariably have a better understanding than customers of the technical language of the insurance contract, and the legal framework and judicial culture in which it will be interpreted. Insurers see the full spectrum of marginal cases, but the customer with a claim typically knows little beyond the facts of her own case. In the courts, on the one hand, insurers are repeat players. This gives them many strategic options: they can choose which claims to litigate to obtain favourable precedents, and which cases to settle quietly and so avoid the creation of unhelpful precedents in the courts. They can choose in which order different aspects of the law are litigated, and so tell a consistent story to the same judges. The customer, on the other hand, usually has just a single claim: she is a one-shot player, and so has few strategic options.

Over time this asymmetry of legal options between repeat players and one-shot players gives rise to what have been called (originally in an employment law context) *losers' rules*.[26] Losers' rules

---

[26] The terms *repeat player* and *one-shot player* come from Galanter (1974), a classic law review article which has more than 3,500 citations. The term *losers' rules* comes from Gertner (2012).

are a series of precedents favourable to insurers, generated from the tiny minority of cases which are selected by insurers for litigation because of their insurer-friendly facts. For example, an insurer might choose to litigate non-disclosure where the policyholder was brazenly dishonest; the resulting precedent can then be cited to reject claims for non-disclosure where the policyholder was merely confused or careless. Even if each individual case which insurers select to present to the court is fairly decided on its merits, the asymmetry of options in the legal process creates over time a substantial bias towards repeat players such as insurers.

The asymmetry of information about claims handling suggests the possibility of *insurer-side adverse selection*.[27] This arises where some insurers handle claims honestly and fairly, while others are stingy and deceptive, and the asymmetry of information about claims handling means that prospective customers cannot tell the difference between honest and deceptive insurers. Over time the deceptive insurers, because they can offer lower prices, come to dominate the market; and customers assume (eventually correctly) that all insurers cheat on claims.

Insurer-side adverse selection is an obvious mirror image of conventional customer-side adverse selection, but it is largely ignored in insurance economics. Adverse selection and asymmetric information are concepts deployed selectively to criticise the weak and the poor; they are seldom directed against the strong and the rich.

Bias: Asymmetric Assumptions about Behaviour

Insurance economics is unrelentingly cynical about the behaviour of insureds, but curiously naïve about the behaviour of insurers. It stresses that customers sometimes act in ways which are deceptive or lacking in good faith, but largely ignores that insurers also do this.

---

[27] This concept comes not from an economist but from a lawyer. see Schwarcz (2009).

On the one hand, it is stressed that high-risk customers may conceal what they know about their risks (non-disclosure), buy more insurance if they know their risk is high (adverse selection) or take fewer precautions because they hold insurance (moral hazard). These possibilities have been comprehensively theorised in hundreds or perhaps thousands of papers.

On the other hand, little attention is given to the deception and bad faith often evident in the actions of insurers. Insurers' business models are typically accepted at face value: the collection of risk-based premiums to offer real cover for real risks, and prompt compensation for losses suffered by the policyholder when they occur. But the most profitable and attractive business for insurers is often where the cover is carefully defined so as to be largely illusory, or where the insurance contract contains small-print terms carefully contrived to enable the insurer to avoid paying claims which any reasonable observer would expect to be paid. Extended warranties on consumer durables, payment protection insurance (creditor insurance) and many add-on policies sold with car or home insurance are all examples of how insurers' most commercially successful products provide largely illusory cover; to a lesser extent the same principle underlies critical illness insurance, where a detailed but limited list of diseases appears designed to create an illusion of comprehensive cover.[28]

One recent paper which does engage with the reality that insurers systematically under-compensate legitimate claims is 'Fraudulent claims and nitpicky insurers', published in 2014 in the *American Economic Review*. In this paper, 'nitpicking' refers to insurers reducing payments on claims which are not fraudulent, and where the customer is not in any way at fault. But rather than being

---

[28] The dread diseases typically include cancer, heart attack, stroke, kidney failure, organ transplantation, paralysis of two or more limbs and total permanent disability (the assessment of the last being at the insurer's discretion). The details vary across the jurisdictions where critical illness insurance has achieved some market success, including South Africa, the UK and parts of Asia.

critical of nitpicking, the paper contrives an argument that it is socially optimal. In the acknowledgements section of the paper, one of the authors discloses a 5-year research grant from the French insurance company AXA.[29]

Myth: Tax Transfers are Superior to Risk Classification Bans (Concern Trolling)

Economic accounts of restrictions on risk classification typically allow that they may have desirable 'distributional' consequences (e.g. they may enable people in poor health to receive some medical care). But they also typically argue that all restrictions have negative 'efficiency' consequences. Informally, it is claimed that risk classification bans always 'reduce coverage' (not true if coverage is correctly measured on a risk-weighted basis, i.e. by loss coverage). More technically, Pareto-type arguments are used to suggest that hypothetical schemes of transfers from low to high risks through taxes and benefits are always superior to risk classification bans.

The following extracts from a recent survey article 'Economic effects of risk classification bans'[30] coauthored by a former editor of *The Journal of Risk and Insurance* give a flavour of such arguments:

> So, while a social planner could, on distributional grounds, reasonably prefer a straight ban on risk classification to the pure free market outcome with legal risk classification, any welfarist social planner would strictly prefer a regime with legal risk classification and such a tax/subsidy scheme.
>
> Even when banning risk classification furthers some distributional objective, imposing a ban is a suboptimal way to achieve this objective.

[29] Bourgeon and Picard (2014). That the research grant is disclosed at all reflects a new policy recently introduced by the American Economic Association, publishers of the *American Economic Review*, in response to criticisms of economists' conflicts of interest following the 2008 financial crisis.
[30] Dionne and Rothschild (2014).

> Insofar as these sorts of taxes are within the purview of
> the social planner, then, one can conclude that bans on risk
> classification are never strictly desirable, regardless of
> distributional concerns.

Since these remarks are from a survey article, I can reasonably treat them not as idiosyncratic claims of the particular authors, but rather as illustrative of orthodoxy in insurance economics. In my opinion the claimed superiority of tax-and-subsidy schemes is illusory, for at least three reasons: infeasibility, inconsistency and stigma.

> *Infeasibility.* Restrictions on risk classification are generally much easier
> to agree, implement and police than new taxes. This difference in
> feasibility is reflected in the fact that while restrictions on risk
> classification are common, tax-and-subsidy schemes to offset
> unfairness in risk classification are unknown in the real world.[31]
>
> *Inconsistency.* In most contexts, economists tend to emphasise that all
> taxes are costly to administer, that complexity increases these costs,
> that high taxes inhibit economic growth and so on. The cost of raising
> an additional £1 of tax revenue is commonly estimated at somewhere
> between £1.20 and £2.00.[32] Yet when considering the specific
> problems of risk classification, economists ignore their general
> critique of complexity and costs in taxation, and enthusiastically
> advocate complicated new schemes of taxes and benefits.
>
> *Stigma.* Bans on risk classification by specific variables, on the one hand,
> have the great advantage that the banned variables do not need to be
> revealed to the insurer, the employer, the State authorities or the
> world at large.[33] Tax-and-subsidy schemes, on the other hand, imply
> that those with a disadvantageous risk profile must reveal their

---

[31] One limited exception: the actuary David Wilkie recalls that when he was a pilot on National Service with the Royal Air Force in the 1950s, the Air Ministry paid 75% of the extra life insurance premiums attributable to flying risks. But this was a limited scheme for an occupational risk directly imposed by the State, not a comprehensive scheme.

[32] Boadway (1997) says this is the range suggested by the economics literature.

[33] Some banned variables such as gender can be inferred with moderately high probability from other information, such as forenames. But most sensitive variables, such as genetic test results, can remain reliably private if they are banned.

disadvantaged status to receive the subsidy. It would not be surprising or unreasonable if many people were hesitant to reveal an adverse genetic profile or a hidden disability to an employer, an insurer, the State or the world at large. Even if the revelation gives entitlement to some subsidy in its immediate context, an individual may quite reasonably fear the consequences in other contexts or at future times of such a revelation.

Economists' habitual advocacy of tax-and-subsidy schemes in preference to risk classification bans often has the appearance and effect of a tactic known as 'concern trolling'. Concern trolls exploit the proverb that the best is the enemy of the good. They ostensibly express support for (or at least do not oppose) some desired ends, such as some redistribution towards people in poor health; but at the same time they gurgle endlessly about their 'concerns' with the obvious practical means, and advocate instead other quite impractical means. The elaborate voicing of 'concerns' with the obvious practical means does not lead to the adoption of better means; it just promotes inertia and doubt, and so lessens the chance that anything will be done.

Summary

This chapter has been critical of the unreality of the standard account of adverse selection in insurance economics. In fairness, I should acknowledge that in recent years this unreality has started to be acknowledged by some economists. 'Adverse selection: an exaggerated threat' might have been a good title for this book, if it had not already been used as the title of a paper by the economist Peter Siegelman in 2004; and his 2010 paper with Alma Cohen on 'Testing for adverse selection' was a useful source for Chapter 8.[34] Another example is a book *Insurance and behavioral economics: improving decisions in the most misunderstood industry*.[35] As implied by the 'behavioral economics' in the title, the book's main theme is that insurers and their customers often do not act in line

---

[34] Siegelman (2004) and Cohen and Siegelman (2010).
[35] Kunreuther et al. (2013).

with the predictions of economic theory. These departures from theory are characterised as 'anomalies', and policy recommendations take the form of 'nudges' intended to make messy real-world behaviour conform better to pristine theory.

My critique is directed at theory itself, rather than corralling insurers and customers to conform. In my opinion, insurance economics gives too much credence to concepts which are not substantiated in real insurance markets: Rothschild–Stiglitz as a broadly representative model; a high likelihood of market collapse if high risks are 'too small' a fraction of the population; universally negative adverse selection; deductibles as screening devices; 'rationing' of cover for low risks; unrestricted cover for high risks; uniform endowments; and the superiority of tax-and-subsidy schemes over restrictions on risk classification. Insurance economics also incorporates various systematic biases: asymmetric assumptions about information, asymmetric assumptions about behaviour, and a tendency to semantic stretches in response to weak or contradictory evidence on adverse selection.

Although my critique is made from a social perspective, the shortcomings of insurance economics are also evident from a commercial perspective. Perhaps the strongest evidence of the unreality of concepts such as deductibles as screening devices, rationing of insurance for low risks and unrestricted cover for high risks is that to the best of my knowledge, these concepts are not salient to actuaries or others involved in insurance pricing or marketing. While economic models are generally not intended to be directly useful to practitioners, a good model's main premises and predictions ought to be recognisable in reality in some form.[36]

---

[36] I am aware that there may be a methodological preference in economics for modelling what actuaries do, rather than what we say; and also of the notion, usually attributed to Milton Friedman, that a theory should be judged on the accuracy of its predictions rather than the realism of its assumptions; but I think that the Rothschild–Stiglitz paradigm does poorly on both these criteria.

11   Contexts Where Adverse Selection May Be Stronger

Key Ideas:

information edge; Kelly criterion; repetition (independent transactions in sequence); diversification (independent transactions in parallel); time average; ensemble average; probability neglect

The first of the three main claims stated in Chapter 1 was 'Adverse selection in insurance is usually weaker than most commentary suggests.' But this does not mean that adverse selection is always unimportant, or equally overstated across all contexts. We have already seen in Chapter 8 that the strength of evidence for adverse selection varies considerably across different markets. This chapter works towards explanations for this variation.

The general approach in this chapter is to treat adverse selection as a decision problem for the customer, who is assumed to have some private knowledge of her own risk. From the customer's perspective, I ask the following questions. First, what circumstances make it more or less attractive to engage in adverse selection, framed as a 'bet' against the insurer? Second, where the size of the contract can be varied, as in life insurance and annuities, what is the optimal size of the bet?

Personally, I believe that very few customers would actually make such calculations. Nevertheless, the approach in this chapter can be justified in at least three ways. First, the *minority argument*: to the extent that a few people *actually* make such calculations (or some rough equivalent thereof), these few may be an important driver of any adverse selection we observe. Second, the *proxy argument*: people may tend to act *as if* they make such calculations, even if they do not do so explicitly. Third, the *thought experiment argument*: even if we do not believe that people actually make such calculations (or tend to act as if they do), insurers seem to worry that people might, and so it is interesting to explore the consequences if they do.

There are two main conditions which make using private information about risk to bet against an insurer more attractive to the customer. Either:

(a) the information gives the customer a *large information edge*, defined as the difference of a true probability based on the customer's private information, and a probability used by the insurer to set premiums; or

(b) the customer can engage in *multiple independent transactions*, either in sequence (*repetition*) or in parallel (*diversification*).

Information Edge

Many adverse selection stories are predicated on predictions that anyone with some private knowledge of their higher risk will wish not just to buy insurance, but to buy *very large* amounts of insurance. Such predictions are typically supported by assertions that the insurance is a 'good investment' for the customer, but numerical justifications are seldom given. In Chapter 9, under the heading *Fallacy of the One-Shot Gambler*, I suggested that a large bet on a small favourable edge is not attractive if the bet can be made only once. But if we can make the bet many times, either in sequence (*repetition*) or in parallel (*diversification*), and limit the size of the bet in each instance, such propositions can become more attractive. I now examine these possibilities in more detail.

For case of recognition, I use the similar symbols as before, μ for the risk and π for the premium charged, but their interpretation now is slightly different. In this chapter, the focus is on the decisions of a single customer (so we do not need the i-subscript from previous chapters), who can vary the size of the insurance contract (which is not fixed at 1 as in previous chapters). The risk μ is the customer's accurate assessment of the probability of loss, informed by private information (say family history, or a genetic test). The insurer does not have the private information, and so sets a premium $\pi < \mu$, which is too low. This gives the customer an information edge:

$$\text{Information edge} = \mu - \pi \qquad (11.1)$$

Assuming that the customer views the insurance with an information edge as a bet or investment (I use these terms synonymously), what fraction of her total wealth should the customer invest?

As an example, consider the one-shot gamble proposed in Chapter 9: a true risk $\mu = 20\%$ over some period, which the insurer underprices at $\pi = 4\%$. The expected outcome is maximised by betting all our wealth on this gamble. But if we do this, we are very likely – 80% likely, on the true probability – to just lose all our wealth. Personally, I would make only a very small bet on this proposition; but for a single contract over a single period, considered in isolation, it is difficult to suggest a robust principle to decide *how* small.[1]

It becomes easier to suggest a robust principle if we assume a context where the customer can engage in multiple transactions, either in sequence (*repetition*) or in parallel (*diversification*). Each of these is considered below.

Repetition (Independent Transactions in Sequence)

The context of multiple independent transactions in sequence (repetition) can be provided by assuming that after the term of the insurance contract, there will be a sequence of other favourable investment opportunities in future. This may seem a strange concept for life insurance (you only live once). But we can make sense of the concept by focusing on *dynastic wealth*. This means that the life insured and his or her dependants and descendants are all

---

[1] If I was pressed to express a view, I would say 'no more than the Kelly fraction' (as described subsequently in this chapter). My rationale is that there is a game-theoretic argument that the Kelly fraction is 'competitively optimal' even for a single investment over a single period, in the sense that in a contest between two investors, it will outperform with probability of at least 0.5 (Bell and Cover, 1980, 1988).

regarded as forming a single economic family unit (a dynasty). Wealth can then be viewed as having the same value to the dynasty irrespective of the survival of the particular life currently insured. If the life survives the term of the insurance, a new contract on that life can be bought; or if the life dies and the insurance pays out, other insurances or investments can then be bought by the family.

To keep things simple, I assume that apart from mispriced term life insurance, the family has only one other possible investment, cash. What fraction of dynastic wealth should this family invest in mispriced term life insurance?

Clearly the family should not invest *all* its wealth in mispriced term life insurance, because if death does not occur during the term, all wealth will be lost. So the answer is to invest only part of the wealth and keep the rest in cash.

More precisely, a sensible answer is to invest the fraction of wealth which maximises the *expected rate of growth* of the family's total wealth. This is equivalent to maximising the *expected logarithmic return* on total wealth. Maximising expected logarithmic return, not expected return, is optimal because of the nature of compound growth: logarithmic returns, not returns, are additive over time.[2] This approach is well known in some investment circles under names such as 'capital growth theory' or 'Kelly betting'. It has many favourable properties (and a few unfavourable ones), and there

---

[2] To understand the importance of the distinction between expected return and expected logarithmic return, consider the following toy example: an investment which is equally likely to rise 50% or fall 40% in each year. The expected return is $(1.5 + 0.6)/2 = 1.05$, or +5%, which looks satisfactory. But if we invest all our wealth in this investment every year, we shall eventually go broke, because (intuitively) $1.5 \times 0.6 = 0.9$. Reflecting this unfavourable prospect, the expected logarithmic return on total wealth is negative: $\{\log 1.5 + \log 0.6\}/2 = -5.27\%$. To give a positive expected logarithmic return on total wealth, we need to restrict the investment to fraction $f < 0.5$ of our total wealth in each period and keep the rest in cash (or other safe assets). The Kelly optimal policy is found by maximising $\{\log [1.5f + (1 - f)] + \log[0.6f + (1 - f)]\}/2$ over f; this leads to $f = 0.25$, giving an expected logarithmic return on total wealth of $+0.621\%$. For an adverse selector, similar considerations limit the sensible size of the bet which should be made on the mispriced insurance contract.

are good arguments that it is superior to *any* alternative strategy for a long-term investor.[3]

Another way of describing the distinction between maximising expected logarithmic return rather than expected return is to say that the family should maximise the *time average* rather than *ensemble average* of the rate of growth of total wealth. The time average is the limit as $T \to \infty$ of the *single path* over which wealth evolves over *many periods*. The ensemble average is the limit as $N \to \infty$ of *many paths* (hypothetical 'parallel universes') over which wealth evolves over a *single period*. Repetition of transactions implies that the family experiences a single path of wealth over time; it does *not* imply that the family experiences many parallel universes. For repetition of transactions, the time average is therefore a more decision-relevant concept than the ensemble average.

Suppose the family invests fraction f of its wealth in single premium term life insurance mispriced at π when the true probability of death during the term is μ. The remaining fraction $(1 - f)$ of wealth is kept in cash.

Then if death occurs (probability μ), at the end of the term we shall have our initial wealth of 1, *plus* the payout on the insurance f/π, *less* the premium paid f. If no death occurs (probability $(1 - \mu)$), we shall have $(1 - f)$. Summing over these two possibilities, the expected logarithmic return on total wealth over the term of the insurance is[4]:

---

[3] Good and bad properties of the Kelly criterion are discussed in Ziemba (2003) and Maclean et al. (2010). A discussion and rebuttal of some critiques of the Kelly criterion are given in Ziemba (2015). A colourful history of the use of the Kelly criterion by successful investors is given in Poundstone (2005).

[4] For simplicity, I assume 0% interest on cash, and that if the life dies in the term of the insurance, the claim is paid only at the end of the term. These assumptions simplify the presentation; making them more realistic does not change the pattern of results. If we had $n > 1$ possible risky investments, the same 'maximise expected log' principle would still apply: we allocate our wealth across the n investments and cash to maximise the expected logarithmic return on total wealth in each period. But the calculations become much harder, because for n investments, we have an n-variable stochastic nonlinear programming problem.

$$E[\log \text{ return}] = \mu\log\left[1 + \left(\frac{1}{\pi} - 1\right)f\right] + (1-\mu)\log[1-f] \qquad (11.2)$$

Differentiating with respect to f and setting to zero, we obtain the optimal fraction f^* of wealth to invest in mispriced term life insurance as:

$$f^* = \frac{(\mu - \pi)}{(1 - \pi)} \qquad (11.3)$$

and the second derivative is negative (given $\mu < 1$ and $\pi < 1$), showing that we have a maximum point.

I make the following observations on the Kelly fraction f^* as given by Equation (11.3).

(a) As $\pi \to 0$ from above, $f^* \to \mu$ from below.

In other words, the optimal fraction of wealth to bet is *always less than the true risk*. For most realistic life insurance scenarios, this point alone ensures that the optimal fraction to bet is small; this limits the scale of sensible 'over-insuring' by the customer.

(b) If π is small, $f^* \approx (\mu - \pi)$.

In other words, in a typical term life insurance scenario, the optimal fraction of wealth to bet depends mainly on the information edge $(\mu - \pi)$, that is the *difference* between the true probability and the insurance price. Contrary to many people's casual intuition, a high *ratio* of μ/π does not, in itself, justify a large over-insurance.

For example, if of $\mu = 0.04$ and $\pi = 0.01$, the insurer's premium is 'wrong by a factor of 4', but this does *not* justify a large bet on the mispriced insurance. The optimal bet as per Equation (11.3) is only $(0.04 - 0.01)/(1 - 0.01) = 3.03\%$ of wealth.

(c) For a given information edge, $(\mu - \pi)$, the optimal fraction f^* is larger for larger π.

In other words, for a given information edge, adverse selection is more attractive to the customer for contracts involving risk events with high probabilities (e.g. annuities) than for those involving risk events with low probabilities (e.g. life insurance). For annuities, 'risk events' refer to events such as predeceasing one's spouse, or surviving long enough for the value of an increasing annuity to exceed that of a level annuity.

These are events on which the customer can select by choosing appropriate annuity features. The probability of such events is typically much higher than the probability of death under a term life insurance contract.

(d) Also note:

$$\frac{\partial f^\star}{\partial \mu} = \frac{1}{1-\pi} > 1 \tag{11.4}$$

which says that with the insurance price π held constant, the optimal fraction of wealth to invest increases more than proportionately with increases in the true probability μ of the risk event. This is again consistent with the idea that adverse selection is more attractive for the customer when the risk events have higher probabilities (e.g. annuities rather than life insurances).

(e) Similarly, note:

$$\frac{\partial f^\star}{\partial \pi} = -\frac{1-\mu}{(1-\pi)^2} < 0 \tag{11.5}$$

which says that with the true probability μ of the risk event held constant, the optimal fraction of wealth to invest falls as the insurance price π rises. This is consistent with intuition.

(f) Also note that the absolute size of the expression in Equation (11.5):

$$\left| -\frac{1-\mu}{(1-\pi)^2} \right| \tag{11.6}$$

is smallest when $\pi \to 0$ and largest when $\pi \to \mu$. This says that
 – the optimal fraction of wealth to invest rises slowly in response to falls in the insurance price π when π is already close to zero (because we have already invested almost all of the fraction μ of our wealth); and
 – the optimal fraction of wealth to invest rises quickly in response to falls in the insurance price π when π is only just below the true probability μ (because at that point we have so far invested only a tiny fraction $(\mu - \pi)/(1 - \pi) \approx 0$ of our wealth).

To illustrate the observations (a) to (f) above, Figure 11.1 shows contours of the optimal $f^\star$ plotted on the (μ, π) plane. All contours lie below the 45° line: in other words, a bet is made only if the

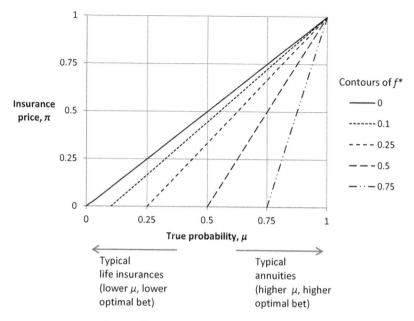

FIGURE 11.1 Repeated transactions: contours of optimal fraction f^* of wealth to invest in mispriced insurance

insurance price is less than the true risk.[5] Note that for small values of μ towards the left of the graph, such as are typical for risk events relating to life insurances, the optimal f^* shown by the contour is small. For large values of μ, towards the right of the graph, such as are typical for risk events relating to annuities, the optimal f^* shown by the contours is large.[6]

The theoretically optimal fraction f^* as illustrated by the contours in Figure 11.1 should be regarded as an *upper limit* on the sensible size of the bet. Betting *larger* than one's estimate of the Kelly

[5] Of course in reality, most insurance buyers are willing to pay a price higher than their true risk (they pay insurance premiums which include expense loadings). This observation confirms that most people do *not* approach insurance as a bet against the insurer, to be made only if private information about the risk suggests it is a good bet. To recap, this chapter assumes the latter framing only for the reasons given in the third paragraph: the minority argument, the proxy argument and the thought experiment argument.

[6] The linear pattern of the contours can be validated by rearranging Equation (11.3) to give π as a function of μ. For given f^*, the function is linear.

fraction is never sensible, because progressive increases above this level involve more risk for a progressively *lower* expected logarithmic return, until eventually the expectation goes negative. For example, if $\pi = 0.01$ and $\mu = 0.05$, the optimal bet is about 4% of wealth; but betting more than about 13% of wealth gives *negative* expected logarithmic growth in Equation (11.2). Thus Kelly is not a cautious betting strategy but an upper limit, the boundary between an adventurous strategy and a merely foolish one.

A further reason for regarding the Kelly fraction as an upper limit is that while betting this amount has some favourable properties in the long run, it can lead to a very erratic growth path, with large 'drawdowns'. A 'fractional Kelly' strategy, betting say one-quarter of one's estimate of the Kelly fraction, provides a smoother path, and a safety margin for errors in the probability estimates.[7]

To summarise this section on repeated transactions, if under-priced insurance is approached as a bet against the insurer, the optimal fraction of wealth to bet is always less than the true risk. This implies a very small bet for most risk events relating to insurances, but a possibly larger bet for some risk events relating to annuities.

Diversification (Independent Transactions in Parallel)

Instead of *repeating* transactions, we could instead seek to *diversify* transactions, that is to enter into many instances of independent transactions over the same time period, investing a small part of our wealth in each transaction.

As the number of independent transactions across which we diversify increases, the law of large numbers implies that the variance of the return on the entire portfolio of transactions declines. With a sufficiently large number of transactions, we can be very confident

---

[7] Baker and McHale (2013) give a formal justification of the need for a safety margin: optimised utility (full Kelly) is an upward-biased estimator of out-of-sample expected maximum utility, and so it can be further optimised by bet rescaling. For risk-averse utility functions and plausible bet parameters, the required rescaling is always a fraction less than 1.

of getting a portfolio return close to the expected return over all the individual transactions.

Note that in this set-up of diversification, unlike the previous set-up of repetition, the ensemble average (rather than time average) of the individual transactions is decision-relevant. This is because the investor *actually* experiences many 'parallel universes', in the form of the different outcomes from insurances on different lives. So for individual transactions to add value to the portfolio of transactions, we require only that they have a positive expected return. This is a less stringent requirement than the positive expected *logarithmic* return on total wealth which we needed under repeated transactions, where time average was the decision-relevant concept.[8]

This is the principle on which an insurer operates: diversification across a large portfolio of risks. However, it is generally difficult for an insurance customer to apply this principle. An individual or household can typically insure only one life, or at best perhaps a small number of lives (say life insurance for both earners in a household).

In theory, more substantial diversification may be possible via so-called life settlement or viatical transactions, whereby the original insured lives sell on their policies to a third-party investor. The expenses of such a scheme and the logistical obstacles may be considerable. But to explore the theoretical scope for adverse selection when an investor can diversify, let's assume that it is possible to engage in many independent transactions, where the prices paid for the policies are say half the true risk. We can then ask: over how many such 'half-price' insurances would an investor in viatical transactions need to diversify to be reasonably certain of making a profit?

The graph in Figure 11.2 shows answers to this question for three values of the investor's required probabilities of profit, $a = 50\%$,

---

[8] Of course, if we envisage repeating the exercise of investing in a diversified portfolio of insurance transactions over more than one time period, then at the level of the whole portfolio, the previous analysis of repetition still applies.

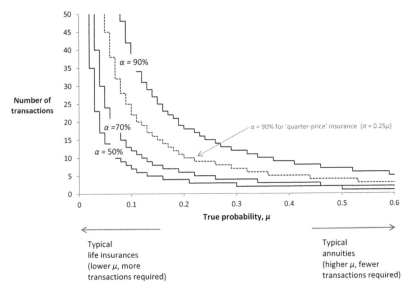

FIGURE 11.2 Diversified transactions: number of independent transactions on 'half-price' insurance required to give Prob{profit > 0} ≥ α

70% and 90% (the three solid stepped lines in the graph), and a range of values of the true probability μ from 0 to 0.6 along the x-axis. The values are calculated using the exact binomial distribution.[9]

I make the following observations on Figure 11.2:

(a) The stepped pattern of the lines reflects the discrete nature of the binomial distribution.

(b) Towards the left of the graph, for small values of $\mu < 0.15$ (that is, events which are quite unlikely), the numbers of simultaneous transactions required to be reasonably certain of making a profit are too large to be practical for a single individual or family. Note that $\mu < 0.15$ corresponds

---

[9] The mathematical details are as follows. Let X be the number of claims from a portfolio of n independent insurance contracts, each with unit sum assured and true probability of claim μ, mispriced at rate π ($\pi < \mu$). Then X has a binomial distribution: $X \sim \text{Binomial}(n, \mu)$. The total profit on the portfolio of insurances is $X - n\pi$. We find the lowest n such that $\text{Prob}(X > n\pi) \geq \alpha$. The figures are calculated from the exact binomial distribution (using a Wolfram Alpha Widget). A normal approximation to the binomial does not work well for low numbers of contracts n or low probabilities μ.

to the probability of the relevant event (death) for term life insurance for typical ages and terms.

(c) Towards the right of the graph, for high values of $\mu > 0.5$ (that is, events which are more likely than not), we need only one or two transactions to be reasonably confident of making a profit. Note that $\mu > 0.5$ corresponds to the probability of the relevant event for some aspects of product choice for annuities (e.g. survival of a spouse after the annuitant's death, or survival to a high enough age to benefit from an increasing annuity). So this analysis of diversified transactions is suggestive of greater opportunities for selection in annuities compared with insurances, the same pattern as in our earlier analysis of repeated transactions.

(d) As the required probability of profit α increases, the required number of transactions increases. The increase is much larger as α moves from 70% to 90% than from 50% to 70%. This reflects the fact that for $\alpha = 50\%$ or 70%, only one claim is needed; but for $\alpha = 90\%$, at least two claims are needed.[10]

(e) The three solid stepped lines in the graph are based on an insurance price of half the true risk, i.e. $\pi = 0.5\mu$. For the 50% and 70% lines, it makes no difference if the insurance price is even lower than half the true risk (e.g. $\pi = 0.25\mu$, say): we still need only one claim in order for total receipts to exceed the total premiums paid. For the 90% line, a more advantageous insurance price implies that we spend less in total on premiums, and therefore need only one claim to make a profit, rather than two claims as explained in (d) above. So in this case the step function with a more advantageous insurance price is a bit lower, as shown by the dotted line ($\alpha = 90\%$ with $\pi = 0.25\mu$). The limited sensitivity of results to the ratio (μ/π) despite its intuitive relevance is loosely analogous to the same pattern found in our earlier analysis of repeated transactions.

---

[10] To understand why profit with probability $\alpha = 90\%$ requires at least two claims, consider the case where the true risk $\mu = 0.10$. The insurance price is half the true risk, so $\pi = 0.05$. If we buy 20 policies, we have spent $20 \times 0.05 = 1$ on premiums. But the binomial distribution gives the probability of at least one claim from 20 policies as only 88%. We therefore need to carry on and buy more policies; but once we go past 20 policies, we shall have spent more than 1 on premiums, so generating a profit will then require at least a second claim. When we have bought 38 policies, we shall have spent 1.9 on premiums; and with 90.4% probability, we shall have received two claims.

The overall conclusion from Figure 11.2 is that to obtain a reasonable probability of profit from a portfolio of mispriced life insurances, we need more independent transactions than would typically be viable for a single household. The required number of transactions is smaller for risk events involving high probabilities (typical annuities) than for risk events involving low probabilities (typical insurances).

Some Comments on Psychological Realism

Probability Neglect

Apart from being theoretically sound under the framing that the customer aims to make an optimal 'investment' decision, stronger adverse selection where risk events have higher probabilities also has psychological plausibility. Most people probably give more attention to calibrating probabilities over likely future states of the world than over very unlikely states. For probabilities below some low threshold, many people may not calibrate probabilities at all, and so will not change their actions in response to changes in probabilities or prices, even if the *proportional* changes are large (say a doubling or trebling of probabilities). This well-documented psychological phenomenon has been called *probability neglect*.[11]

Most accounts of probability neglect suggest that this unresponsiveness to variations in low prices and low risks amounts to cognitive error. However, it may be sensible to give very little consideration to optimising your decisions over low-probability states of the world, particularly if attention given to preparing for unlikely states reduces preparedness for more likely states. At least to some degree, the latter trade-off always applies: if I direct all my attention or spend all my money on preparing myself for the world to end tonight, I shall be very unprepared if the sun rises again tomorrow.[12]

---

[11] See Sunstein (2002) or Kahneman (2011).
[12] A formal version of this argument is made in Mackowiak and Widerholt (2011).

In the specific context of insurance, some evidence for probability neglect has been found in experimental studies of purchasing decisions. One study questioned people about insurance to cover the risk of death caused by toxic discharge from a chemical plant. It found essentially the same willingness to pay for risks which were *one-tenth* the risk of car travel, or *ten times* the risk of car travel. It made no difference whether risks were expressed as a probability or as a dollar insurance premium.[13] Another study found that willingness to pay for insurance against a probability of loss of 0.01 was bimodal: people either said they were not willing to pay anything (effectively choosing to ignore the risk), or they were willing to pay much more than the stated risk of 0.01.[14] In summary, many people seem to be substantially unresponsive to variations in probabilities or prices below some arbitrary low threshold; this unresponsiveness makes adverse selection less likely for insurances involving small probabilities.

Repeated Transactions and Learning

The discussion of multiple transactions above was framed mainly in terms of life insurance and annuities, which are usually long-term contracts. For annually renewable insurances such as health insurance or farm crop insurance, repetition may also be advantageous for another reason: it allows time for new information to emerge and for the 'adverse selector' to learn. Adverse selection requires that customers have some idea of either (a) how their probabilities of loss compare with insurance prices; or perhaps, as a proxy, (b) how their probabilities of loss compare with other customers' probabilities of loss. They may not have much idea initially, but if they repeat a particular type of insurance transaction every year, they may develop a better idea with time.

---

[13] Kunreuther et al. (2001, p. 109).
[14] McClelland et al. (1993).

Explaining Differences in Adverse Selection across Different Insurances and Annuities

Applying the two concepts above – the size of the information edge and the feasibility of repeating or diversifying transactions – can help to explain some of the empirical results on adverse selection in insurance which were detailed in Chapter 8. To recap, studies of life insurance generally find little evidence of adverse selection (after insurer underwriting).[15] There is some evidence for adverse selection in annuities, but predicated on shrewd choice of contract features (e.g. rate of increase, guarantee period, spouse's benefits) rather than on the size of the initial annuity.[16] There is some evidence for adverse selection in some commercial insurances such as crop insurance for farmers in the USA.[17]

These empirical results are broadly consistent with the theories in this chapter. To recap, on the one hand, the low probabilities which are typically relevant to risk events in life insurance give rise to low information edges $(\mu - \pi)$, so the customer's theoretically optimal bet on any mispricing is therefore small. On the other hand, the larger probabilities which are typically relevant to risk events in annuities can give rise to large information edges, even where an insurer's probability estimate contains only a small proportional error. Also, it is psychologically realistic that people give greater attention to variations in probability estimates for likely events (typically relevant for annuities) than for unlikely events (typically relevant for life insurances).[18]

---

[15] E.g. Cawley and Philipson (1999).

[16] E.g. Finkelstein and Poterba (2004) and Mitchell and McCarthy (2010).

[17] Quiggin et al. (1993), Just et al. (1999) and Makki and Somwaru (2001).

[18] In exceptional cases, high probabilities may be relevant to risk events in life insurance. For example, if an insurer asks no health questions whatsoever when selling term life insurance, it might be bought by people with terminal illnesses who have only a few months to live. For these 'deathbed proposals', μ is close to 1 and π is close to 0; so the optimal bet $(\mu - \pi)/(1 - \pi)$ is large. But such exceptional cases do not negate the generalisation that for most customers, term life insurance typically involves risk events with low probabilities, and an annuity typically involves some risk events with higher probabilities.

In farm crop insurance and health insurance, the relevant probabilities are typically well above those for life insurance, although lower than those for annuities. It seems psychologically realistic that farmers give considerable thought to the likely outcome of the year's harvest, and patients to their likelihood of needing medical treatment in the near future. In both cases, the annually renewable nature of the contracts provides some opportunities for learning.

While this book is principally concerned with insurance, adverse selection is also often said to occur in other markets. Indeed, there seems to be better evidence for it in some other markets. Examples include eBay and other online exchanges for second-hand goods,[19] online stamp auctions[20] and loans packaged and resold to investors by banks under the 'originate-to-distribute' lending model.[21] In all these markets, the parties with superior information engage in a large number of transactions every year. Thus the better evidence for adverse selection in these markets as compared with insurance is consistent with the theory that the ability to engage in multiple independent transactions tends to facilitate adverse selection.[22]

Summary

This chapter has highlighted circumstances in which adverse selection may be stronger than suggested in earlier chapters. The main points are as follows.

Large information edge. The optimal bet on a mispriced insurance or annuity increases with the information edge: the difference

---

[19] Ghose (2009).

[20] Dewan and Hsu (2004).

[21] Berndt and Gupta (2009).

[22] Another superficial contrast is that in all these other markets, the party which is hypothesised to exploit superior information is the seller (not the buyer, as in insurance). But this is not a fundamental distinction: a *buyer* of insurance is arguably a *seller* of risk. The important distinction is between parties who have many opportunities for diversification or repetition and those who do not.

(not the ratio) between the probability of a risk event as assessed by the customer given her private information, and the probability of the same risk event given only the insurer's information. Higher probabilities give more scope for a large information edge. This suggests that adverse selection may be stronger where the relevant risk events have high probabilities, such as in annuities. Conversely, adverse selection may be weaker where the relevant risk events have low probabilities, such as in term life insurance. In the latter case, probability neglect – that is, the psychological tendency to neglect variations in low probabilities – may also suppress selective behaviour.

Multiple independent transactions. Adverse selection may be stronger where the customer can engage in multiple independent transactions. There are two versions of multiple independent transactions: sequential (repetition) and parallel (diversification). For repetition, to maximise the multiperiod rate of growth in wealth (the time average), the customer needs to limit the fraction of wealth exposed to risk in each transaction; this limits the scale of a sensible adverse selector's 'bet' against the insurer. For diversification, the number of independent transactions required to ensure that the single period rate of growth in wealth (the ensemble average) exceeds zero with reasonable probability is more than would typically be viable for an individual household. The required number of transactions is lower for risk events involving high probabilities (typical of annuities) than risk events with low probabilities (typical of term life insurance). So again, this suggests that adverse selection may be stronger in annuities than in insurances.

12 Risk Classification and Moral Hazard

Key Ideas:

precaution neglect; overconsumption; optimal moral hazard; optimal risk-taking; third-party moral hazard

The central ideas of this book were stated in Chapter 1 as follows:

(a) Adverse selection in insurance is usually weaker than most commentary suggests.

(b) From a public policy perspective, 'weak' adverse selection is a good thing. This is because a degree of adverse selection is needed to maximise loss coverage, the expected losses compensated by insurance for the whole population.

(c) To induce the degree of adverse selection which maximises loss coverage, some restrictions on risk classification are a good thing in some insurance markets.

Moral hazard does not impinge directly on these three claims. In the account of loss coverage given in Chapters 3–6, moral hazard was assumed to be nil. This assumption was merely convenient for exposition; it was not essential.[1]

However, moral hazard is often mentioned in almost the same breath as adverse selection, and is typically portrayed in an equally negative light. An author who downplays the negative perception of adverse selection, while assuming away moral hazard in his exposition, may attract the critique that his treatise fails to consider moral hazard.

---

[1] Moral hazard manifests as a positive correlation between risk and insurance cover, the same as adverse selection. In principle, we could define adverse selection to be the effect net of any correlation attributable to moral hazard. But the distinction, although clear in principle, may be hard to measure in practice. For expository purposes in Chapters 3–6, it was simpler just to assume no moral hazard.

This chapter therefore considers moral hazard. As with adverse selection, my main theme is to question the perception that moral hazard is always a bad thing.

Three Meanings of Moral Hazard

The term moral hazard is used with at least three meanings in insurance. The most widely applicable is the idea that once insured, a person may be inclined to neglect precautions and take more risks, and hence the fact that a loss has been insured can increase the probability of that loss. This is the notion of moral hazard as *precaution neglect* (sometimes called *ex ante* moral hazard, because it operates before the loss event).

The term moral hazard is also used with a slightly different meaning in health insurance. Because illness is disagreeable independent of its financial costs, it seems fanciful to suggest that after buying insurance, people take more risks of becoming ill (precaution neglect). Instead moral hazard in health insurance usually refers to the idea that insured persons, for whom medical services are free or nearly free at the point of use, will tend to use more medical services than they would have used if they paid for all treatment out of their own pockets at the point of use. This is the notion of moral hazard as *overconsumption* (sometimes called *ex post* moral hazard, because it operates after the loss event, such as becoming ill).

The third meaning of moral hazard is explicitly 'moral': an allusion to increased claims or other costs to the insurer which arise from the *bad character* of the insured person. Fraudulent claims, accidents caused by illegal drugs and other criminal behaviour are all examples of this explicitly 'moral' notion of moral hazard.[2]

All three notions of moral hazard are concerned with the *hidden action* of the insured. This contrasts with adverse selection, which is concerned with the *hidden information* of the insured.

---

[2] For a history of the meanings of 'moral hazard' in practitioner and academic contexts, see Rowell and Connelly (2012).

Economists usually use the term moral hazard to mean precaution neglect or overconsumption (the first or second meanings above); any notion of moral censure (the third meaning above) is often specifically disavowed. But this declaration of moral neutrality often appears insincere, because despite their formal disavowals, economists tend to use the term in ways which are clearly censorious of the insured. One textbook on *Insurance economics* makes a typical declaration:

> Moral hazard has little to do with morality.
>
> (Zweifel and Eisen, 2012, p. 268)

But on the very next page, the same text asserts that moral hazard is practically indistinguishable from fraud:

> In its extreme form, moral hazard turns into criminal activity. Indeed, for a substantial subset of insurance buyers, there is only a thin line separating moral hazard from insurance fraud ... the distinction between insurance fraud and moral hazard is difficult to draw. (p. 269)

As with adverse selection, there seems to be strong presumption that the phenomenon of moral hazard must always be bad, and a reluctance to consider it neutrally, even when some token declaration of neutrality is made. In my view, moral hazard is not always a bad thing. This can be seen by examining the details of the 'overconsumption' and 'precaution neglect' notions of moral hazard. (I shall not consider further the third notion of moral hazard as criminal behaviour.)

Moral Hazard in Health Insurance: Overconsumption

Moral hazard in health insurance usually refers to overconsumption. In the standard economic analysis,[3] people are said to be motivated

---

[3] The standard reference is Pauly (1968). Subsequently, Pauly (1983) acknowledged that his earlier analysis applied only to 'routine physicians' visits, prescriptions, dental care, and the like', and that 'the relevant theory, empirical evidence and policy analysis for moral hazard in the case of serious illness have not been developed'. But these qualifications are glossed over in most texts.

to buy insurance by *financial risk aversion*: they prefer pay a fixed premium rather than be exposed to possible medical costs which are actuarially equivalent (that is, have the same expected value), but are also highly uncertain. Indeed, this preference is sufficiently strong that people are prepared to pay a bit *more* than the actuarial equivalent (and so insurers are able to make a profit). Once a person has paid the premium, the effective price of medical services to that person is greatly reduced. This is said to lead to 'overconsumption' of medical services: the person uses more medical services than if they paid out of pocket at the point of use. The 'overconsumption' raises the price of insurance, so that people who expect to need little medical care buy less insurance than if there were no moral hazard. This reduction in purchasing is said to be inefficient.

The story is similar to adverse selection, except that rather than higher purchasing of insurance by people who have private knowledge of their risk of becoming ill ('hidden information'), it is higher utilisation of insurance benefits by those who do become ill ('hidden action') that causes the increase in price.

As with adverse selection, the quantum of these effects is usually claimed to be very large. One widely cited paper in the *Journal of Political Economy* claims that imposing a copayment rate of two-thirds – that is, requiring everyone with health insurance to pay two-thirds of all medical costs themselves – would increase the aggregate welfare of the population.[4] A more recent study of 'the trade-off between risk sharing and moral hazard' published in the same journal concluded that a 50% copayment rate would be optimal.[5] In effect, orthodox insurance economics says that health insurance cover should be dramatically restricted compared to typical levels; people should be forced to pay most healthcare costs out of their own pockets after they become ill.

The overconsumption idea fails some basic common sense checks. Medical services are not like most other services, because in

[4] Feldstein (1973).
[5] Manning and Marquis (1996).

general the more expensive a medical service is, the more disagreeable it is to consume. Very rich or well-insured people probably do
on average consume more medical services, for a given level of
health, than poor or uninsured people; but they do not check into
the hospital for a heart transplant instead of going on holiday, to the
opera or to the golf course. Some medical investigations or services
are less cost-effective than others, but most people do not have
much idea which is which; it is hard (and implausible, given the disagreeable nature of most medical services) to *choose* to consume
only frivolous services.

Another problem with the standard account of health insurance and moral hazard outlined above is the idea that insurance
purchase is motivated principally by financial risk aversion (preferring a certain premium to actuarially equivalent uncertain costs).
Many major medical procedures cost more than most people's net
worth. For such procedures, the framing of demand for insurance as
an alleged preference for a 'certain premium' rather than 'uncertain
costs' makes no sense, because it involves an impossible counter-
factual (that if you became ill, you would pay for major medical
procedures out of your own pocket).

A Better Theory of Health Insurance: Redistribution

A more sensible theory of health insurance is given in John
Nyman's book *The theory of demand for health insurance.*[6]
Nyman suggests that the primary motive for buying insurance is
not, as orthodox insurance economics has it, *financial risk aversion*
(preferring a certain premium to actuarially equivalent uncertain
costs), but rather *desire to participate in redistribution*. People want
to shift income from possible future states in which they are well to
possible future states in which they are ill. Therefore before knowing which future state will apply, they voluntarily join a scheme for
redistribution from the healthy to the ill (i.e. buy insurance). Those

[6] Nyman (2003).

who become ill consume more medical services than they would have consumed absent the scheme for redistribution. But this is not 'overconsumption': it is an intended and preferred outcome, which *ex ante* benefits the population as a whole.

Another way of putting this is that the transfer of resources through health insurance increases the effective income of the ill, and this effect causes an *upward shift in the demand curve* for medical services. This is distinct from a second effect, the *movement along the demand curve* arising from the lower effective point-of-use price of medical services, when part or all the price is paid by the individual's insurer. The first effect is beneficial to the population in aggregate; only the second effect may have problematical aspect. Nyman estimates that around 70% by value of the moral hazard in US health insurance represents the first effect, making moral hazard a net benefit to the system overall.

Moral Hazard in Other Classes of Insurance: Precaution Neglect

In other classes of insurance besides health insurance, moral hazard usually has a different meaning from the 'overconsumption' concept described above. In other classes of insurance, moral hazard usually refers to precaution neglect: the idea that once insured, a person has less incentive to take other precautions against risk, and hence the fact that a loss has been insured can increase the probability of that loss.

Precaution neglect seems most plausible where the potential loss is purely economic, and so can be wholly rectified by monetary compensation. In practice, this is seldom the case. Most types of loss cannot be wholly compensated by money, particularly not an uncertain amount of money, which may or may not be received after extended delay and dispute. But some types come closer to being purely economic than others. In particular, losses of commercial firms may be largely economic, so precaution neglect may be more likely in insurances held by such firms than in personal insurances.

But for most personal insurances, the event insured against is usually sufficiently unpalatable, for non-financial as well as financial reasons, so as to contain any precaution neglect to a limited scale. Precaution neglect can also be limited by contract terms such as co-insurance (requiring the insured to pay part of any loss), or requirements for the insured to implement specific precautions (e.g. fire alarms, locks, etc.).

Moral hazard in the precaution-neglect sense thus seems likely to be a weak effect for most classes of insurance. To the extent that it may prevail, it is usually seen as a bad thing. But this overlooks the point that in some cases it may be socially desirable to substitute insurance for other precautions against risk. Also, some individual risk-taking generates positive externalities, and absent moral hazard, the amount of such risk-taking may be too low. Some examples are as follows:

(a) *Professional indemnity insurance.* This helps to align the interests of professional advisers and clients. Without insurance, professional advisers typically have negatively skewed payoffs: they face a large downside risk (when clients suffer bad outcomes, advisers may be sued), and not much upside (when clients enjoy good outcomes, advisers merely retain their fees). Without insurance, professionals might therefore practise very defensively. In high-risk professions such as obstetric medicine, they might be reluctant to practise at all. Insurance and its consequent precaution-neglect moral hazard promote the availability of professional services in high-risk professions, and the provision of realistic and useful rather than excessively defensive professional advice.

(b) *Third-party liability car insurance.* This allows people to approach driving as an everyday routine which demands only reasonable levels of care and attention. Without liability insurance, some people might be reluctant to drive at all, because of the constant threat of a potentially ruinous lawsuit from any injured third party. Facilitating everyday mobility is a good consequence of moral hazard.

(c) *Life insurance.* Precaution neglect does not seem plausible to any great extent in life insurance, because the insured event is so unpalatable.

But if it happens to a limited extent, this is not dysfunctional, it is one of the purposes of insurance: to enable people to live life, if they so choose, as a daring adventure, free from constant worry about highly improbable catastrophes.

Optimal Moral Hazard

The discussions of overconsumption and precaution neglect above suggest an analogy between adverse selection and loss coverage on the one hand, and moral hazard and risk-taking on the other. Some degree of adverse selection is generally needed to optimise loss coverage. Similarly, some degree of moral hazard is generally needed to optimise use of medical services, and to optimise risk-taking. Any overconsumption and any precaution neglect will always be seen as bad things by insurers, but some degree of each is optimal for society as a whole.

Another way of looking at this is to note that if individuals' use of medical services and allocation of effort to loss-prevention activities is socially optimal in a world where there is no insurance, it is unlikely to be socially optimal for individuals to behave in exactly the same way in a world where the institution of insurance exists. Some change in individual behaviour following the introduction of risk-sharing and redistribution mechanisms is not pathological, as most commentary on moral hazard seems to suggest. It is optimal behaviour for society as a whole.

Note that while moral hazard increases the expected losses compensated by the insurer, we do *not* say that moral hazard increases loss coverage. Under moral hazard, there is an increase in expected compensation paid by the insurer *arising from newly created risk*, which is created by the overconsumption or precaution neglect which moral hazard implies. This newly created risk is not necessarily a bad thing (for reasons I outlined above). But moral hazard does not increase the expected compensation paid by the insurer *arising from pre-existing risk*. Loss coverage is always defined by reference to the pre-existing risks, that is, risks before any increase from moral hazard.

When Might Moral Hazard be Excessive?

Third-Party Moral Hazard

The standard account of moral hazard involves a change in behaviour of the insured – the second party to the insurance contract – after the insurance contract is signed. But it is plausible that third parties also change their behaviour in the presence of insurance. For example, professional indemnity insurance may allow a professional adviser to practise in a less risk-averse manner; but the presence of insurance may also encourage third parties (e.g. aggrieved clients) to claim against the perceived 'deep pockets' of the insured party, in circumstances where the client might not pursue the professional adviser if there was no insurance.

Third-party moral hazard probably has a significant effect on the practical operation of tort law. Tort claims are made mainly against parties who carry compulsory insurance, for example drivers and employers in the UK. Around 80% of tort claims in England and Wales in 2011–12 were for road accidents, and 8% for accidents at work.[7] This is despite the fact that these areas constitute at most half of all accidents, and possibly much less than this (one survey in Australia suggested that they were less than 20% of all accidents).[8] Accidents in the home or in leisure activities or sport are more common, but very few of these result in a damages award. This may sometimes be because fault is less obvious in these contexts; but it is also because of the absence of compulsory insurance and hence third-party moral hazard in these contexts.

Third parties are more remote from the insurer than the insured. This remoteness may make third-party moral hazard harder for an insurer to anticipate than the conventional second-party moral hazard, and also harder to control by terms in the insurance contract. The difficulty of anticipating and controlling third-party

---

[7] Statistics from Department of Health Compensation Recovery Unit. www.gov.uk/dwp

[8] Australian survey quoted in Lewis and Morris (2012).

moral hazard suggests that it might be more problematic than second-party moral hazard.

But again, as with conventional second-party moral hazard, facilitating some change in behaviour is one of the purposes or functions of insurance, from the viewpoint of society as a whole. The belief of our society, as expressed in its laws, is that third parties who suffer loss caused by a negligent driver or employer *should* be able to obtain some compensation. To some extent, third-party moral hazard which increases the chance that such compensation will be sought is a feature, not a bug.

Displacement of Operational Risk Reduction Measures

Moral hazard might be a bad thing from society's viewpoint if it takes the form of insurance displacing operational risk reduction measures. For example if the existence of insurance for a sporting event leads the organisers not to take reasonable precautions to ensure the safety of competitors and crowds, that might be a bad thing. But in practice the influence of insurance on risk reduction is often in the other direction. Insurance tends to promote risk reduction, because the insurer advises or mandates it in the terms of the insurance contract, or encourages it by offering discounts if the relevant measures are taken (a sort of 'reverse moral hazard').

If moral hazard is significant, there seems no reason why insurers should not price for it. If people who buy insurance *ipso facto* have higher probability of loss, the price of insurance can reflect that. Only *unanticipated* moral hazard behaviour can create a problem for insurers. As noted above, third-party moral hazard may be harder to anticipate than second-party moral hazard.

Why Is Nyman's Health Insurance Theory Neglected?

John Nyman seems correct in pointing out that the standard economic account of health insurance, where demand arises from risk aversion and moral hazard causes inefficient 'overconsumption' of healthcare, is unrealistic. His alternative account, in which demand arises from a desire to participate in redistribution, and most moral hazard represents an efficient transfer of resources from the lucky healthy to unlucky sick, seems compelling. Yet the theory has received very little attention. Why is this? Two possible reasons are as follows.

First, Nyman's theory of health insurance demand may be ideologically unappealing to some economists. It emphasises that people buy health insurance because they wish to participate in a scheme of redistribution. This is an entirely commercial arrangement. But once the widespread desire for redistribution from the lucky healthy to the unlucky ill is acknowledged, it becomes obvious to ask whether redistribution by the State might be more universal, more effective and cheaper than a commercial arrangement.

Second, the notion of moral hazard as overconsumption may be an example of a one-way hash argument as described in Chapter 10. The argument superficially conforms to widely held beliefs about the relationship between cost and demand. Common sense affirms that if a service is free at the point of use, it will tend to be overconsumed. The neglected nuance in healthcare is that the service is generally disagreeable to consume, which limits the overconsumption even if the service is free.

Summary

The term moral hazard is used to describe three phenomena: precaution neglect, overconsumption and criminal activity. Only the third meaning carries an explicit connotation of wrongdoing, but the prejudicial terminology tends to lead to disapproval of the others as well.

Overconsumption moral hazard in health insurance is, on closer examination, generally a good thing. It can be split into two elements, one arising from a transfer of resources and one from a reduction in effective prices:

– a transfer of resources from the lucky well to unlucky ill, which causes an *upward shift in the demand curve* for medical care (this is clearly good); and

– a reduction in the effective price of medical care at the point-of-use, which causes an *upward movement along the demand curve* (this is less clearly good, and may lead to wasteful consumption).

The net effect of overconsumption moral hazard is the sum of these two elements. The good from the first element may often outweigh any harm from the second element.

Precaution-neglect moral hazard is not always a good thing. But it can be a good thing, if precautionary behaviour in the absence of insurance is at excessive levels. This may often be true in relation to professional indemnity insurance: without some moral hazard and hence precaution-neglect arising from the insurance, professionals might give excessively cautious and hence not very useful advice.

Overall, as with adverse selection, moral hazard tends to be exaggerated and excessively maligned in many policy discussions. Moral hazard is not always a bad thing.

13 Risk Classification and Big Data

Key Ideas:
blind auditions; statistical stereotyping; big data and loss coverage; broken promises of privacy; political defences; technical defences; identity diversification

Like many people in the UK, I have groceries home-delivered by one of the larger national supermarkets. I am vaguely uneasy about the detailed purchasing histories which these firms collect, and the possibility that the data may one day be used in ways I do not anticipate, perhaps by entities quite remote from the supermarket. Already Tesco in the UK is reported to be using individual supermarket loyalty card data to price car and home insurance; Lloyds Bank in the UK uses bank statements to assess 'fiscal responsibility' when pricing other products; and in the USA, records of prescriptions processed by pharmacists are sold to insurers and often used to reject life and health insurance applicants.[1] Consequently, I now buy most groceries with payment cards which do not bear the name on the front of this book, and are not registered to the address where groceries are delivered.

I engage in this and a range of other precautions – or perhaps protests – against commercial surveillance not because I have something to hide, but because I have nothing to gain. It is convenient when buying groceries to have private access to a shopping list of my regular purchases. But I see no material advantage, and some

---

[1] 'Insurers mine customers' finance records to set premiums', *Financial Times* 12 July 2014; 'Insurers warned to use big data responsibly', *Financial Times* 1 February 2015; 'They know what's in your medicine cabinet', *Bloomberg Businessweek* 22 July 2008.

quite sinister possible disadvantages, in such records being linked to my other data across a range of contexts and tied forever to a single identity. So as a matter of principle and prudence, I try to make it more difficult for organisations to do this. I do not expect my precautions to be completely robust, and I am inconsistent and imperfect in my application of them. But privacy is a dial, not a switch; and turning that dial a little against the snoopers, at least some of the time, does something to reduce my vague sense of unease.

My unease about an ecology of pervasive commercial and State surveillance relates to issues of intellectual and political freedom which are beyond the scope of this book, so this paragraph gives only a sketch. As regards intellectual freedom, I subscribe to Thomas Huxley's maxim that 'every great advance in natural knowledge has involved the absolute rejection of authority'.[2] What would have happened to this principle if every book written in the past 500 years had been reporting its readers to contemporary authorities? Efforts to associate all web page visits with particular IP addresses may be today's equivalent of this. As regards political freedom, monitoring of private communications has been a tactic of control in most oppressive regimes. Efforts to store all communications metadata and to compromise or ban encryption may be today's equivalents of this. More generally, history offers no evidence for – and quite a lot of evidence against – the proposition that the surveillance apparatus of totalitarianism is consistent with a functioning democracy.[3]

The surveillance aspirations of insurers are only a small part of the worrying ecology of pervasive surveillance, and their mundane commercial ambitions can seem remote from existential issues of intellectual and political freedom. But this apparent remoteness

---

[2] Huxley wrote this in 1866 in his essay *On the advisableness of improving natural knowledge*. Reprinted in Bibby (1971).

[3] For a compelling expansion of the concerns sketched in this paragraph, see the series of lectures given by law professor Eben Moglen at www.snowdenandthefuture.info, last accessed 24 December 2015.

may be illusory, because it can be nullified by a complementary remoteness between the ostensible purposes for which data are collected, and the unrelated and unlimited purposes for which data can later be used.

If we focus on insurers' commercial ambitions, there are at least three ways in which they might seek to use big data: risk classification, non-risk price discrimination (price optimisation) and fraud detection. Consistent with the theme of this book, this chapter focuses on risk classification and not the other potential uses.[4] It considers how insurers might use big data in risk classification; how this behaviour might be regulated (strategic, political or top-down responses); and some defences which individuals might adopt (tactical, technical or bottom-up responses).

What Is Big Data?

Although 'big data' is an immediately recognisable label for the topic of this chapter, it is a vague term, often bandied around indiscriminately by consultants with something to sell. My interpretation is that 'big data' describes databases which are *too unstructured* or *too large* to be analysed using everyday tools such as Microsoft Excel or Access.

An 'unstructured' database lacks any obvious organisation relevant to the prediction task in hand, such as a distinction between independent and dependent variables. Unstructured data are typically text-heavy, buy may also contain numbers, dates, images, videos and other formats.

A 'large' database contains *many variables*, or *many observations*, or both. *Variables* are the categories of information, such as age, gender, blood pressure, mileage, etc. *Observations* are the values which the variables take for particular persons, or at particular times. The distinction between *many variables* and *many observations*

---

[4] For a discussion of non-risk price discrimination (price optimisation) and public policy, see my paper Thomas (2012). For a discussion of big data and insurance fraud, see Srinivasan and Arunasalam (2013).

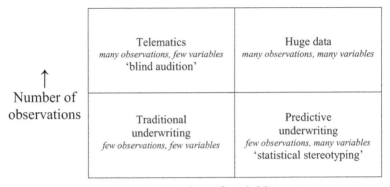

FIGURE 13.1 Big data: many observations, or many variables, or both

recurs throughout this chapter, so it may help to give some examples, which are also illustrated in Figure 13.1.

- Suppose a car insurer installs a 'black box' in each customer's car, which periodically transmits location, speed and acceleration to the insurer. This is big data, in the form of *many observations* for each customer on *few variables* (in this case, three variables). The three variables have obvious relevance (sometimes called 'face validity') to car insurance risk. I characterise this 'many observations, few variables' approach as a *blind audition*.
- Suppose a life insurer obtains for all customers 50 items of demographic data (age, address, occupation, social media sites used, etc.) and 50 items of financial and purchasing data (credit cards held, current balance on each card, shops patronised, gym memberships, frequency of cash withdrawals, etc.). This is big data, in the form of *few observations* for each customer on *many variables*. Not all of the variables have obvious relevance to life insurance risk. I characterise this 'few observations, many variables' approach as *statistical stereotyping*.

Figure 13.1 schematically illustrates the *observations-variables* dimensions of traditional underwriting, telematics and predictive underwriting. For logical completeness, Figure 13.1 also shows the upper-right fourth quadrant *many observations, many variables*, which might be deemed 'huge data', but I say nothing more about this.

Blind Auditions versus Statistical Stereotyping

As far as I know, the term *blind audition* is original in the context of risk classification, but it is well known in the selection of musicians for professional orchestras. New members for orchestras were traditionally selected by solo auditions in which they played one or more pieces of music before an expert panel. The success rate for women in these auditions was much lower than for men. The success rate for women improved substantially after a change in practice whereby a visual screen was placed between the candidate and the expert panel. This created a blind audition, allowing *many observations* on a *few variables* (or here just one variable, the sound) with obvious relevance to the task of selecting musicians.[5]

For the orchestra selection task, a *statistical stereotyping* approach would involve selecting musicians for whom a *few observations* closely match existing orchestra members on *many variables*. The many variables might include schools and universities attended, courses studied, number of siblings, occupations of parents, residential tenure, age, height, weight, eye colour and so on. Note that most of these *many variables* have little obvious relevance to selecting musicians; but if such variables appear to reliably characterise the existing orchestra members, the lack of face validity is of no concern to a selector who relies on statistical stereotyping.

Risk classification has always involved some degree of statistical stereotyping. But traditionally, statistical stereotyping typically used relatively few variables, and was relatively transparent to the customer. The customer knew the scope of the information sought by the insurer (e.g. as requested on an application form), and in many cases would also have some knowledge of how that information might affect premiums. The influence of variables such as gender, age,

---

[5] The economists Goldin and Rouse (2000) document the higher success rate for women when blind auditions are used. The blind audition concept was also promoted by a lawsuit in the early 1970s against the New York Philharmonic Orchestra by Art Davis, a black double bass player (he lost the case, but it nevertheless prompted changes in practice).

occupation and disability on insurance prices was widely discussed in newspapers and elsewhere, and so operated with some degree of transparency and social consent. Big data make statistical stereotyping potentially less transparent in three ways: many more variables (including abstract 'manufactured variables') may now be used, many of the new variables have little face validity and many of the variables are collected without the consent or even knowledge of the customer.

Blind Audition Example: Telematics

One example of a blind audition using big data for risk classification is telematics in car insurance, that is 'black box' tracking of location, time, speed and acceleration. The black box transmits to the insurer many observations on a few variables, which have obvious relevance to car insurance risk. Many people may consider the focus on a few relevant variables fairer than traditional approaches to pricing car insurance, which rely on statistical stereotyping on less obviously relevant variables such as age, gender and occupation. But while the blind audition technology arguably gives a fairer risk assessment, it also encroaches on privacy: the insurer and potentially other parties – police, other State agencies, the insurers' employees, civil litigants, private detectives, hackers – can access a detailed record of where and when the vehicle was driven.

At the time of writing, telematics is cost-effective only for niche markets such as young drivers, where the difference in price for a lower risk driver compared with a higher-risk driver can amount to hundreds of pounds. For older drivers, for whom premiums are lower overall, the difference in price which the insurer can profitably offer (after telematics costs) is generally not worthwhile. It might become worthwhile if the costs of installing telematics hardware in the vehicle are reduced or circumvented, for example as part of car manufacturing.

While telematics is the most salient form of blind audition technology in insurance today, other analogous technologies are being developed, and might be used in insurance pricing. Personal monitors of heart rate, exercise levels, sleep patterns and other bio-metric data might be used in life or health insurance. Fire sensors and other detectors in homes might monitor the prevalence of 'near miss' events such as smoke and gas escapes, or doors and windows left unlocked for long periods. Note that in every case, these tech-nologies are akin to blind auditions: they collect many observations on few variables with obvious relevance to the risk.

Statistical Stereotyping Example: Predictive Underwriting

One salient example of statistical stereotyping using big data for risk classification is predictive underwriting in life insurance. Traditional life insurance underwriting in the UK involves observations gener-ated from a costly combination of medical questionnaire, GP (family doctor) report and perhaps a medical examination arranged by the insurer. In predictive underwriting, the insurer takes say 10,000 'fully underwritten' cases which have gone through the traditional under-writing process, and attempts to predict the underwriting decision for each customer from a few observations on many variables, many of which may not have obvious relevance to the risk. Note that typi-cally, underwriting decisions (offer insurance at standard rates, higher rates or decline), rather than actual deaths, are the predicted variable. This is because there are very few actual deaths in the early years of life insurance policies, so the full record may take decades to emerge.

The *many variables* might include electoral rolls and driver licensing records; credit reference agency databases; other purchased marketing databases; supermarket, banking, and credit card records held by the insurer's affiliates; the pattern of the individual's access to the insurer's website, including incoming link, time spent on site, hardware, browser, etc.; and data gathered from social media.[6]

---

[6] Tweets and Facebook likes have been shown to predict properties of individuals such as the 'big five' personality traits (neuroticism, extraversion, agreeableness, conscientiousness, openness) much better than chance (Kosinski et al., 2013). Perhaps some of these properties can also be shown to be correlated with risk level for some types of insurance.

Once an adequately predictive model of the full underwriting decisions is found, this can thereafter be used for most new cases without obtaining the traditional medical questionnaire, GP report and medical examination. The slower and more expensive traditional underwriting can then be reserved for any unusual cases identified either by the model itself, or by a very limited number of questions asked of applicants (e.g. 'have you had any illness in the past 5 years requiring more than a month off work?').

Predictive underwriting can be used not just for reactive assessment of insurance applicants, but also to proactively identify marketing prospects. It might also be used to create individualised marketing messages for different types of prospect. Fear and dread can be promoted to the neurotic, prudent protection to the conscientious, bargain offers to the thrifty and so on. And all this can be done without exposing the individualised messages to public or regulatory scrutiny.

Public Policy Concerns

Statistical stereotyping using big data as described above potentially invokes most of the possible objections to risk classification which I outlined in Chapter 7. The following concerns seem particularly pertinent to predictive underwriting.

(a) *Unfairness.* Statistical stereotyping using big data will typically use many variables which have no obvious relevance to the risk. This lack of face validity strengthens the intuition that even if statistical discrimination is accurate at the group level, it may be unfair to many individuals.

(b) *Transparency.* In traditional underwriting, where applicants complete an application form and give consent for a medical report, it is reasonably clear what variables are being used. In predictive underwriting, applicants will usually not know what variables are being used, and indeed may not know that observations on these variables exist.

(c) *Consent.* Applicants who are assessed using big data drawn from their supermarket, credit card or bank account records have probably not given consent – and certainly not informed consent – to having their data used in this way. Many people resent such snooping on their private purchasing behaviour – 'creepy' is the typical affective reaction – and insurers who are trialling such techniques usually seem anxious to keep quiet about them.

These concerns make many people feel more uneasy about statistical stereotyping in the context of big data than they feel about traditional underwriting (statistical stereotyping in the context of limited data). Bringing big data into underwriting promises benefits to insurers, and to some subjects of prediction; it also threatens to impose costs on other subjects of prediction, particularly those who are excluded from insurance or charged higher prices. There is no obvious reason why society should automatically be content with this allocation of costs and benefits.

Technical Shortcomings of Big Data

The discussion above implicitly assumes that big data will be highly effective for insurers. It is often claimed that more data will always lead to more accurate predictions, and that theories of causation will be less important in future because 'with enough data, the numbers speak for themselves'.[7] This is less obvious than many people think.

Correlations found in big data can be either valid or spurious. They are 'valid' if they persist in repeated observations of the same (or similar) populations. They are 'spurious' if they reflect a mere chance association peculiar to a particular set of observations.

In any database containing observations on many variables, some high but spurious correlations will be observed between any designated 'dependent' variable (say occurrence of loss) and some subset of all the other variables. As the number of variables considered is increased, the distribution of the maximum observed spurious correlation shifts to the right; in other words, the problem becomes worse.[8] The number of valid correlations observed may

---

[7] One influential and widely quoted advocate of this claim is the editor of *Wired* magazine (e.g. Anderson, 2008).

[8] See Fan et al. (2014).

also increase, but quite possibly at a lower rate. Loosely speaking, we can summarise these problems by saying that as the number of variables grows, noise may grow faster than truth.

These problems may be less acute for blind auditions which use just a few variables which appear to have face validity, as in car insurance telematics. But I have so far seen no convincing evidence that car insurance telematics either improves driving behaviour (the 'reverse moral hazard' effect), or materially improves predictive performance compared with traditional underwriting. A recent literature review from the Transport Research Laboratory found 'no sufficiently robust direct evidence that telematics affects accident rates of young and novice drivers'.[9] The lack of 'robust' evidence is partly due to methodological limitations; and absence of evidence is not, of course, conclusive evidence of absence. But I suspect that the predictive value of telematics for car insurance risk classification will turn out to be like the predictive value of genetics for life insurance risk classification: weaker and less useful than typical narratives about adverse selection suggest. (Telematics might, however, be useful to insurers for purposes other than risk classification, such as resolving claim disputes, detecting fraud and early notification of accidents, which are economically important for controlling claims costs.)

Big Data and Loss Coverage

For the reasons just given, large and rapid improvements in predictive performance from big data seem to me rather unlikely. I certainly

[9] Tong et al. (2015), 3. A much earlier attempt to use a measure of 'driving skill' to predict accidents was reported over 40 years ago by the Transport and Road Research Laboratory (Hoinville et al., 1972). They used questionnaires to collect around 40 variables and 3-year accident records for people who had passed or failed the advanced driving test of the Institute of Advanced Motorists. Those who had passed had 25% fewer accidents in the 3 years after taking the test than those who had failed. But in a multivariate model – effectively a primitive insurance rating model – several variables were more important than the IAM test results, including urban location, annual mileage, driver age and interest in DIY car maintenance. The study population in this study – people who have either passed or failed the IAM test – is a small and motivated subset of drivers compared with most insurers' clienteles.

do not see any pattern of rapid progress in the predictive power of big data comparable to Moore's Law for computing power.[10] Nevertheless, it does seem plausible that advances in the use of big data, either blind auditions or statistical stereotyping, may at the margin enable insurers to classify risks more accurately in future. Using the terms defined in Chapters 6 and 8, competitive adverse selection may reduce the inclusivity of risk classification. From a public policy perspective technological advances in risk classification could reduce adverse selection too much, and thus reduce loss coverage from current levels. Advances in the use of big data may therefore become a possible reason for imposing some new limits on risk classification.[11]

Broken Promises of Privacy

Concerns about privacy and consent in relation to insurers' use of big data are mediated by trust. If we trust the organisation using big data, we are likely to be less demanding about transparency, and more inclined to acquiesce in whatever use the organisation wishes to make of our data. Trust is likely to be lower in circumstances where data are disseminated outside of the organisation which collected them, or used for a very different purpose from that for which they were collected.

---

[10] Moore's Law is the historical observation that the number of transistors in an integrated circuit has doubled approximately every 2 years; or loosely speaking, that computing power has doubled every 2 years. Casual awareness of this phenomenon seems to mislead many people into a mistaken perception that rapid progress is already occurring, or will soon occur, in other quite unrelated technologies.

[11] Contrary to this argument, some economists suggest that improvements in risk prediction by insurers may promote inclusivity, rather than leading to greater separation (Siegelman (2014), based on Villeneuve (2005)). In their model, insurers using big data know each individual's risk level, but the individuals initially do not know their risk level themselves. If an insurer then offers a low-risk individual a lower (but still profitable) price than the price for complete pooling, this offer 'signals' to the individual that she is low-risk; the individual can then infer from the offer that she is a member of the group with low true risk, and so shop around for a still lower price exactly equivalent to that risk. This implies there is no advantage for an insurer in offering the lower price in the first place, so it will not do so. But I am not persuaded by this ingenious argument, because the inferential powers and bargaining skills it assigns to individuals seem wholly unrealistic.

One example of such circumstances is the commercial use of individual medical records. In 2013 the Hospital Episode Statistics, a complete record of all treatment provided in National Health Service (NHS) hospitals in the UK over 13 years, were sold for a nominal sum to a group funded by the Institute and Faculty of Actuaries. The group used the data to demonstrate that incidence rates for most diseases were higher in socially deprived areas, and reported that 'Overall we would conclude that the use of geodemographic profiling could refine critical illness pricing bases'.[12] In plain English, they suggested that insurers should charge higher prices to people living in poor areas. When this was publicised on the front page of the *Daily Telegraph* in 2014, many people were astonished that individual medical records had been sold outside the NHS, for commercial purposes wholly unrelated to providing or improving healthcare.[13]

Those who seek to defend such scandals often refer to precautions such as removing names, partial addresses and partial dates of birth. In the case just described, the Institute and Faculty of Actuaries asserted in a press release that 'Individuals cannot be identified from this data',[14] and to *Wired* magazine that the data were 'totally anonymous'.[15] The problem with such assertions is demonstrated by an earlier experiment in open data in Massachusetts in the mid-1990s, when the hospital attendance records of all state employees covered by health insurance were released to researchers. The Governor of Massachusetts, William Weld, gave public assurances that the data were 'totally anonymous', because obvious identifiers such as names and exact dates of birth had been removed. But a graduate student in computer science (Latanya Sweeney, now a

---

[12] Banthorpe et al. (2013, p. 13).

[13] 'Hospital records of all NHS patients sold to insurers', *Daily Telegraph* 24 February 2014.

[14] *Telegraph article rebuttal*. Press release dated 25 February 2014. www.actuaries .org.uk, accessed 23 October 2015

[15] 'NHS: Oops, we already gave your medical records to insurers', *Wired* 25 February 2014.

professor at Harvard University) theatrically demonstrated that these assurances were misplaced: she quickly identified Governor Weld's own records in the released data, including his diagnoses and prescriptions, and sent them to his office.

As shown by this anecdote, re-identification of supposedly 'anonymised' data is easier than common intuitions suggest. Censoring identifiers such as names and dates of birth generally does not provide effective anonymity. Given a large 'anonymised' database, re-identification typically requires only a few snippets of 'outside' data (facts about an individual sourced from outside the database).

Suppose we have a national database of anonymised health records, and we wish to find the entire records of an individual, say David. We also have a little 'outside data': two dates on which David was seen attending an outpatient clinic in a particular hospital. Then we can search the national database for records which include male gender and outpatient attendances at the relevant hospital on the two dates. There will probably be at most a few such records, and if we examine them in detail, and subjectively compare other fields such as age with David's general appearance, we can probably identify David's record. This matching of a very few items of external data to a unique internal record is known as a 'jigsaw attack', but the metaphor arguably makes the task sound harder than it is. We do not need to piece together hundreds of pieces of David's data. Once we match a couple of items in the database with a couple of items of external data, the rest of David's data immediately follows from the internal structure of the database.

In one study of a large anonymised credit card database, just four items of outside data were sufficient to re-identify uniquely 90% of individuals.[16] Reducing the resolution of the data by suppressing certain fields, for example day and month for birthday, inhibits re-identification, but the effect is counter-intuitively small: the ease

[16] De Montjoye et al. (2015).

with which individuals can be re-identified typically declines only as a one-tenth or one-hundredth power of the resolution of the data.[17]

Ease of re-identification might not matter if we could place confidence in assurances from data controllers not to seek to re-identify individuals. But such assurances, and privacy policies in general, are typically so riddled with exceptions that nobody can place much confidence in them. The typical organisational privacy policy comprises a series of what have pithily been called *bullshit promises*.[18] This is where an organisation uses promissory language ostensibly to make a commitment – for example to keep data confidential – but elsewhere reserves the right not to fulfil that commitment, or to alter the terms of the commitment unilaterally at any time when it sees fit. Similarly, national laws which prohibit re-identification may offer little comfort, if large organisations could easily carry out the re-identification in some less regulated jurisdiction.

Given the technical and organisational reasons for distrusting promises of privacy, what can be done to limit privacy intrusions by insurers and other organisations? There are two broad approaches: political (strategic, collective or top-down) and technical (tactical, individual or bottom-up).

Limits on Surveillance: Political Defences

Conceptually, there are two main approaches which data regulation can take: it can limit *proactive collection*, or it can limit *particular usages and outcomes*. In the UK, the ban on insurers asking about genetic test results is a ban on proactive collection, but some outcomes from usage are allowed (if the customer volunteers the information and asks for it to be taken into account). On the other hand, the European Union's ban on gender classification in premium

---

[17] De Montjoye et al. (2013). 'The ease with which individuals can be re-identified' is technically defined as the *unicity* of the database. Unicity of degree d is the percentage of records which can be re-identified with d items of outside data.

[18] Bridgeman and Sandrik (2008).

setting is a ban on a particular usage and outcome (different premiums for otherwise identical people of different gender), but proactive collection for other usages such as reserving and reinsurance pricing is allowed.

Insurers would probably prefer that any controls are narrowly focused on particular usages and outcomes. But policing usages and outcomes can be technically difficult, because the details are often buried in mathematical models. Big data models can create a digitised bureaucracy which is harmful in effect (say discriminatory against legally protected minorities) without *ex ante* intent on the part of the human developers, and possibly even without their *ex post* awareness. In this context, the concept of direct discrimination (in US terminology, disparate treatment) is unlikely to be much help. Regulators may instead need to consider indirect discrimination (in US terminology, disparate impact).[19] Instead of attempting to assign intent to human developers, it may be more fruitful to regard models as autonomous agents, which should themselves be subject to regulation.

Regulation of organisations' proactive collection or particular usages and outcomes of data is probably more socially efficient than widespread adoption of the technical defences discussed below, which require individuals to take the trouble to obscure or obfuscate their data. But effective regulation may be hard to enact, because of the classical problem of collective action. A few insurers and other organisations expect to benefit greatly from surveillance (although they may be mistaken); most individuals expect to lose only a little (in some cases they may be mistaken too), and wealthy and influential individuals may not lose at all. So support for surveillance is focused, but resistance to surveillance is diffused.

---

[19] Under the Equality Act 2010, direct discrimination is differential treatment based explicitly on a forbidden classification. 'Indirect discrimination' is not explicitly based on a forbidden classification, but nevertheless disproportionately disadvantages a protected group; it is unlawful unless the discriminator can show that it is 'a proportionate means of achieving a legitimate aim'.

Limits on Surveillance: Technical Defences

What technical defences can individuals adopt against excessive surveillance by insurers and other organisations? Some possibilities are discussed below. None of these simple measures is completely secure, and for many people, the marginal personal benefits may not justify the effort required. But if such measures are adopted by a sufficient fraction of the target population, they may create a form of herd immunity, by making statistical stereotyping less reliable and hence less attractive to commercial organisations. They may also help to subvert the restrictions on intellectual and political freedom which modern authoritarians seek to impose upon us. So even if you think that the measures below are not worthwhile for you on a personal cost–benefit basis, they may be justified as pro-social activities.

Discretion

Discretion is the simplest privacy technique. It helps to use private settings in social media, and to be prudently circumspect in open publication. More generally, to protect against identity theft as well as surveillance, one should decline unnecessary requests for highly identifying information. Vendors may need your credit card number, but they generally do not need your date of birth, telephone number or official registration numbers of any kind.

Although discretion is the simplest privacy technique, it is sometimes an inconvenient one. It is difficult to make your personal data less visible to unwanted surveillance without also reducing your visibility to those with whom you wish to communicate. Different people will make this trade-off in different ways; as I said earlier privacy is a dial, not a switch. Where simple discretion becomes too limiting, there is a more sophisticated alternative: identity diversification.

Identity Diversification

In simple terms, identity diversification means using different identifying information in different contexts.

Most people diversify their identities to some extent in everyday social life. You probably adopt a different style of dress and manner of speech when attending a job interview or giving evidence in court, compared with relaxing at home or meeting friends in a bar. To achieve equivalent diversification in a world of pervasive surveillance, identifiers such as name and date of birth need to be thought of as flexible aspects of self-presentation, in much the same way as style of dress and manner of speech.

In many instances, unnecessary and intrusive requests for identifiers can be satisfied with entirely transient responses. When a telephone number is requested, often any number will do; the same goes for email address, name, date of birth and so on. Alternatively, where the context – such as repeated logins to an online service – requires persistent identity, the login name and password which you use for each service or group of services can be thought of as a separate 'identity legend'. Multiple passwords can be maintained by always applying the same simple rules (e.g. reverse the login name and prefix with a standard numeral and symbol). With a little technical knowledge, internet metadata such as browser cookies or IP addresses can easily be obfuscated.

The purpose of identity diversification is not to gain advantage by assuming any specific identity, but rather to maintain some prudent separation between different contexts and networks. Identity diversification may initially seem to add unnecessary complication to life, but more careful consideration shows that it can actually make many decisions easier. Identity diversification enables you to quickly decide to trust a particular organisation in a single mutually beneficial interaction. You do not need to decide whether to trust that organisation with the ability to aggregate, mine, sell, share or leak all your past and future data and spy on you forever.

Summary

Big data are potentially useful to insurers for risk classification in two main contexts: blind auditions, which use *many observations* on *few variables*, all with obvious relevance to the risk (e.g. car insurance telematics); and statistical stereotyping, which uses *few observations* on *many variables*, many of which may have no obvious relevance to the risk (e.g. life insurance predictive underwriting).

For blind auditions, the main public policy concern is the potential encroachment on privacy through collection of many observations on the few variables. For statistical stereotyping, privacy of personal data is one concern, but there are also other concerns: the perceived unfairness of discriminating against some customers on the basis of variables which do not have any obvious relevance to the risk, the lack of transparency and the lack of customer consent.

There is little evidence to date of large improvements in risk prediction from big data, and certainly no discernible pattern of rapid progress comparable to Moore's Law. Nevertheless, it does seem plausible that technological advances in the use of big data, either blind auditions or statistical stereotyping, will at least to some degree enable insurers to classify risks more accurately in future.

To the extent that use of big data does enable insurers to reduce the inclusivity of risk classification, this could reduce loss coverage, if adverse selection is reduced too much. Hence awareness of loss coverage may provide a possible justification for imposing some limits on the use of big data in risk classification.

Part IV Conclusion

14 Summary and Suggestions

Key Ideas:

main ideas of this book; suggestions for public policymakers; suggestions for economists; suggestions for actuaries

This chapter first summarises main ideas of this book. It then makes some suggestions: first for public policymakers, then for economists, and then for actuaries.

The Main Ideas of This Book

The main ideas, summarised in the order presented, are as follows.

(a) (Chapters 1, 2, 8) Adverse selection in insurance is usually weaker than most commentary suggests.

(b) (Chapters 1, 3–5) From a public policy perspective, 'weak' adverse selection is a good thing. This is because a degree of adverse selection is needed to maximise loss coverage, the expected losses compensated by insurance for the whole population.

(c) (Chapters 1, 3–5) To induce the degree of adverse selection which maximises loss coverage, some restrictions on risk classification are a good thing in some insurance markets.

(d) (Chapter 6) The extent to which a risk classification scheme differentiates between different risks can be indexed by the *separation* of the risk classification scheme, or its complement of *inclusivity* (one minus separation).

(e) (Chapter 7) Risk classification may be objectionable for two distinct reasons:

(i) *insufficient inclusivity* – too much risk classification overall, resulting in a suboptimal degree of adverse selection according to (b) above or

(ii) *misguided methods* – even if the overall degree of classification is optimal according to (i) above, particular classification methods may be objectionable on various grounds: unfairness, inaccuracy, reinforcement of prejudice, reinforcement of pre-existing disadvantage, controllability, transparency, privacy, socially perverse incentives, legitimacy creep and risk classification as blame.

(f) (Chapter 8) Empirical investigations of adverse selection, typically undertaken by applied economists, support my contention at (a) above that adverse selection in insurance is generally weaker than economic theory suggests. Where adverse selection does occur, it is often driven more by insurers introducing innovations in risk classification ('competitive adverse selection'), rather than by insureds having private knowledge of their own risks ('information adverse selection'). In other words, adverse selection often arises from games insurers play with each other rather than games customers play with insurers.

(g) (Chapter 9) Insurance rhetoric promulgates myths about adverse selection through four mechanisms:
   (i)   genuine misperceptions (naïve cynicism, actuarial paranoia, fallacy of composition, fallacy of the one-shot gambler);
   (ii) strategic exaggerations (cartoons, barricades and signals);
   (iii) other rhetorical devices (semantic stretches, one-way hash arguments, presumption of privilege, devaluation of the disadvantaged, affectations of virtue, emo-phobia); and
   (iv) cognitive capture (industry funding, career incentives for researchers).

(h) (Chapter 10) Insurance economics gives too much credence to concepts which are not substantiated in real insurance markets: Rothschild–Stiglitz as a broadly representative model; adverse selection always representing 'efficiency losses'; a high likelihood of market collapse if high risks are 'too small' a fraction of the population; deductibles as screening devices; 'rationing' of cover for low risks; unrestricted cover for high risks; uniform endowments; and the superiority of tax-and-subsidy schemes over restrictions on risk classification. Insurance economics also incorporates various systematic biases: asymmetric assumptions about information, asymmetric assumptions about behaviour and a tendency to semantic stretches in response to weak or contradictory evidence on adverse selection.

(i) (Chapter 11) Adverse selection is stronger in some contexts than others. Theoretically, opportunities for adverse selection are larger where (i) the customer has a large information edge or (ii) the customer can engage in multiple independent transactions, either in sequence (repetition), or in parallel (diversification). Multiple transactions also offer opportunities for customer learning. These theories are broadly consistent with empirical evidence on adverse selection in different contexts.

(j) (Chapter 12) Like adverse selection, moral hazard is exaggerated and excessively maligned. Over consumption moral hazard in health insurance is usually a good thing. In other types of insurance, precaution-neglect moral hazard is sometimes a good thing.

(k) (Chapter 13) Big data are potentially useful to insurers in risk classification, but there are technical pitfalls which can be loosely summarised by the maxim that as the number of explanatory variables is increased, noise may grow faster than truth. To the extent that big data do enable insurers to reduce the inclusivity of risk classification, this could reduce loss coverage, if adverse selection is reduced too much. Hence technological advances in big data may justify imposing some new limits on risk classification.

Typically, the policies purportedly justified by adverse selection arguments are policies which exclude or otherwise discriminate against the sick, the disadvantaged and the poor. Hence the exaggeration of adverse selection arguments often leads to policies which are cruel and regressive. While this book presents a technical argument against such policies, it can also be read as an appeal for kindness.

Suggestions for Public Policymakers

Implicit in most policy discussions about risk classification is the idea that compensation of losses by insurance is a 'good thing'. It follows that one of policymakers' objectives in most insurance markets should be to raise the expected fraction of the population's losses that is compensated by insurance, that is to raise loss coverage.[1]

---

[1] I say 'most' insurance markets because there may be a few unusual insurance markets where policymakers may appropriately prefer to adopt a neutral or even negative stance towards increasing loss coverage: for example, insurance of pet animals or insurance against the cost of regulatory penalties. In the UK, the Financial Conduct Authority bans authorised firms from insuring against these costs (see paragraph GEN 6.1.5 of FCA handbook, www.fca.org.uk, last accessed 31 May 2015).

In a few markets, this objective may appropriately be ensured by the draconian expedient of making insurance compulsory. Examples are compulsory third-party liability cover in car insurance and employer's liability insurance in the UK, and to some extent the individual mandate under the Patient Protection and Affordable Care Act 2010 (Obamacare) in the USA.

For the majority of markets where the importance of loss coverage is not sufficient to justify the infringement of freedom which compulsory insurance implies, a different approach is needed. Policymakers should aim to raise loss coverage to the maximum level consistent with individual freedom of choice over whether to buy insurance or not. This can be achieved by increasing the inclusivity of risk classification, so as to induce the 'right' level of adverse selection – the level which maximises loss coverage.

How much restriction is required? This depends on insurance demand elasticities for higher and lower risk-groups in particular markets. Extant empirical work (as summarised in Table 5.1) shows that insurance demand elasticities are often less than one. Theoretical models then suggest the possibility that even a complete ban on risk classification may increase loss coverage compared with fully risk-differentiated prices. Alternatively, partial risk classification may give the highest loss coverage (as in the central region in Figure 6.1).

Apart from increasing loss coverage, there are two further justifications for advocating some restrictions on risk classification.

First, there are other policy objectives to consider beyond optimising aggregate outcomes in the insurance market. These other objectives may include: limiting the perceived unfairness to individuals of statistical stereotyping; promoting public health (e.g. by maximising uptake of HIV and genetic tests); promoting equality of opportunity (by lessening cumulative disadvantage to individuals or families); and ameliorating the other objections to risk classification which were discussed in Chapter 7. To the extent that these objectives cannot be achieved without some restrictions on risk classification, they are further reasons why a degree of adverse selection should be tolerated, possibly beyond the level which maximises loss coverage.

Second, there is the dismal record of exaggeration and dogmatism about adverse selection by other commentators that was outlined in Chapters 2, 9 and 10. Most commentators assert that public policy should always seek to reduce adverse selection as much as possible; in aggregate, this commentary has a malign effect on public policy. Because of this, strong statements of opposing arguments backed up by specific proposals are likely to improve political outcomes, even if the proposals cannot yet be precisely calibrated.

Fortified by the arguments in the two previous paragraphs, I now advance a range of specific proposals for restrictions on risk classification. These are not presented as a package all to be implemented at once (which is in any case politically quite infeasible). Rather they are presented as a menu, from which policymakers might choose some proposals to take forward, depending on local political priorities and constraints. Provided the proposals initially implemented have a benign effect, further proposals can be considered at a later date.

Ban Questions about Pre-symptomatic Genetic Tests

My first specific recommendation to policymakers is that insurers should be banned from asking about prospective customers' pre-symptomatic genetic tests. *De facto* bans already apply in many countries, either by legislation (e.g. Mexico, Israel, Italy, Norway, Switzerland) or by agreement (e.g. Japan, UK). In the USA, the federal Genetic Information Nondiscrimination Act 2008 applies a ban for health insurance only; a few states including California, Vermont and Oregon also apply a ban in life, long-term care and disability insurance. Where bans are currently by agreement, they should now be given statutory force. A ban is justified by

(a) the extensive evidence from both theoretical models and experience that a ban is unlikely to have a large effect on insurance premiums;

(b) the likelihood, validated in a number of surveys,[2] that worries about future insurability deter people from undergoing tests which may lead to useful advice or further monitoring or prophylactic treatment; and

---

[2] Armstrong et al. (2003) and Phoenix Strategic Perspectives (2013). See also 'Fearing punishment for bad genes', *New York Times* 7 April 2014.

(c) the intrinsic undesirability of encouraging and normalising new forms of discrimination which are (i) morally offensive to many people in that they relate to an individual's essential identity or heritage and (ii) uncomfortably reminiscent of the early stages of now discredited past misadventures in eugenics (not just in Germany, but also in Scandinavia and the USA).[3]

If restricting use of pre-symptomatic genetic tests raises premiums only by a small amount, it also raises loss coverage only by a small amount. So this recommendation is driven more by the ban's *lack* of consequences for insurance markets, coupled with the undesirable consequences *avoided* under (b) and (c) above, rather than by any expectation that a ban will significantly increase loss coverage.

In this proposal, the term 'pre-symptomatic' is an important qualification. It means tests carried out on a healthy person because of a family history of disease, or as part of broad population screening; it excludes tests carried out as part of the investigation of existing symptoms. The line is drawn in this way mainly for pragmatic reasons. Assuming that symptoms and medical treatments themselves continue to have to be disclosed by insurance applicants, a ban on disclosing just one element of treatment may be ineffective and administratively cumbersome. Alternatively, if such a ban is actually effective in preventing all disclosure of a current treatment, it may have a much larger effect than banning only pre-symptomatic tests. The simpler and safer course is to focus a ban only on pre-symptomatic tests.

Ban Questions about Family History

In some jurisdictions such as the Netherlands, the ban on questions about pre-symptomatic genetic tests also extends to limits on questions which can be asked about the family history of insurance

---

[3] Edwin Black's aptly titled book *War against the weak* describes the influence of eugenic thought in America in the first half of the twentieth century (Black, 2003).

applicants (e.g. the ages of death and causes of death for parents and other relatives).[4] Since a ban on family history questions appears to work satisfactorily in the countries concerned, it may be attractive to adopt in other jurisdictions. The effect on premiums and loss coverage is likely to be somewhat larger than a ban on pre-symptomatic tests, but any rise in average premium will still probably be modest. One study suggested that in the mortgage-related term insurance market, the rise in average premium would probably be less than 10%.[5]

Banning the use of pre-symptomatic genetic tests stymies the growth of a new form of discrimination which on current evidence appears unnecessary for the successful operation of insurance, and is particularly offensive to many people because of its association with essential identity, and with discredited twentieth-century initiatives in eugenics. Banning family history is a natural extension of this. Neither of these bans is likely to have a large effect on insurance premiums or loss coverage. The bans would greatly benefit a minority of unfortunate individuals, at little cost to the whole population of insurance customers.

After these obvious easy wins, further recommendations are less obvious. Some of the possible restrictions below could have a larger effect on insurance markets, and could conceivably increase adverse selection *beyond* the point which maximises loss coverage. This would need to be weighed against other possible social benefits of the restrictions.

---

[4] In the Netherlands, permissible questions about family history for policies below a threshold sum assured are limited to questions about cardiovascular disease, diabetes and mental illness in parents and siblings. Wider questions encompassing cancers and other diseases cannot be asked (Hudson, 2008).

[5] Macdonald (2003) calculated this 'probably less than 10%' estimate for the effect of a ban on family history in mortgage-related term insurance in the UK. Adverse selection by size of sum assured is unlikely in mortgage-related insurance, because the sum assured is set by reference to the size of the loan. In the UK, the mortgage-related term insurance market represents at least 40% by number of total term life insurance sales (Swiss Re, 2014).

Bans on Other Specific Risk Variables

Most jurisdictions ban insurers from using certain risk variables. In principle this is usually not targeted solely at insurance risk classification; rather the usual principle is that the ban applies across many contexts – public services, private goods and services, employment – and exceptions may or may not be made for insurance risk classification. In the UK, the principle applies without exceptions for racial discrimination. The Race Relations Act 1968 outlawed direct discrimination by race in the supply of all goods and services, and the Race Relations Act 1976 outlawed indirect discrimination[6]; there has never been any question of an exemption for insurance.

One way of increasing adverse selection and (potentially) loss coverage would be to ban further risk variables. Some possibilities are gender, postal address, credit score, age and disability.

In jurisdictions where risk classification by gender is currently permitted, this is *not* an area I would prioritise for change. In the European Union (EU), risk classification by gender was banned for new policies after from 21 December 2012, so the change has now been made. The ban's impact on prices has been much smaller than many earlier predictions (see Chapter 2). Overall, a ban on gender classification is probably benign. But how much does it improve the world? Nobody was excluded from insurance before the ban by reason of gender. Differences in insurance prices between men and women were modest, with some difference such as in annuities favouring men and others such as in life insurance and car insurance favouring women; most individuals would experience both over their lifetimes. Classification by gender expends no resources on underwriting (gender is observable at zero cost to insurers). It has none of the collateral impacts, for example on privacy or public

---

[6] 'Indirect discrimination' occurs where a criterion is not explicitly racial, but nevertheless disadvantages a disproportionate fraction of some racial group, and the discriminator cannot show that the discrimination is 'a proportionate means of achieving a legitimate aim'. It is similar to the notion of 'disparate impact' in US federal law.

health, which other classifications sometimes have. The changeover to a ban incurs transitional costs. Overall, a ban on gender seems to me a poor bargain from the available menu of restrictions on risk classification, which should attract lower priority than some of the ideas below. But where the transitional costs have already been paid, I would not advocate incurring further transitional costs to reverse a gender ban.

A ban on postal address or credit score will in principle be economically progressive: for most insurance policies, people living in poor areas or people with poor credit scores (usually poor people) are charged more as a result of these risk variables. But except for home and car insurance, the effect size is fairly small.[7]

Bans on age or disability are likely to have a larger effect in life or health insurance than any of the other risk variables discussed above. A complete ban on either of these variables may be viable in some types of insurance such as car insurance (particularly if risk assessment by telematics monitoring becomes commonplace). But in other types of insurance such as life insurance, a complete ban may increase adverse selection too much. If age and disability were completely banned, loss coverage in life insurance might be reduced to coverage of mainly very elderly persons or those in very poor health; this would almost certainly represent 'too much' adverse selection, and hence suboptimal loss coverage.

In implementing any of the above possible bans on particular risk variables, policymakers need to consider whether priority should be placed on *procedural* or *substantive* exclusion of the banned variable. This amounts to a choice between a *method of omission* versus a *method of averaging*.

---

[7] In principle, risk-differentiated pricing also implies that pension annuities should be cheaper for people living in poor areas, and some annuity providers do offer such discounts. But this does not have much practical effect. People with small pension savings often do not appreciate that they can shop around when buying an annuity with their accumulated fund, and they are not of much interest to financial advisers; so they often accept expensive 'default' annuity offers from their pension provider.

Under the *method of omission*, insurers are required simply to *omit* the banned variable and then re-estimate their pricing models. The models will then place increased weight on any remaining risk variables which are correlated with the banned variable, so that part of its impact is replicated by increased contribution from the correlated variables. For example, if gender is omitted from a car insurance pricing model, an increased weight will be placed on variables such as engine size and occupation, which are correlated with gender. The EU ban on gender requires omission, and the European Commission guidance explicitly acknowledges that correlated risk variables may then capture some of the gender effect.[8]

Under the *method of averaging*, insurers are required to follow a two-step procedure. First, estimate the pricing model with all variables, including the banned ones. Second, set the contribution to total risk from each banned variable to its *average* value across the whole population used to estimate the model, and re-estimate the weights for all other variables. This method ensures that correlated variables do not act as proxies for the banned variables.[9]

Partial Limits on Disability as a Risk Variable

Limits on disability as a risk variable merit some further discussion. For pre-symptomatic genetic tests, family history and gender, the moderate impact of these variables on prices means that the polar solution of a complete ban is an obvious way to calibrate restrictions. Banning disability as a risk variable potentially has much wider scope and a larger effect on prices in some types of insurance, so calibrating any restrictions is harder. But the essential merit of *some* restrictions is already recognised in many jurisdictions.

In the UK, the extant restriction takes the following form. The Equality Act 2010 (originally the Disability Discrimination Act 1995)

---

[8] Paragraph 17 of European Commission (2011).

[9] For a full description of the method of averaging see Pope and Sydnor (2011). I am not aware of any instances where this method has actually been specified by a regulator.

prohibits discrimination in the supply of goods and services by any of nine protected characteristics (age, disability, gender reassignment, marriage and civil partnership, pregnancy and maternity, race, religion or belief, sex and sexual orientation). The exemption for insurance (in Schedule 3, Part 5) provides that in relation to disability discrimination, it is permitted to do anything in connection with insurance if:

> (a) that thing is done by reference to information that is both relevant to the assessment of the risk to be insured and from a source on which it is reasonable to rely, and (b) it is reasonable to do that thing.

This prohibits only uninformed or 'taste-based' discrimination by insurers. The Act may have encouraged a more evidence-based approach, and so increased loss coverage slightly by comparison to the pre-1995 position. But to increase loss coverage significantly is likely to require further restrictions.

Some possible further restrictions on disability as a risk variable are as follows.

(a) *Higher standards for evidence*. More specific and stringent requirements for evidence might be mandated to justify any discrimination. Rather than 'information', the acceptable evidence might be limited to actuarial or statistical data in peer-reviewed publications, so that insurers could not rely on mere opinions of their own staff or consultants, or similar 'information'. (This does not deny that information of this type may often have some predictive validity; it is just a pragmatic redrawing of the boundary between permitted and unpermitted discrimination in a way which may help some people with disabilities, and also increase loss coverage.)

(b) *Permit disability discrimination only for specific classes of insurance*. The possible relevance of some types of disability to assessment of risk in income protection or life insurance is obvious and substantial. The relevance of disability to assessment of risk in say car insurance or home insurance is much less obvious. It may be reasonable to ban the use of disability as a risk variable in general, *except* for classes such as income protection and life insurance where it is specifically permitted. This is unlikely to have a discernible effect on car insurance and home insurance average prices, and would remove any lingering suspicion that insurers do discriminate by disability in those classes.[10]

Allow Loadings, Ban Rejections

A variant on banning all use of a particular risk variable is to allow its use to adjust individual premiums, but ban its use as a reason for automatic rejection. Many insurers currently refuse to quote for travel insurance or life insurance for older people. While higher premiums may be reasonable for older people, automatic refusal to quote is probably not. For variables such as age or disability, which are sometimes associated with very large variations in individual risk, a ban on automatic exclusion may be a better calibrated measure than a total ban.

Mandatory Quote Requirements

The mandatory quote requirement is an extension of the 'no rejections' idea. Rather than banning use of a particular variable to justify rejections, a mandatory quote requirement means that *no* variable or combination of variables can justify rejection. In other words, for any contract marketed to the general public, the insurer must quote a price for that contract to any applicant. If the risk is high or little information is available, the price can be very high; but the insurer cannot simply refuse to quote. In practice, insurers might be allowed to satisfy the mandatory quote requirement by referring unusual risks onwards to a specialist insurer; the requirement would then be to *facilitate* a quote for any applicant.

---

[10] Such suspicions can arise from insurers' insensitivity or carelessness. One example is that many car insurers have a blanket policy of refusing to quote for cars which have 'modifications' from the manufacturer's standard specification. The motivation is presumably to avoid insuring 'boy racers' whose cars often have modifications. However, the cars of many disabled drivers also have modifications (e.g. left foot accelerator pedal for a right-leg amputee, or hand controls instead of pedals, etc.). Refusing to quote for cars with such 'modifications' is unlawful unless it can be justified with evidence pursuant to the Equality Act 2010 (which seems most unlikely). One disabled driver has sued several UK insurers on this point, leading to settlements ranging from £500 upwards to £4,000 (*The Observer* 30 August 2009).

A less stringent variant of the mandatory quote requirement would be to allow an insurer to reject some risks, but with an upper limit on the percentage of applicants rejected every year. Some flexibility in the limit in a particular year could be provided by allowing any excess or shortfall against the limit to be carried forward and used to adjust the limit for subsequent years.

Maximum Price Ratios

Maximum price ratios are limits of the following form on premiums for a particular type of insurance:

(a) a maximum ratio (e.g. 4 times) for the highest to the lowest premium rates an insurer can quote in any calendar year to any applicant who approaches the insurer; or

(b) a maximum ratio (e.g. 3 times) for the highest 5% to the lowest 5% of premium rates the insurer actually charges over a calendar year.

Alternatively, such limits might apply not to the total variation in premium rates, but to the variation by reference to a particular risk variable. One example of this is the Patient Protection and Affordable Care Act (Obamacare) in the USA, which allows premiums to vary for age by a maximum factor of 3 times, and for smoking status by a maximum factor of 1.5 times.[11] To be effective, controls such as these generally need to be combined with some form of mandatory quote requirement, since otherwise the insurer could improve its price ratio simply by refusing to quote for the highest (or lowest) risks.

Maximum Number of Risk-Groups

Insurers could be restricted to using five say risk-groups and hence premium rates (lowest, low, medium, high, highest) for a particular type of insurance. Under this approach, each insurer would be free to set its own five premium rates, and would allocate individual

---

[11] Section 2701 of the Patient Protection and Affordable Care Act 2010.

risks to risk-groups using any criteria of its choice. This approach would not prevent a large variation from the lowest to highest rates. But it would limit the 'arms race' of competitive adverse selection leading to ever-increasing fragmentation of risk-groups, which is a negative-sum activity (after costs) from the viewpoint of society as a whole (or indeed the insurance industry as a whole).

Suggestions for Economists

Economics is a notoriously imperialistic discipline,[12] in which intellectual exporters attract more prestige than intellectual importers (a mercantilist fallacy in epistemology!), and the opinions of an actuary may be of scant interest. Nevertheless, since Chapter 10 is critical of aspects of insurance economics, it seems appropriate to offer a few suggestions.

My first suggestion is to reconsider the dogma that adverse selection in insurance is always inefficient. This view does not seem reasonable where the shift in coverage towards higher risks more than compensates for the fall in insurance demand, so that loss coverage is increased. In these circumstances, adverse selection implies an increase in the quantum of risk voluntarily traded, and an increase in losses compensated by insurance.

Economists usually evaluate different risk classification schemes using a criterion of social welfare (often abbreviated to just 'welfare'). In many discussions the precise meaning of this criterion is not clearly stated, but usually implicit is a utilitarian approach where social welfare is a (possibly weighted) sum of expected utilities over all members of the population (so an increase in one person's utility can offset a decrease in another person's utility).[13] For power utility functions (and hence iso-elastic insurance demand),

---

[12] E.g. Stigler (1984), Becker (1992) and Lazear (2000).

[13] The alternative approach of characterising optimal social welfare only by the non-existence of a Pareto improvement or Kaldor–Hicks improvement seems less useful than utilitarian formulations for comparing risk classification schemes. This is because (a) risk classification schemes usually produce both winners and losers and (b) the winners, in practice, never compensate the losers.

utilitarian social welfare and loss coverage both give the same rank ordering of different risk classification schemes.[14]

In my view loss coverage has some significant advantages over social welfare as a criterion for assessing risk classification schemes, which I hope economists will consider and explore more fully:

– First, loss coverage is based solely on observable claims, whereas social welfare requires unobservable utilities. In a broader context, economic policies target observable quantities such as national output, not national utility. To say that risk classification policy should maximise social welfare is like saying that it should maximise happiness: theoretically attractive, but it provides no basis for action.
– Second, loss coverage is a simpler concept, and hence more conducive to wide understanding in policy discussions.
– Third, and as discussed in Chapter 12, the 'expected utility' framing where insurance is driven by a preference for 'certain premiums' over 'uncertain losses' seems unsuited to the many cases where the potential loss is large, so that there is no realistic option of bearing it uninsured: without insurance the surviving dependants would be destitute, or the expensive medical treatment would never be received. In such cases, the motivation for insurance may be better understood as a desire to participate in redistribution.[15] Loss coverage makes no assumptions about the motivation driving individual insurance decisions. (It does assume that the compensation of losses by insurance is a good thing; but I believe this is an assumption which commands wide policymaker and public support, provided that insurance is voluntary.)

As regards the Rothschild–Stiglitz model and derivative models based on alternative equilibrium concepts,[16] these should be subjected to a reality check. As I described in Chapter 10, my impression

[14] This is shown in Hao et al. (2016b). The social welfare measure is necessarily standardised to negate the possibility of a 'utility monster' dominating social welfare (Nozick, 1974).

[15] This means to gain access to a scheme where transfers will be made from those who are lucky in the future to those who are unlucky in the future. It does not necessarily imply any desire for redistribution in the sense of equalising pre-existing endowments.

[16] E.g. Miyazaki (1977), Wilson (1977), Spence (1978), Riley (1979), Grossman (1979) and Dasgupta and Maskin (1986).

is that the main premises and predictions of these models – separation of risk-groups via menus of contracts with different deductibles, rationing of insurance for low risks, instability of markets with small fractions of high risks – appear unfamiliar and grossly counter-factual to actuaries and other insurance practitioners.

On the models in Chapters 3 to 5, much more work could be done. The only insurance demand function for which a comprehensive analysis of loss coverage has so far been published is the iso-elastic function used in most examples in this book.[17] Loss coverage could be comprehensively evaluated under a variety of alternative insurance demand functions (e.g. those briefly introduced in Appendix A). All analysis to date has been based on loss coverage defined as the *expectation* of losses compensated by insurance; it may be interesting to investigate the variance and possibly higher moments. Empirical work is needed on estimating insurance demand functions, so that we can calibrate the degree of restriction of risk classification which will maximise loss coverage in particular markets.[18]

The notion of separation of risk classification outlined in Chapter 6 could be further developed and applied. In that chapter, the set-up for *partial classification* was that insurers observed the risk (probability of loss) for every individual, and then because of regulation *deliberately* set premiums which did not fully reflect differences between individuals' risks. Another possibility is that insurers sometimes make mistakes, assigning a high risk to a low premium or vice versa, either through error or because of deception by the customer; we might call this *mis-classification*. A third possibility is that insurers cannot observe the risk of individuals, but can observe some attribute (say gender) which is imperfectly correlated with their risks, and use that attribute to assign individuals to

---

[17] Hao et al. (2016a).

[18] This need for empirical validation of course implies that at the moment, broadly similar criticisms regarding lack of empirical evidence as I make of Rothschild–Stiglitz could also be made of loss coverage. But loss coverage is a new idea, not a paradigm which has dominated insurance economics for the past 40 years.

premiums; we might call this *imperfect classification*. Some risk classification schemes may be especially prone to error, or may create particularly strong incentives for customers to misrepresent their risk status. These three concepts (partial classification, misclassification and imperfect classification) and the relationships between them could be explored.

As regards empirical work on adverse selection as in Chapter 8, this should in future focus on quantifying the extent of adverse or advantageous selection in different markets, and explaining variations between markets by reference to product, customer and institutional characteristics. I acknowledge that much work is already being done in this area.[19] One possible direction arising from this book is that in Chapter 11 I suggested two conjectures about circumstances which might make adverse selection stronger: (i) the customer has a large information edge or (ii) the customer can engage in multiple transactions.

My final suggestion to economists is this admonition: *own your rhetoric*. Economic rhetoric about adverse selection typically conflates all of the following elements: 'asymmetric information ... higher risks ... reduced cover ... inefficiency'. The rhetoric is implicitly, and sometimes explicitly, disparaging about higher risks (which in many contexts means the sick and the poor).[20] When I question some of these rhetorical elements – for example by pointing out that under 'reduced cover' the quantum of risk voluntarily traded can be increased, and it seems surprising that this is deemed 'inefficient' – economists sometimes respond that despite the

---

[19] A good survey is Einav et al. (2010).

[20] While such disparagement is most florid in informal discussion, it also features in some of the seminal papers in insurance economics. For example Rothschild and Stiglitz (1976, p. 638): 'The presence of the high-risk individuals exerts a negative externality on the low-risk individuals. The externality is completely dissipative ... If only the high-risk individuals would admit to their having high accident probabilities, all individuals would be better off.' All this is technically correct within the Rothschild–Stiglitz model. But its rhetorical effect in the real world is an unjustified insinuation that high risks should be blamed not only for their own problems, but even for the problems of others.

rhetoric, reduced cover is not the essence of their concerns about adverse selection, which really focus on the mere existence of asymmetric information (why is this 'adverse'?), or hypothetical Pareto improvements, or Kaldor–Hicks improvements, or something else. But if your rhetoric about adverse selection habitually conflates several elements, you should be able to defend all of those elements. Disavowing whichever element of your rhetoric a particular criticism targets is a response which can be deployed against any succinct criticism; but deployed frequently, it is a response which becomes tiresome and unconvincing. *Own your rhetoric.*

Suggestions for Actuaries

Parts of this book have been critical of historical commentary and predictions by actuaries on risk classification in the context of HIV, genetics and gender discrimination. The Institute and Faculty of Actuaries promulgated predictions for deaths from AIDS in the UK which were between 10 times and 30 times too high; its warnings that critical illness insurance would no longer be sold if insurers' access to pre-symptomatic genetic tests was banned have not been borne out; its predictions for increases in car insurance prices for young women after a ban on gender classification were up to 5 times the actual increases.[21] As one lawyer has put it: 'actuaries are sometimes like the boy who cried wolf when it comes to adverse selection'.[22]

As well as tending to make overstated predictions about adverse selection, actuaries sometimes give the impression of being disgruntled with contemporary anti-discrimination norms. In particular, they often appear disapproving of the social trend towards some limits on statistical discrimination. Their standard argument is that restrictions on insurance discrimination will increase adverse selection, and therefore lead to an unending spiral of rising prices and declining coverage.

[21] These predictions were detailed in Chapter 2.
[22] Hall (1999).

One can imagine an alternative world in which this argument is mathematically decisive: a world where adverse selection is a strong and relentless force, so that any restriction on risk classification in an insurance market leads inevitably to the collapse of that market, as actuaries often appear to suggest. In such a world, conventional adverse selection arguments would eventually be vindicated. But the real world is nothing like this. Adverse selection is a weak force in most insurance markets; in moderation, it can increase loss coverage; and even where it does not, it may be a price worth paying for other social benefits. In this real world, doctrinaire aversion towards anti-discrimination norms will not lead to eventual vindication; it may instead lead to actuaries being increasingly side-lined and ignored, at least as far as public policies on risk classification are concerned.

Actuaries' aversion to anti-discrimination norms in the context of insurance underwriting is a product of the analytical framework within which they have traditionally understood risk classification. The syllogism still taught to every actuarial student runs as follows: adverse selection is bad; restrictions on risk classification cause adverse selection; therefore restrictions on risk classification are bad. The fact that policymakers and wider society seem broadly to welcome some restrictions on risk classification is inexplicable in this framework. For actuarial doctrine and contemporary social norms to be reconciled, the traditional framework now needs to be extended. Every actuarial student should learn about loss coverage.

Keynes famously claimed in the final paragraph of his *General theory* that public policymakers are usually unconsciously driven by the ideas of 'some academic scribbler of a few years back'.[23] But not all theorists enjoy such influence, only those whose theories address the concerns of the policymakers of the day. In a world where policymakers increasingly endorse a moral principle of some limits on discrimination, the theorists (and professions) with

[23] Keynes (1936).

influence will be those who can reconcile their theories with that principle. The concept of loss coverage provides an actuarial theory which allows that some limits on risk classification sometimes have merit. It provides a means of quantifying how far such restrictions should go, and the disadvantages of taking them too far. It is, if you like, a way of reconciling traditional insurance concerns with the anti-discrimination concerns which preoccupy modern society: an actuarial idea for our times.

APPENDIX A Alternative Demand Functions

Key Ideas:

negative exponential demand; generalised negative exponential demand; exponential power demand

The 'iso-elastic' property of the demand function used in Chapter 5 implies that demand elasticity does not change as the premium changes. This is the simplest possible specification and is mathematically tractable, but it is arguably unrealistic: the usual pattern for most goods and services is that demand elasticity increases as price increases. To accommodate this, more flexible demand specifications are needed.

Negative Exponential Demand

As the first alternative to demand elasticity being determined by membership of a risk-group and invariant to changes in the premium (that is, iso-elastic), suppose that demand elasticity is an increasing function of the premium π, and the same irrespective of the individual's risk-group. One example of this is represented in Figure A.1. The linear relationship shown between demand elasticity and premium is assumed to apply identically for both high and low risk-groups.

In Figure A.1, the values of 0.2 and 0.8 marked by the two circles are the demand elasticities corresponding to premiums of 0.01 and 0.04, respectively. Assuming the true risks are 0.01 and 0.04 as in Chapter 5, these values of 0.2 and 0.8 represent the *fair-premium demand elasticities* for low and high risks, respectively.

The particular linear relationship in Figure A.1, where the straight line representing demand elasticity passes through the

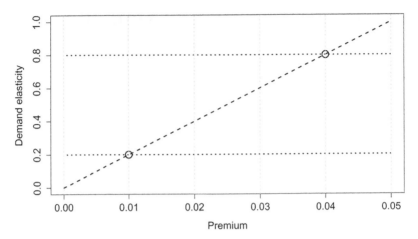

FIGURE A.1 Demand elasticity linear in premium (leads to negative exponential demand)

origin, amounts to saying that the fair-premium demand elasticities λ_i vary in proportion to the corresponding fair premiums μ_i (for risk-groups $i = 1, 2$), that is:

$$\frac{\lambda_2}{\lambda_1} = \frac{\mu_2}{\mu_1} \tag{A.1}$$

A suitable model for demand elasticity $\varepsilon(\pi)$ is then:

$$\varepsilon(\pi) = \frac{\lambda_1}{\mu_1}\pi = \frac{\lambda_2}{\mu_2}\pi \tag{A.2}$$

Recalling that demand elasticity can be written as the log–log derivative:

$$\varepsilon(\pi) = -\frac{\partial \log\left[d(\mu_i, \pi)\right]}{\partial \log \pi} \tag{A.3}$$

We can then equate Equations (A.2) and (A.3) and solve to obtain the *negative exponential demand* function:

$$d(\mu_i, \pi) = \tau_i \exp\left\{ \left(1 - \frac{\pi}{\mu_i}\right)\lambda_i \right\} \tag{A.4}$$

where

- $\tau_i = d(\mu_i, \mu_i)$ is the 'fair-premium demand' for population i, that is the proportion of risk-group i who buy insurance at an actuarially fair premium, that is when $\pi = \mu_i$
- μ_i is the risk (probability of loss) for members of risk-group i
- λ_i is the *fair-premium demand elasticity* for members of risk-group i, that is the demand elasticity when an actuarially fair premium $\pi = \mu_i$ is charged.

This demand function satisfies the axioms for a demand function which were stated in Chapter 5.

Negative exponential demand has the characteristic property that the second derivative is the first derivative squared, divided by the original function.

Generalised Negative Exponential Demand

Now suppose that instead of the linear function shown in Figure A.1, demand elasticity is an increasing but *nonlinear* function of the premium, and the same irrespective of the individual's risk-group. Two cases are shown in Figure A.2. For a continuous demand function, demand elasticity must go to zero when the premium goes to zero; so a straight line between the two points representing high and low risks' fair-premium demand elasticities in these plots would not give a sensible model. Instead, we need to fit a nonlinear curve which passes through the two points and the origin. Suitable nonlinear curves can be fitted such that:

$$\varepsilon(\pi) = \lambda_1 \left(\frac{\pi}{\mu_1}\right)^n = \lambda_2 \left(\frac{\pi}{\mu_2}\right)^n, \quad \text{for some } n \qquad (A.5)$$

Observing that $\varepsilon(\mu_1) = \lambda_1$ and $\varepsilon(\mu_2) = \lambda_2$, where the λ_i are defined as the fair-premium demand elasticities as earlier, we can find n as:

$$n = \frac{\log(\lambda_2/\lambda_1)}{\log(\mu_2/\mu_1)} \qquad (A.6)$$

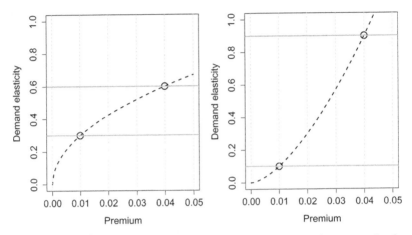

FIGURE A.2 Demand elasticity curvilinear in premium (leads to generalised negative exponential demand)

The parameter n can be interpreted as the 'elasticity of elasticity', also known as the 'second-order elasticity'.

In this specification, demand elasticity as a function of premium is: for $n = 1$, linear (as in the previous example, Figure A.1); for $0 < n < 1$, concave (as in the left-hand panel of Figure A.2); and for $n > 1$, convex (as in the right-hand panel of Figure A.2).

Equating Equation (A.5) to the definition of demand elasticity in Equation (A.3) and solving, we obtain the *generalised negative exponential demand* function:

$$d(\mu_i, \pi) = \tau_i \exp\left\{ \left[1 - \left(\frac{\pi}{\mu_i}\right)^n \right] \frac{\lambda_i}{n} \right\} \tag{A.7}$$

Note that the demand functions discussed earlier are both special cases of this generalised negative exponential demand function: $n = 1$ corresponds to negative exponential demand, and $n \to 0$ corresponds to iso-elastic demand.

Exponential Power Demand

The exponential power demand function corresponds to the generalised negative exponential demand formula, but with $n = \lambda_i$. It is a very flexible, but rather intractable, formulation which allows a wide range of levels and curvatures for the demand curve to be specified. Exponential power demand is specified as follows:

$$d(\mu_i, \pi) = \tau_i \exp\left\{ 1 - \left(\frac{\pi}{\mu_i}\right)^{\lambda_i} \right\} \tag{A.8}$$

This specification was suggested in De Jong and Ferris (2006), and I adopted it in my early papers on loss coverage (Thomas, 2008, 2009). With hindsight it would have been better to use a more tractable specification, such as iso-elastic demand.

Table A.1 summarises the functional form and demand elasticity for each of the four demand functions discussed above. In the right-hand column of Table A.1, the specification of demand elasticity as a function of λ_i becomes increasingly sophisticated as one moves down the page.

The differences between the four demand functions can also be understood graphically. Figure A.3 plots the four demand functions for a single risk-group with $\mu = 0.01$ and the specimen parameter values $\lambda = 0.5$ (the top curve in each panel), $\lambda = 1.0$, and $\lambda = 1.5$

Table A.1. *Functional form and demand elasticity for common demand functions*

Demand model	Functional form of $d(\mu_i, \pi)$ (multiplier $\tau_i p_i$ omitted in each case)	Corresponding demand elasticity
Iso-elastic	$\left(\frac{\pi}{\mu_i}\right)^{-\lambda_i}$	λ_i
Negative exponential	$\exp\left\{ \left(1 - \frac{\pi}{\mu_i}\right)\lambda_i \right\}$	$\frac{\lambda_i}{\mu_i}\pi$
Generalised negative exponential	$\exp\left\{ \left[1 - \left(\frac{\pi}{\mu_i}\right)^n\right]\frac{\lambda_i}{n} \right\}$	$\lambda_i\left(\frac{\pi}{\mu_i}\right)^n$
Exponential power	$\exp\left\{ 1 - \left(\frac{\pi}{\mu_i}\right)^{\lambda_i} \right\}$	$\lambda_i\left(\frac{\pi}{\mu_i}\right)^{\lambda_i}$

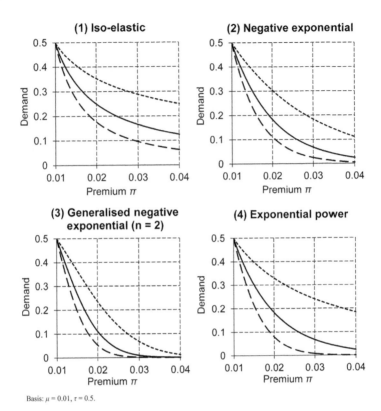

Basis: $\mu = 0.01$, $\tau = 0.5$.

FIGURE A.3 Plots of four demand functions for a single risk-group for $\lambda = 0.5$ (top line), $\lambda = 1.0$ (middle line) and $\lambda = 1.5$ (bottom line)

(the bottom curve in each panel). It can be seen that the lower right panel showing exponential power demand has the most flexible specification: as the λ-parameter is changed from 0.5 to 1 to 1.5, the demand curve 'sweeps' across a wide area, and exhibits a large change in curvature. The first three panels in Figure A.3 – iso-elastic, negative exponential and generalised negative exponential demand – are all particular cases of generalised negative exponential demand (for $n \to 0$, $n = 1$ and $n = 2$, respectively). It can be seen that as n increases from panel (1) to panel (3), demand decreases at all premium levels.

Unlike the other demand functions in this chapter, exponential power demand is not predicated on demand elasticity being the same function of premium irrespective of risk-group (as shown in Figures A.1 and A.2). Therefore loss coverage under this demand function cannot be plotted against a single demand elasticity at the equilibrium premium, as was done for other demand functions shown in Figure 5.8). However, using a slightly different interpretation of 'demand elasticity at the equilibrium premium', we can obtain a similar inverted-U shaped graph, showing that loss coverage is maximised by intermediate demand elasticity. The details are given in Thomas (2009).

APPENDIX B Multiple Equilibria: A Technical Curiosity

Key Ideas:

multiple equilibria

For some parameter values, the zero-profit condition when using the demand models described in Chapter 5 and Appendix A can be satisfied by more than one equilibrium premium. In other words, the profit as a function of premium has *multiple roots* (I shall use this term throughout this appendix). This is mainly a technical curiosity, because the parameter values required to generate multiple roots are unlikely to arise in practice. This appendix explains how multiple roots can arise, and states conditions for the parameter values which are required.

Throughout this appendix, I shall use the same iso-elastic demand function from Chapter 5 as an example. Proofs of all results in this chapter and similar analyses for other demand functions are given in MingJie Hao's PhD thesis.

How Multiple Roots Can Arise

Graphically, a root of the profit equation is determined where the expected profit crosses the x-axis. Figure B.1 illustrates this for the typical parameters $(\mu_1, \mu_2) = (0.01, 0.04)$, $\alpha_1 = 0.9$ and $\lambda_1 = \lambda_2 = 1$. Note that as the actual premium increases above the equilibrium level, insurers make progressively increasing profits; and as the premium decreases, insurers make progressively increasing losses. The monotonic nature of the profit function implies that the equilibrium shown is stable and well-defined. Under deviations from equilibrium, profit is negative when equilibrium requires an increase in premium and vice versa (that is, the profit 'signal' always has the 'right sign').

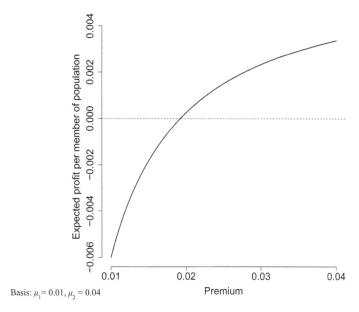

Basis: $\mu_1 = 0.01, \mu_2 = 0.04$

FIGURE B.I Profit function for $(\lambda_1, \lambda_2) = (1, 1)$: single root

Now suppose we change the parameters to $\alpha_1 = 0.992$, $\lambda_1 = 5$ and $\lambda_2 = 1$. Note that these values are extreme, in particular the high risk-group is extremely small, and there is a very large difference in demand elasticities between risk-groups. The result is shown in Figure B.2. In the left panel, the y-axis has the same scale as in Figure B.1. In the right panel, the y-axis has a 10× zoom.

In the left panel, notice that profit is nearly zero over the full range of potential premiums (that is, a 'wrong' premium leads to only a weak profit 'signal'). In the zoomed right panel, note that the profit function has three roots, representing three potential equilibria. At the 'middle' root, small increases in premium above this level initially lead to increasing losses for insurers and vice versa (that is, the profit signal has the 'wrong sign'). These features in combination – a weak profit signal, possibly with a 'wrong sign' – are suggestive of an unstable market.

Figure B.3 shows the profit function with parameters as per Figure B.2, but with five curves corresponding to five values of the low-risk fair-premium demand-share α_1. It can be seen that multiple

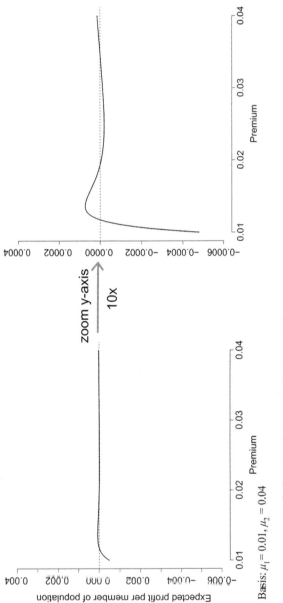

FIGURE B.2 Profit function for $(\lambda_1, \lambda_2) = (5, 1)$: multiple roots

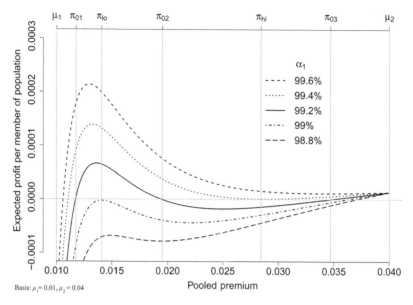

FIGURE B.3 Profit functions for $(\lambda_1, \lambda_2) = (5, 1)$ and five values of α_1

roots arise only when α_1 falls within a narrow range of high values. In more detail:

- For any $\alpha_1 < 0.99$, there is a unique root close to μ_2.
- For $\alpha_1 = 0.99$, in addition to a root close to μ_2, the profit curve attains a local maximum, which is also a root, at π_{lo}.
- For $0.99 < \alpha_1 < 0.994$, the profit curve has three roots $(\pi_{01}, \pi_{02}, \pi_{03})$, where $\mu_2 < \pi_{01} < \pi_{lo} < \pi_{02} < \pi_{hi} < \pi_{03} < \mu_2$.
- For $\alpha_1 = 0.994$, the profit curve has a root below π_{lo}, but attains a local minimum at a root π_{hi}.
- For any $\alpha_1 > 0.994$, there is a unique root close to μ_1.

Statement of Results

The conditions for multiple roots exemplified in Figure B.3 can be stated formally as follows:

(a) For the iso-elastic demand function as used in Chapter 5, there exist three roots of the profit function in the range $[\pi_{lo}, \pi_{hi}]$ if and only if

$$\lambda_1 - \lambda_2 \geq \frac{\sqrt{\mu_1} + \sqrt{\mu_2}}{\sqrt{\mu_2} - \sqrt{\mu_1}} \tag{B.1}$$

and

$$\frac{\alpha(\pi_{lo})}{1 + \alpha(\pi_{lo})} = \alpha_{lo} \leq \alpha_1 \leq \alpha_{hi} = \frac{\alpha(\pi_{hi})}{1 + \alpha(\pi_{hi})} \tag{B.2}$$

where

$$\alpha(\pi) = \left(\frac{\mu_2 - \pi}{\pi - \mu_1}\right) \left(\frac{\mu_2^{\lambda_2}}{\mu_1^{\lambda_1}}\right) \pi^{(\lambda_1 - \lambda_2)} \tag{B.3}$$

and (π_{lo}, π_{hi}) solves

$$\pi^2 - \left(\mu_1 + \mu_2 + \frac{\mu_2 - \mu_1}{\lambda_2 - \lambda_1}\right)\pi + \mu_1 \mu_2 = 0 \tag{B.4}$$

Result (a) highlights that multiple roots arise only if we have *both* an implausible divergence of demand elasticities (large $\lambda_1 - \lambda_2$) *and* an extreme population structure (α_1 in a narrow range of high values). So provided α_1 is *less* than the lower end α_{lo} of this range, we have a unique root *irrespective* of demand elasticities. This is summarised by the following result:

(b) Given (μ_1, μ_2), define $c = \frac{\sqrt{\mu_1} + \sqrt{\mu_2}}{\sqrt{\mu_2} - \sqrt{\mu_1}}$. Then if:

$$\alpha_1 < \frac{\left(\sqrt{\frac{\mu_2}{\mu_1}}\right)^{c+1}}{1 + \left(\sqrt{\frac{\mu_2}{\mu_1}}\right)^{c+1}} \tag{B.5}$$

there exist no multiple roots.

Application of Results

For $(\mu_1, \mu_2) = (0.01, 0.04)$, Equation (B.1) evaluates as 3 and Equation (B.5) as 0.941. That is, provided *either* $\lambda_1 - \lambda_2 < 3$ *or* $\alpha_1 < 0.941$, multiple roots can be ruled out.

Even if neither of these conditions is satisfied, multiple roots will arise only if α_1 falls within the narrow range (lying somewhere above 0.941) specified by Equation (B.2). For $(\lambda_1, \lambda_2) = (5, 1)$, the required narrow range for α_1 evaluates as (0.99, 0.994), as previously illustrated in Figure B.3.

Writing relative risk $\beta = \mu_1/\mu_2$ as usual, the expression c in Equation (B.5) can also be written as:

$$c = \frac{(1 + \sqrt{\beta})}{(\sqrt{\beta} - 1)} \tag{B.6}$$

Table B.1 evaluates the conditions in Equations (B.1) and (B.5) for various values of relative risk β. It can be seen that as one condition becomes less extreme, the other becomes more extreme and vice versa. Overall, multiple roots are very unlikely to be an issue in practice.

The feature that multiple roots can arise when α_1 is very high (but not too high) – roughly speaking, when high risks form a very small fraction of the population – is vaguely reminiscent of the 'no equilibrium' result in the Rothschild–Stiglitz model, which I criticised in Chapter 10. However, the interpretations placed on the two results are very different. For the Rothschild–Stiglitz analysis, a typical interpretation is that the problem may be very significant for real insurance markets. For the models in this book, multiple roots arise only if in addition to a very small (but not too small) fraction

Table B.1. *Conditions sufficient to rule out multiple roots for various relative risks*

	Either condition is sufficient to rule out multiple roots	
β Relative risk	Demand elasticity condition: $c = (\lambda_1 - \lambda_2)$ less than	Population structure condition: α_1 less than
2	5.82	0.914
3	3.73	0.931
4	3.00	0.941
5	2.61	0.948
6	2.38	0.954

of high risks, there is also an implausible divergence of demand elasticities. My interpretation is that the problem is *not* likely to be significant for real insurance markets.[1]

---

[1] Another way dispensing with the problem of multiple roots is to say that the lowest root represents the only 'true' equilibrium, by reason of the following argument given by Hoy and Polborn (2000). The middle equilibrium is unstable because on either side of it, the profit signal has the 'wrong sign', and so causes insurers to diverge from the middle equilibrium. If we are at the highest equilibrium, some enterprising insurer can undercut all other insurers by switching to a price slightly above the lowest equilibrium, and thus attract all the customers and make large profits. Arguably therefore, the lowest equilibrium is the only 'true' equilibrium. However, for this argument to work requires some insurer to *know* that the situation is one of the multiple roots, where it can make a large profit by a large reduction in price; in other words, it requires *global knowledge* of the demand curve. If insurers have only *local knowledge* of the demand curve – such as can be obtained from small experiments with the price – then the highest equilibrium could be stable. For this possibility, the analysis in this appendix provides further reassurance.

References

Acerbi, C. (2002) 'Spectral measures of risk: a coherent representation of subjective risk aversion', *Journal of Banking and Finance*, 26(7): 1505–18.

Akerlof, G. (1970) 'The market for lemons: quality uncertainty and the market mechanism', *Quarterly Journal of Economics*, 84: 488–500.

American Academy of Actuaries (2011) *On risk classification*. www.actuary.org, last accessed 23 April 2016.

American Council of Life Insurers (2014) *Life insurers factbook*. www.acli.org, last accessed 23 April 2016.

Anderson, C. (2008) 'The end of theory: the data deluge makes the scientific method obsolete', *Wired*, 23 June 2008. www.wired.com/2008/06/pb-theory, last accessed 23 April 2016.

Armstrong, K., Weber, B., FitzGerald, G. et al. (2003) 'Life insurance and breast cancer risk assessment: adverse selection, genetic testing decisions and discrimination', *American Journal of Medical Genetics*, 120A: 359–64.

Arrow, K.J. (1963) 'Uncertainty and the welfare economics of medical care', *American Economic Review*, 53: 141–9.

Association of British Insurers (2005) *Statement of best practice for income protection cover*. www.abi.org.uk, last accessed 23 April 2016.

Association of British Insurers (2011) *Statement of best practice for critical illness cover*. www.abi.org.uk, last accessed 23 April 2016.

Association of British Insurers (2014) *Life insurance – key facts 2014*. www.abi.org.uk, last accessed 23 April 2016.

Auerbach, A.J. and Kotlikoff, L.J. (1991) 'The adequacy of life insurance purchases', *Journal of Financial Intermediation*, 1: 215–41.

Avraham, R., Logue, K.D. and Schwarz, D. (2014) 'Towards a universal framework for insurance anti-discrimination laws', *Connecticut Insurance Law Journal*, 21: 1–52.

Babbel, D. (1985) 'The price elasticity of demand for whole life insurance', *Journal of Finance*, 40(1): 225–39.

Baker, R.D. and McHale, I.G. (2013) 'Optimal betting under uncertainty: improving the Kelly criterion', *Decision Analysis*, 10(3): 189–99.

Banthorpe, P., Cleverley, P., Fairall, C. et al. (2013) *Extending the critical path*. www.sias.org.uk, last accessed 23 April 2016.

Baronoff, E. (2003) *Risk management and insurance*. John Wiley & Sons.

Becker, G. (1992) *The economic way of looking at life*. Nobel Prize Lecture, www.nobelprize.org, last accessed 23 April 2016.

Bell, R. and Cover, T.M. (1980) 'Competitive optimality of logarithmic investment', *Mathematics of Operations Research*, 5: 161–6.

Bell, R. and Cover, T.M. (1988) 'Game-theoretic optimal portfolios', *Management Science*, 34: 724–33.

Berndt, A. and Gupta, A. (2009) 'Moral hazard and adverse selection in the originate-to-distribute model of bank credit', *Journal of Monetary Economics*, 56: 725–43.

Bernheim, B.D., Formi, L., Gokhale, J. and Kotlikoff, L.J. (2003) 'The mismatch between life insurance holdings and financial vulnerabilities: evidence from the health and retirement study', *American Economic Review*, 93: 354–65.

Bibby, C. (1971) *T.H. Huxley on education*. Cambridge University Press.

Black, E. (2003) *War against the weak: eugenics and America's campaign to create a master race*. Dialog Press.

Black, K.B., Skipper, H.D. and Black, K. (2013) *Life insurance*, 14th edn. Lucretian LLC.

Blumberg, L., Nichols, L. and Banthin, J. (2001) 'Worker decisions to purchase health insurance', *International Journal of Health Care Finance and Economics*, 1: 305–25.

Boadway, R. (1997) 'Public economics and the theory of public policy', *Canadian Journal of Economics*, 30(4a): 753–72.

Bond, E.W. (1982) 'A direct test of the lemons model: the market for used pickup trucks', *American Economic Review*, 72(4): 836–40.

Bourgeon, J.M. and Picard, P. (2014) 'Fraudulent claims and nitpicky insurers', *American Economic Review*, 104: 2900–17.

Brackenridge, R.D.C., Croxson, R.S. and Mackenzie, R. (2006) *Brackenridge's medical selection of life risks*, 5th edn. Palgrave Macmillan.

Bridgeman, C. and Sandrik, K. (2008) 'Bullshit promises', *Tennessee Law Review*, 76: 379–404.

Buchmueller, T.C. and Ohri, S. (2006) 'Health insurance take-up by the near-elderly', *Health Services Research*, 41: 2054–73.

Butler, J.R. (1999) 'Estimating elasticities of demand for private health insurance in Australia', Working Paper No. 43. National Centre for Epidemiology and Population Health, Australian National University, Canberra.

Canadian Institute of Actuaries (2014) *Statement on genetic testing and insurance*. www.actuaries.ca, last accessed 21 July 2015.

Cardon, J.H. and Hendel, I. (2001) 'Asymmetric information in health insurance: evidence from the National Medical Expenditure Survey', *Rand Journal of Economics*, 32: 408–27.

Carpenter, D. and Moss, D.A. (2014) *Preventing regulatory capture: special interest influence and how to limit it*. Cambridge University Press.

Cawley, J. and Philipson, T. (1999) 'An empirical examination of information barriers to trade in insurance', *American Economic Review*, 89: 827–46.

Chade, H. and Schlee, E. (2016) 'Insurance as a lemons market: coverage denials and pooling', Working Paper. www.public.asu.edu/~hchade/papers/Exclusion_June.pdf, last accessed 23 July 2016.

Chernew, M., Frick, K. and McLaughlin, C. (1997) 'The demand for health insurance coverage by low-income workers: can reduced premiums achieve full coverage?', *Health Services Research*, 32: 453–70.

Chiappori, P.-A. (2000) 'Econometric models of insurance under asymmetric information', in *Handbook of insurance*, ed. Dionne, G. North-Holland.

Chiappori, P.-A. and Salanie, B. (1997) 'Empirical contract theory: the case of insurance data', *European Economic Review*, 41: 943–50.

Chiappori, P.-A. and Salanie, B. (2000) 'Testing for asymmetric information in insurance markets', *Journal of Political Economy*, 108: 56–78.

Cohen, A. (2005) 'Asymmetric information and learning in the automobile insurance market', *Review of Economics and Statistics*, 87: 197–207.

Cohen, A. and Siegelman, P. (2010) 'Testing for adverse selection in insurance markets', *Journal of Risk and Insurance*, 77: 39–84.

Confused.com (2013) *Gender gap opens on car cover costs*. www.confused.com, last accessed 9 November 2014.

Cosmides, L., Clark Bennett, H. and Tooby, J. (2010) 'Adaptive specializations, social exchange and the evolution of human intelligence', *Proceedings of the National Academy of Sciences*, 107: 9007–14.

Cowen, T. and Tabarrok, A. (2015) 'The end of asymmetric information?', *Cato Unbound*, April 2015. www.cato-unbound.org, last accessed 23 April 2016.

Crocker, K.J. and Snow, A. (1986) 'The efficiency effects of categorical discrimination in the insurance industry', *The Journal of Political Economy*, 94: 321–44.

Cummins, J.D. and Doherty, N.A. (2006) 'The economics of insurance intermediaries,' *Journal of Risk and Insurance*, 73(3): 359–96.

Cummins, J.D., Smith, B.D., Vance, R.N. and VanDerhei, J.L. (1983) *Risk classification in life insurance*. Springer.

Cutler, D.M. and Reber, S.J. (1998) 'Paying for health insurance: the trade-off between competition and adverse selection', *Quarterly Journal of Economics*, 113(2): 433–66.

Dasgupta, P. and Maskin, E. (1986) 'The existence of equilibrium in discontinuous economic games, ii: applications', *The Review of Economic Studies*, 53: 27–41.

Daykin, C.D., Akers, D.A., Macdonald, A.S. et al. (2003) 'Genetics and insurance – some social policy issues', *British Actuarial Journal*, 9: 787–874.

Daykin, C.D., Clark, P.N.S., Eves, M.J. et al. (1988) 'The impact of HIV infection and AIDS on insurance in the United Kingdom', *Journal of the Institute of Actuaries*, 115: 727–837.

De Jong, P. and Ferris, S. (2006) 'Adverse selection spirals', *ASTIN Bulletin*, 36(2): 589–628.

De Meza, D. and Webb, D.C. (2001) 'Advantageous selection in insurance markets', *Rand Journal of Economics*, 32: 249–62.

De Montjoye, Y.-A., Hidalgo, C.A., Verlayen, M. and Blondel, V.D. (2013) 'Unique in the crowd: the privacy bounds of human mobility', *Scientific Reports*, 3: 1376.

De Montjoye, Y.-A., Radaelii, L., Singh, V.K. and Pentland, A. (2015) 'Unique in the shopping mall: on the reidentifiability of credit card metadata', *Science*, 347: 536–9.

Department of Health (2001) *Government response to the report from the House of Commons Science and Technology Committee: genetics and insurance.* HMSO.

De Ravin, J. and Rump, D. (1996) 'The right to underwrite', *Quarterly Journal of the Institute of Actuaries of Australia*, September 1996: 16–58.

Dewan, S. and Hsu, V. (2004) 'Adverse selection in electronic markets: evidence from online stamp auctions', *Journal of Industrial Economics*, 52(4): 497–516.

Dionne, G., Gourieroux, C. and Vanasse, C. (2001) 'Testing for evidence of adverse selection in the automobile insurance market: a comment', *Journal of Political Economy*, 109: 444–73.

Dionne, G. and Rothschild, C.G. (2014) 'Economic effects of risk classification bans', *Geneva Risk and Insurance Review*, 39: 184–221.

Doiron, D., Jones, G. and Savage, E. (2007) 'Healthy, wealthy and insured? The role of self-assessed health in the demand for private health insurance', *Health Economics*, 17: 317–34.

Doll, R. and Hill, A.B. (1954) 'The mortality of doctors in relation to their smoking habits', *British Medical Journal*, 228: 1451–5.

Dorfman, M.S. (2002) *Introduction to risk management and insurance*, 7th edn. Prentice Hall.

Einav, L., Finkelstein, A. and Levin, J. (2010) 'Beyond testing: empirical models of insurance markets', *Annual Review of Economics*, 2: 311–36.

European Commission (2011) *Guidelines on the application of Council Directive 2004/113/EC to insurance, in the light of the Court of Justice of the European Union in Case C-236/09 (Test-Achats)*. www.ec.europa.eu, last accessed 17 August 2015.

Fan, J., Han, F. and Liu, H. (2014) 'Challenges of big data analysis', *National Science Review*, 1(2): 293–314.

Fang, H., Keane, M. and Silverman, D. (2008) 'Sources of advantageous selection: evidence from the medigap insurance market', *Journal of Political Economy*, 116(2): 303–50.

Feldstein, M.S. (1973) 'The welfare loss of excess health insurance', *Journal of Political Economy*, 81: 251–80.

Finkelstein, A. and McGarry, K. (2006) 'Multiple dimensions of private information: evidence from the long-term care insurance market', *American Economic Review*, 96: 938–58.

Finkelstein, A. and Poterba, J.M. (2002) 'Selection effects in the United Kingdom individual annuities market', *The Economic Journal*, 112: 28–50.

Finkelstein, A. and Poterba, J.M. (2004) 'Adverse selection in insurance markets: policyholder evidence from the UK annuity market', *Journal of Political Economy*, 112: 183–208.

Finkelstein, A. and Poterba, J.M. (2014) 'Testing for asymmetric information using 'unused observables' in insurance markets: evidence from the UK annuity market', *Journal of Risk and Insurance*, 81: 709–34.

Flegal, K.M., Kit, B.K., Orpana, H. and Graubard, B.I. (2013) 'Association of all-cause mortality with overweight and obesity using standard body mass index categories: a systematic review and a meta-analysis', *Journal of the American Medical Association*, 309(1): 71–82.

Friedland, J. (2013) *Fundamentals of general insurance actuarial analysis*. Society of Actuaries.

Galanter, M. (1974) 'Why the "haves" come out ahead: speculations on the limits of legal change', *Law and Society Review*, 9: 95–160.

Gertner, N. (2012) 'Losers' rules', *Yale Law Journal*, 122: 109–24.

Ghose, A. (2009) 'Internet exchanges for used goods: an empirical analysis of trade patterns and adverse selection', *MIS Quarterly*, 33(2): 263–91.

Gini, C. (1921) 'Measurement of inequality of incomes', *Economic Journal*, 31: 124–6.

Goldin, C. and Rouse, C. (2000) 'Orchestrating impartiality: the impact of blind auditions on female musicians', *American Economic Review*, 90: 715–41.

Goodwin, B.K. (1993) 'An empirical analysis of the demand for multiple peril crop insurance', *American Journal of Agricultural Economics*, 75(2): 424–34.

Gray, R.J. and Pitts, S. (2012) *Risk modelling in general insurance*. Cambridge University Press.

Grossman, H.I. (1979) 'Adverse selection, dissembling, and competitive equilibrium', *Bell Journal of Economics*, 10: 330–43.

Hall, M. (1999) 'Restricting insurers' use of genetic information: a guide to public policy', *North American Actuarial Journal*, 3(1): 34–46.

Hammond, E.C. (1958) 'Smoking and death rates: report on forty-four months of follow-up of 187,783 men', *Journal of American Medical Association*, 15 March 1958: 1294–308.

Hao, M., Macdonald, A.S., Tapadar, P. and Thomas, R.G. (2016a) 'Loss coverage under restricted risk classification: the case of iso-elastic demand,' *ASTIN Bulletin*, 46(2): 265–91.

Hao, M., Macdonald, A.S., Tapadar, P. and Thomas, R.G. (2016b) 'Insurance loss coverage and social welfare', University of Kent Working Paper. https://kar.kent.ac.uk/54235, last accessed 10 July 2016.

Hao, M., Tapadar, P. and Thomas, R.G. (2015) 'Loss coverage in insurance markets: why adverse selection is not always a bad thing', Paper presented at *International Actuarial Association Colloquium*, Oslo, June 2015. guythomas.org.uk, last accessed 17 April 2016.

Häring, N. and Douglas, N. (2013) *Economists and the powerful*. Anthem Press.

Harsanyi, J.C. (1955) 'Cardinal welfare, individualistic ethics, and interpersonal comparisons of utility', *Journal of Political Economy*, 63: 309–21.

Hately, P. (2011) 'Life in the fast lane', *The Actuary*, August: 34–5.

Health Protection Agency (2004) 'Cumulative data to end June 2004', *AIDS/HIV quarterly surveillance tables*, 63. http://webarchive.nationalarchives.gov.uk, last accessed 23 April 2016.

Heen, M. (2009) 'Ending Jim Crow life insurance rates', *Northwestern Journal of Law and Social Policy*, 4: 360–99.

Hemenway, D. (1990) 'Propitious selection', *Quarterly Journal of Economics*, 105: 1063–9.

Hemenway, D. (1992) 'Propitious selection', *Journal of Risk and Uncertainty*, 5: 247–51.

Hendren, N. (2013) 'Private information and insurance rejections', *Econometrica*, 81(5): 1713–62.

Hirshleifer, J. (1971) 'The private and social value of information and the reward to inventive activity', *American Economic Review*, 61: 561–74.

Hoinville, G., Berthoud, R. and Mackie, A.M. (1972) 'A study of accident rates amongst motorists who passed or failed an advanced driving test', Transport and Road Research Laboratory Report LR499. www.trl.co.uk, last accessed 23 April 2016.

Howard, R.C.W. (2014) *Genetic testing model: if underwriters had no access to known results.* www.cia-ica.ca, last accessed 23 April 2016.

Hoy M. (1982) 'Categorizing risks in the insurance industry', *Quarterly Journal of Economics,* 71(10): 321–36.

Hoy, M. (2006) 'Risk classification and social welfare', *Geneva Papers on Risk and Insurance,* 31: 245–69.

Hoy, M., Orsi, F., Eisinger, F. and Moatti, J.P. (2003) 'The impact of genetic testing on health care insurance', *Geneva Papers on Risk and Insurance,* 28: 203–21.

Hoy, M. and Polborn, M. (2000) 'The value of genetic information in the life insurance market', *Journal of Public Economics,* 78: 235–252.

Hoy, M. and Witt, J. (2007) 'Welfare effects of banning genetic information in the life insurance market: the case of BRCA1/2 genes', *Journal of Risk and Insurance,* 74: 523–46.

Hudson, S. (2008) *Legislation – are the underwriter's hands tied?* www.munichre.com, last accessed 9 August 2014.

Human Genetics Commission (2002) *Inside information: balancing interests in the use of personal genetic data.* Department of Health.

Institute and Faculty of Actuaries (1999) *Genetics and insurance position statement.* Copy in author's files.

Institute and Faculty of Actuaries (2001a) *Response to whose hands on your genes? Consultation.* www.hgc.gov.uk via www.archive.org, last accessed 23 April 2016.

Institute and Faculty of Actuaries (2001b) Memorandum submitted to the Select Committee on Science and Technology. www.publications.parliament.uk, last accessed 23 April 2016.

Institute and Faculty of Actuaries (2010) *Press release dated 7 October 2010.* www.actuaries.org.uk, last accessed 20 July 2013.

Institute of Actuaries of Australia (1994) *Insurance & superannuation risk classification policy.* Copy held in author's files.

Insurance Europe (formerly known as Council of European Assurers) (2011) *The use of gender in insurance pricing.* www.insuranceeurope.eu, last accessed 23 April 2016.

Jowell, R., Curtice, J., Park, A. and Thomson, K. (1999) *British social attitudes 16th report.* Ashgate.

Just, R.E., Calvin, L. and Quiggin, J. (1999) 'Adverse selection in crop insurance: actuarial and asymmetric information incentives', *American Journal of Agricultural Economics,* 81: 843–9.

Kahneman, D. (2011) *Thinking fast and slow*. Allen Lane.

Kennedy, S.P.L., Batting, J.P., Courbould, M.C. et al. (1987) 'Report on of the joint working party on discrimination in insurance and pensions', *Transactions of the Faculty of Actuaries*, 41: 271–367.

Kerr, M.G. (1989) 'AIDS and the Actuary', *Journal of the Institute of Actuaries Students Society*, 33: 195–231.

Keynes, J.M. (1936) *The general theory of employment, interest and money*. Macmillan.

Kosinski, M., Stillwell, D. and Graepel, T. (2013) 'Private traits and attributes are predictable from digital records of human behavior', *Proceedings of the National Academy of Sciences*, 110: 5802–5.

Kunreuther, H., Novemsky, N. and Kahneman, D. (2001) 'Making low probabilities useful', *Journal of Risk and Uncertainty*, 23: 103–20.

Kunreuther, H., Pauly, M.V. and McMorrow, S. (2013) *Insurance and behavioral economics: improving decisions in the most misunderstood industry*. Cambridge University Press.

Lazear, E. (2000) 'Economic imperialism', *The Quarterly Journal of Economics*, 115(1): 99–146.

Leigh, S. (1996) 'The freedom to underwrite', Paper presented to the Staple Inn Actuarial Society. www.sias.org.uk, last accessed 23 April 2016.

Lewis, R. and Morris, A. (2012) 'Tort law in the United Kingdom: image and reality in personal injury Compensation', *Journal of European Tort Law*, 3: 1–35.

Li, K.C.-W. (1996) 'The private insurance industry's tactics against suspected homosexuals: redlining based on occupation, residence and marital status', *American Journal of Law and Medicine*, 22: 477–502.

Life Insurance Association of Singapore (2006) *Genetics and life insurance*. www .bioethics-singapore.org, last accessed 23 April 2016.

Life Insurance Market Research Organisation (2013) *Facts about life*. www.limra .com, last accessed 23 April 2016.

Lippert-Rasmussen, K. (2011) '"We are all different": statistical discrimination and the right to be treated as an individual', *Journal of Ethics*, 15: 47–59.

Macdonald, A.S. (2003) 'Moratoria on the use of genetic tests and family history', *British Actuarial Journal*, 9: 217–37.

Macdonald, A.S. (2004) 'Genetics and insurance management', in *The Swedish Society of Actuaries: one hundred years*, ed. Sandstrom, A. Svenska Aktuarieforeningen.

Macdonald, A.S. and Yu, F. (2011) 'The impact of genetic information on the insurance industry: conclusions from the 'bottom-up' modelling programme', *ASTIN Bulletin*, 41: 343–76.

Mackowiak, B. and Widerholt, M. (2011) 'Inattention to rare events', CEPR Working Paper 8626.

Maclean, L.C., Thorp, E.O. and Ziemba, W.T. (2010) 'Long-term capital growth: the good and bad properties of the Kelly and fractional Kelly capital growth criteria', Quantitative Finance, 10(7): 681–7.

Makki, S.S. and Somwaru, A. (2001) 'Evidence of adverse selection in crop insurance', The Journal of Risk and Insurance, 68: 685–708.

Manning, W.G. and Marquis, M.S. (1996) 'Health insurance: the tradeoff between risk pooling and moral hazard', Journal of Health Economics, 15: 609–40.

McClelland, G., Schulze, W. and Coursey, D. (1993) 'Insurance for low-probability hazards: a bimodal response to unlikely events', Journal of Risk and Uncertainty, 7: 95–116.

McGlamery, J.G. (2009) 'Race based underwriting and the death of burial insurance', Connecticut Journal of Insurance Law, 15(2): 531–70.

Mitchell, O.S. and McCarthy, D. (2002) 'Estimating international adverse selection in annuities', North American Actuarial Journal, 6(4): 38–54.

Mitchell, O.S. and McCarthy, D. (2010) 'International adverse selection in life insurance and annuities', in Riding the age wave, Vol. 3, eds. Tuljapurkar, S., Chu, C., Gauthier, A., Ogawa, N. and Pool, I. Springer.

Miyazaki, H. (1977) 'The rat race and internal labour markets', Bell Journal of Economics, 8: 394–418.

Nozick, R. (1974) Anarchy, state and utopia. Basic Books.

Nyman, J.A. (2003) The theory of demand for health insurance. Stanford University Press.

Ohlsson, E. and Johansson, B. (2010) Non-life insurance pricing with generalized linear models. Springer.

Oxera Consulting (2012) Why the use of age and disability matters to consumers and insurers. www.insuranceeurope.eu, last accessed 23 April 2016.

Paltrow, S.J. (2000) 'Insurers stopped offering dual rates in the '60s, but didn't tell customers', Wall Street Journal 27 April 2000.

Paltrow, S.J. (2001) 'Old memos show in black and white Metlife's use of race to screen clients', Wall Street Journal 24 July 2001.

Parodi, P. (2014) Pricing in general insurance. Chapman & Hall.

Pauly, M.V. (1968) 'The economics of moral hazard: a comment', American Economic Review, 58: 531–27.

Pauly, M.V. (1983) 'More on moral hazard', Journal of Health Economics, 2: 83.

Pauly, M.V., Withers, K.H., Viswanathan, K.S. et al. (2003) 'Price elasticity of demand for term life insurance and adverse selection', NBER Working Paper 9925.

Pfleiderer, P. (2014) 'Chameleons: the misuse of theoretical models in finance and economics', Stanford University Business School Working Paper No. 3020.

Phoenix Strategic Perspectives (2013) *Survey of Canadians on privacy-related issues*. Office of the Privacy Commissioner of Canada. www.priv.gc.ca, last accessed 23 April 2016.

Pope, D.G. and Sydnor, J.R. (2011) 'Implementing anti-discrimination policies in statistical profiling models', *American Economic Journal: Economic Policy*, 3: 206–31.

Poundstone, W. (2005) *Fortune's formula: the untold story of the scientific system that beat the casinos and Wall Street*. Hill & Wang.

Proctor, R. (1988) *Racial hygiene: medicine under the Nazis*. Harvard University Press.

Proctor, R. (1999) *The Nazi war on cancer*. Princeton University Press.

Quiggin, J., Karagiannis, G. and Stanton, J. (1993) 'Crop insurance and crop production: an empirical study of moral hazard and adverse selection', *Australian Journal of Agricultural Economics*, 37(2): 95–113.

Rawls, J. (1971) *A theory of justice*. Harvard University Press. (Reissued edition dated 2005.)

Rees, R. and Wambach, A. (2008) *The microeconomics of insurance*. Now Publishers.

Riley, J.G. (1979) 'Informational equilibrium', *Econometrica*, 47: 331–59.

Rothschild, C. (2009) 'Adverse selection in annuity markets: evidence from the British Life Annuity Act of 1808', *Journal of Public Economics*, 93: 776–84.

Rothschild, M. and Stiglitz, J. (1976) 'Equilibrium in competitive insurance markets: an essay on the economics of imperfect information', *Quarterly Journal of Economics*, 90: 629–49.

Rowell, D. and Connelly, L.B. (2012) 'A history of the term "moral hazard"', *Journal of Risk and Insurance*, 79(4): 1051–75.

Saito, K. (2006) 'Testing for asymmetric information in the automobile insurance market under rate regulation', *Journal of Risk and Insurance*, 73: 335–56.

Schatz, B. (1987) 'The AIDS insurance crisis: underwriting or overreaching?', *Harvard Law Review*, 100: 1782–825.

Schelling, T.C. (1960) *The strategy of conflict*. Harvard University Press.

Schwarcz, D. (2007) 'Beyond disclosure: the case for banning contingent commissions', *Yale Law and Policy Review*, 25: 289–336.

Schwarcz, D. (2009) 'Differential compensation and the "race to the bottom" in consumer insurance markets', *Connecticut Insurance Law Journal*, 15: 723–53.

Schwarze, R. and Wein, T. (2005) 'Is the market classification of risk always efficient? Evidence from German third party motor insurance', *German Risk and
Insurance Review*, 4: 173–202.

Siegelman, P. (2004) 'Adverse selection in insurance markets: an exaggerated
threat', *Yale Law Journal*, 113: 1225–71.

Siegelman, P. (2014) 'Innovation and equilibrium in insurance markets with big
data', *Connecticut Insurance Law Journal*, 21: 317–38.

Sinclair, U. (1934) *I, candidate for governor, and how I got licked*, republished by
University of California Press, 1994.

Smith, M. (2014) 'Critical illness: can prices get any lower?', Presentation at
Institute & Faculty of Actuaries conference. www.actuaries.org.uk, last
accessed 23 April 2016.

Somerville, K. (2011) *Evidence, mortality and underwriting*. Swiss Re presentation, www.actuaries.org, last accessed 23 April 2016.

Spence, M. (1978) 'Product differentiation and performance in insurance markets',
Journal of Public Economics, 10: 427–47.

Srinivasan, U. and Arunasalam, B. (2013) 'Leveraging big data analytics to reduce
healthcare costs', *IT Professional*, 15(6): 21–8.

Stigler, G.J. (1955) 'The nature and role of originality in scientific progress',
Economica, 22: 293–302.

Stigler, G. (1984) 'Economics – the imperial science?', *Scandinavian Journal of
Economics*, 86(3): 301–13.

Stiglitz, J.E. (2001) 'Information and the change in the paradigm in economics',
Les Prix Nobel, 2001: 472–540. www.nobelprize.org, last accessed 23 April
2016.

Sunstein, C.R. (2002) 'Probability neglect: emotions, worst cases, and law', *Yale
Law Journal*, 113: 61–107.

Swiss Re (2014) *Term and health watch 2013*. Copy in author's files.

Thomas, R.G. (2001) *Genetics and insurance: an actuarial perspective with a difference*. Response to consultation by the Human Genetics Commission.
www.guythomas.org.uk, last accessed 17 April 2016.

Thomas, R.G. (2008) 'Loss coverage as a public policy objective for risk classification schemes', *Journal of Risk and Insurance*, 75(4): 997–1018.

Thomas, R.G. (2009) 'Demand elasticity, adverse selection and loss coverage:
when can community rating work?', *ASTIN Bulletin*, 39(2): 403–28.

Thomas, R.G. (2012) 'Non-risk price discrimination in insurance: market
outcomes and public policy', *Geneva Papers on Risk and Insurance*, 37(1):
27–46.

Tong, S., Lloyd, L., Durrell, L. et al. (2015) 'Provision of telematics research', Project Report 755. www.trl.co.uk, last accessed 23 April 2016.

Van Hoyweghen, I. and Horstman, K. (2009) 'Evidence-based underwriting in the molecular age: the politics of reinsurance companies towards the genetics issue', *New Genetics and Society*, 28: 317–37.

Villeneuve, B. (2000) 'The consequences for a monopolistic insurance firm of evaluating risk better than its customers', *Geneva Papers on Risk and Insurance Theory*, 25: 65–79.

Villeneuve, B. (2005) 'Competition between insurers with superior information', *European Economic Review*, 49: 321–40.

Viswanathan, K.S., Lemaire, J.K., Withers, K. et al. (2007) 'Adverse selection in term life insurance purchasing due to the BRCA 1/2 genetic test and elastic demand', *Journal of Risk and Insurance*, 74: 65–86.

Wang, K.C., Huang, R.J. and Tzeng, L.Y. (2009) 'Empirical evidence for advantageous selection in the commercial fire insurance market', *The Geneva Risk and Insurance Review*, 34: 1–19.

Ward, D. and Zurbruegg, R. (2000) 'Does insurance promote economic growth? Evidence from OECD countries', *Journal of Risk and Insurance*, 67: 489–506.

Wilson, C. (1977) 'A model of insurance with incomplete information', *Journal of Economic Theory*, 16: 167–207.

Ziemba, W.T. (2003) 'Good and bad properties of the Kelly criterion', *Wilmott Magazine*, March 2003.

Ziemba, W.T. (2015) 'A response to Professor Paul A. Samuelson's objections to Kelly capital growth investing', *Journal of Portfolio Management*, 42(1): 153–67.

Zingales, L. (2013) 'Preventing economists' capture', in *Preventing regulatory capture: special influence and how to limit it*, eds. Carpenter, D. and Moss, D. Cambridge University Press.

Zweifel, P. and Eisen, R. (2012) *Insurance economics*. Springer.

Index